Personality and Psychopathology
FEMINIST REAPPRAISALS

Personality and Psychopathology
FEMINIST REAPPRAISALS

Laura S. Brown
Mary Ballou
Editors

Foreword by Lenore E. A. Walker

THE GUILFORD PRESS
New York   London

© 1992 The Guilford Press
A Division of Guilford Publications, Inc.
72 Spring Street, New York, NY 10012

Printed in the United States of America

This book is printed on acid-free paper.

Last digit is print number: 9 8 7 6 5 4 3 2 1

Library of Congress Cataloging-in-Publication Data

Personality and psychopathology: feminist reappraisals / edited by
Laura S. Brown, Mary Ballou.
   p.   cm.
Includes bibliographical references and index.
ISBN 0-89862-774-5
   1. Feminist therapy.   2. Women—Mental health.   3. Women—
Psychology.   4. Personality.   I. Brown, Laura S.   II. Ballou,
Mary B., 1949–   .
   [DNLM: 1. Mental Disorders.   2. Personality.   3. Psychopathology.
4. Women—psychology.   WM 100 P4668]
RC489.F45P47   1992
616.89—dc20
DNLM/DLC
for Library of Congress   91-38466
                                                                          CIP

Contributors

Mary Ballou, Ph.D., Associate Professor, Counseling Psychology, Northeastern University, Boston, Massachusetts

Laura S. Brown, Ph.D., Clinical Associate Professor, Department of Psychology, University of Washington, and private practice, Seattle, Washington

Oliva M. Espin, Ph.D., Professor, Department of Women's Studies, San Diego State University, San Diego, California

Iris G. Fodor, Ph.D., Professor, Educational Psychology, New York University, New York

Mary Ann Gawelek, Ed.D., Dean, Counseling and Psychology Division, Lesley College, Cambridge, Massachusetts

Deborah Greenwald, Ph.D., Associate Professor, Counseling Psychology, Northeastern University, Boston, Massachusetts

Jean A. Hamilton, M.D., Associate Professor, Department of Psychiatry, University of Texas Southwestern Medical School, and Institute for Research on Women's Health, Dallas, Texas

Margaret Jensvold, M.D., Laboratory of Developmental Psychology, National Institute of Mental Health, Bethesda, Maryland

Ricki E. Kantrowitz, Ph.D., Associate Professor, Department of Psychology, Westfield State College, Westfield, Massachusetts

Hannah Lerman, Ph.D., private practice, Los Angeles, California

Barbara F. Okun, Ph.D., Professor, Counseling Psychology, Northeastern University, Newton, Massachusetts

Jo Romaniello, M.S., private practice, Carlisle, Massachusetts

Maria P. P. Root, Ph.D., private practice, Seattle, Washington

Foreword

The study of the normal personality (and how it differs from that which we label not normal) and pathology has been a hallmark of the discipline of psychology. Although psychologists have contributed numerous theories of personality over the last hundred years or so, each theory is judged independently by its ability to measure up to the scientific data obtained from rigorous empirical studies. How well a theory holds up to such scrutiny often determines its reception in the scientific psychological community although not necessarily its popularity with practitioners or the general public. Feminist psychology has provided both a new understanding of women as well as a critique of the old theories that neglected to include women's lives in their analyses.

In this book, Laura Brown and Mary Ballou give us a new standard by which to judge personality theories and their accompanying definitions of pathology. By adding gender and diversity to the list of important variables to be evaluated, they have put all of us on notice that no longer can we strip context from the understanding of who we are, what we do, and why we do it. It seems like a simple proposition, but, as you will see as you read through these pages, it creates the need for understanding many levels of complexity. Using this standard simply makes it outdated even to consider that any mental disorder has a single cause, whether it be structure, biochemistry, poor parenting, trauma, poverty, racism, sexism, or any other single factor.

The arguments among classical theorists have focused on nature-or-nurture dichotomies, with the *zeitgeist* of the moment often swinging to one or another side of the argument. When women began to enter the male scientific laboratories, with women's perspectives, they immediately recognized the errors made when scientific studies using only male subjects were used as the yardstick with which to measure personality. Despite the new data presented by both women and men scholars, those who control the standards have ignored pleas for adding external context to the understanding of human behavior, and instead have continued to focus on internal deficits, either with biology or personality.

Feminist therapists, many of whom you will meet in this book, have been working for the past two decades to make the standard more balanced. We have scrutinized the therapy techniques to get rid of those that are more obviously sexist and have developed our own, which are more compatible with a feminist perspective. We have studied illnesses that have high prevalence for women to better understand the contribution of gender to their development and maintenance. We have challenged the mental health professions to clean up their own houses, often by learning how to get some little bits of power by using the same political techniques, focusing initially on more egregious misconduct, such as sex between client and therapist. And, when we recognized the magnitude of the impact of all oppression in the environment on mental health, we challenged ourselves to make our feminist theories more culturally sensitive and inclusive of all diversity.

Now, with this book, Brown and Ballou use feminist theory to push us to the front edges once more. Here the authors are challenging the very notion of how healthy personalities develop, carefully pointing out the need to keep any theory of personality relevant to all women's lives. No major theory of psychotherapy currently in use— even the latest revision—meets the test, as the authors here point out. The idea that there is a personality core that is formed early in life simply conflicts too sharply with the knowledge of situations throughout later childhood, adolescence, and adulthood that have continuous impact on our lives. Here is where we must begin to think in layers. Perhaps the early integration of structure, biochemistry, and situational factors—including parenting quality and styles, interpersonal interactions, gender norms, cultural mores, and disposition—begin the formation of layers that continue the individual's development in the same or different directions. Perhaps a wholly new paradigm is needed, and after you read this book, you may let your own creativity play with the ideas for a while.

The impact of situational factors on the abnormal development resulting in what we label pathology is the focus of the second part of this book. Feminist authors have spent much of their careers challenging the androcentric models that have been stripped of any meaningful context including gender, race, ethnicity and culture, sexual orientation, and interpersonal connections with males and females. The editors have chosen to use the most popular nosology system, the American Psychiatric Association's *Diagnostic and Statis-*

tical Manual of Mental Disorders (3rd ed., rev.) (DSM-III-R) as the model with which to anchor their critiques. Their points become clearly focused when you read the research data that were left out of the predominantly white–male–professional psychiatric task force meetings that created this nosology system.

Each disorder studied in this book—schizophrenia, agoraphobia and panic disorders, depression and affective disorders, posttraumatic stress disorders, and the personality disorders—tells the story. Women have different routes by which these disorders are manifested and almost all involve the lack of relative and perceived power in their lives. Socialization experiences that include oppression because of gender, class, race, educational status, and racial, ethnic, and cultural minority-group membership are the factors most common in women who develop these mental disorders.

Read the research and history presented in each of the chapters in the second section. Then, go back to the DSM-III-R and read the descriptions of each disorder discussed here. Now, stop and think about whether these data could possibly have been taken seriously by the framers of the DSM nosology series. Even more frightening is the lack of attention paid to these data by the committees that are currently working on the next revision, the DSM-IV.

In 1985–1986, I was permitted to attend some of the DSM-III-R Task Force meetings. I was present for the discussion of some of the impressive data you will read in this book about women's experiences with victimization and about the natural cycles of women's hormones and the impact on depression and premenstrual mood. The mostly male psychiatrists heard the presentation of data and proceeded to ignore it since it did not fit in with their conceptual model of mental disorder by consensus. Some critics have been allowed to offer their opinions for the DSM-IV, but for the most part it will be as irrelevant to women's lives as the previous diagnostic systems have been.

How can you, the reader, take to heart Brown and Ballou's directive to think diagnostically if indeed diagnosis is not based on the inclusion of some of the most important parts of women's lives? Here the challenge is up to you. Think about the following steps prior to reading this book and then go back and try to do the tasks when you are finished. If you think about a specific person or even yourself it may make this exercise easier to complete.

First, you must choose your own philosophical view of how a person develops.

Then, decide whether you believe that people are more likely to have a positive pull toward healthy growth or a negative pull toward self-destructive tendencies. Each of us, of course, has some positive and some negative influences on our thinking, feelings, and actions at any time. But, your primary philosophical choice will help you select a theory useful to you in your work.

Next, see if you can determine all the possible influences on an individual's current functioning using the symptoms and syndromes that we commonly use to signify maladaptive and pathological behavior. Start with a list and check off each item on it. Be sure to use gender, culture, and other relevant experiences in this analysis. Is your list different from what it might have been before you read this book?

What do your conceptualizations say about guiding therapeutic treatment planning to help the person (or yourself) eliminate the negative, self-destructive influences on life? Will the new learnings be applied externally or come from within the person?

If you have completed this exercise, you have just done what Brown calls *thinking diagnostically*. Obviously, it is just a beginning step in the longer process of making such diagnostic thinking more relevant to our real lives. This book is a major step in that direction.

—Lenore E. A. Walker
Denver, Colorado

Preface

It is a pleasure to introduce this volume of original feminist critiques of the traditional personality theories and models of psychopathology. A synthesis of more than two decades of feminist analyses of traditional psychological theories, the work promises to be a catalyst for the further development of a context-based, feminist psychological theory.

The major thesis of this volume is that traditional, or mainstream, personality theories and views of psychopathology are not adequate from the standpoint of feminist theory. This inadequacy is found in a number of areas in the traditional theories—in their limited views of human nature; their exclusion of the multiple internal and structural forces affecting human development and functioning; their narrowly constructed definitions of mental health and mental disorder, a result of dominant-group collaboration; and, ultimately, their underlying intellectual processes.

It is unusual, particiularly in the United States, to introduce a text on personality theory and psychopathology with a discussion that refers to Western intellectual history, political dominance, and the supporting ideologies of that culture. However, it is precisely this unique approach that feminist analysis provides. The separation of disciplines and levels of discourse typical of mainstream models blocks the understanding of links, patterns, and interactions. Traditional psychology's theories of personality are no exception. Links between dominant intellectual models, views of human nature, and judgments made about belief and behavior are not only real, but related. Ruling classes control threats to their power and domination. They do so in a variety of ways: by making laws, setting forth particular and partial information, maintaining military forces, imposing economic sanctions and manipulations, and defining nonconforming beliefs as uncivilized or illogical and nonconforming behavior as criminal or sick. Ideological domination is not absent from personality theory and models of psychopathology.

Psychology's exclusive focus on the individual, whether framed in terms of intrapsychic forces, behavioral reinforcement, content of schema, mother–child and child–family interactions, innate potential for growth, or Western mythological archetypes—to draw upon the terms of the various theories discussed in this book—serves to obscure the dominant ideology embedded within the theory. The focus on the individual promotes an ideology of individual responsibility, of success or failure by virtue of one's own motivation, skills, or vicissitudes of psychological development. However, viewed from a larger perspective, this focus may well be seen as a mechanism for maintaining social order and conformity. To this end, certain characteritics, predominantly seen in the developmental patterns and structures of selected, dominant groups, are given the status of being marks of health and effective functioning. Those with less of the selected characteristics, for example, people from non-dominant groups, are defined as less healthy or effectively functioning—and eventually as pathological. The individual focus in traditional personality theories serves to hold people accountable for their adjustment to externally imposed criteria for health while avoiding the social/economic/class-based/gender-based/racial/cultural relativity of those criteria.

As long as personality theories focus solely on the individual in a decontextualized state, the links with politics–power and assignments of status will not be seen. Feminist theory calls for personality theories and models of psychopathology set, not in the Western individual–intellectual traditions, but rather in the context of the multifaceted cultural, structural, and interpersonal forces affecting individual functioning and development. A feminist analysis requires multidisciplinary perspectives that articulate these forces, which describe the full range of human characteristics, kinship patterns, and political/social/economic/historical arrangements.

Feminist analysis has developed significantly over the last 3 decades. Building from early concepts of the second wave of U.S. feminism—such as "the personal is political," the pervasiveness of sexism, the importance of lived experience found in "consciousness raising," and the centrality of gender as a category for analysis—have evolved into a complex and sophisticated perspective. For example, "the personal is political" was originally used to emphasize that one's own experience is important and is, in some measure, caused by external factors. Currently, feminist psychologists use this notion as a starting point for understanding the formative influence of sociocultural structures and forces on the individual and his or her sense of self, hence the reformulation: "the political is personal."

Feminist psychological theory has progressed rapidly in its analyses of gender and, more recently, other nondominant characteristics, in particular race, culture, class, sexual orientation, religion, worldview, and values. Progress has also been made in the use of interactive and contextual models for thinking about human nature and development. What some feminist psychologists have been slower to assess in their theorizing are the structural forces within the larger systems that lie outside of the individual. This perspective sees individuals as shaped by and through the structural impositions of the social/cultural/economic/religious/sexual systems, and is derived from the feminist analyses of other disciplines such as sociology, economy, and political science. Feminist psychologists must turn to feminists in other disciplines to learn new perspectives, then use them to construct new psychological theories, thereby avoiding the tyranny of individualistic viewpoints.

Just as feminists must examine the limitations of exclusively rational or empirical intellectual systems for building nonoppresive theories, so must they explore and explain the larger structural forces of sociocultural systems and incorporate their findings into feminist theory. The social fabric, with its mulitple systems, contains oppressive structures that deeply affect and define individuals. Until these structures are defined, not just in clinical practice but in theories of distress and human nature and development, the fullest depths of oppression will remain unexcavated, and theories that provide optimum life spaces will not have been built.

Contents

Feminist Perspectives on Theories of Personality

Introduction

MARY BALLOU

Part I of this volume addresses mainstream personality theories and, in doing so, raises three central questions. The first question asks the reader to critically examine the paradigms used in the traditional understanding of personality and normal development. The second question inquires into the basic views of human nature generated by such theories. The third central question relates to the importance of context as a force in human development and functioning and challenges the arbitrary, individualistic, yet universalized assumptions in mainstream theory regarding the variables, phenomena, and forces that are considered significant in human functioning and development.

These questions at the paradigmatic level represent aspects of the challenges made by feminists within the biological and social sciences to mainstream epistemology and modes of discourse. Chapters by Espin and Gawelek, Kantrowitz and Ballou, and Romaniello each raise doubts concerning the adequacy of mainstream personality theories' ways of knowing. Each chapter points to the limited ways in which knowledge is traditionally generated and accorded validity. Kantrowitz and Ballou, for example, discuss the impact and limits of empiricism as the dominant model of knowledge generation within cognitive–behavioral theories. Similarly, Romaniello identifies Jung's biases, which are integral to his use of rationalism as an epistemic method. Espin and Gawelek, in their chapter on class and culture bias in personality theories, introduce the more recent stance of social constructivism as a necessary aid to feminist attempts at theory decontamination and reconstruction. These three chapters, in particular, address the limits and dangers contained in the use of a single epistemological approach in mainstream personality theories.

The next two questions raised by these authors are essentially metaphysical considerations: What is reality and by whom is it defined? Basic assumptions in personality theories of what is fundamental and real in human experience serve not only as starting points for theory building, but function to include and exclude particular phenomena as well. If, for example, a theory starts with a basic assumption that an innate growth principle in human nature is one important aspect of reality, an assumption Lerman identifies in humanistic theories, then personality theory leads to the concept that the individual is responsible for change. If, as we see in Okun's discussion of object relations theory, early mother–child interactions are held to define reality (as opposed to sexual instincts, as held in classical psychoanalysis), then the mother–child relationship becomes central to the theory. These examples demonstrate that the phenomena held to be "real" by a given theory determine the consequent shape taken by the theory, both in terms of what is defined as being fundamentally important (essentially real) and what is seen as not important (either not real or derivative). The phenomena in the second class, "not important," are shortchanged in the development of a particular theory, because their realness in human nature and development is ignored. The metaphysics, or the reality, accorded to particular phenomena within personality theories is critical to the construction of the theory because it defines what is centrally important within human nature and its development and determines what is excluded from importance.

Taken as a whole, the chapters in the first section of this volume reappraise the limited underlying views of human nature and the exclusion of contextual and structural forces upon human development and functioning within mainstream personality theories. The chapters use feminist analyses of gender, context, and structure to assess the adequacy of the metaphysics in traditional personality theories' assumptions of what is real and important in human nature and functioning.

The major contemporary (mainstream) personality theories discussed in this section were developed within the traditions of Western intellectual history, a period of remarkable achievements, but serious limits, as well. In the latter decades of the 20th century, these limits are being seen, discussed, and countered through epistemology, disciplinary evolution, and politics. Feminist analysis, while certainly not alone, has been a prime force in this movement. The chapters in this volume are a part of the process. In particular, some feminist analyses are epistemologically challenging the idea that exclusive rationalism and/or empiricism are the only acceptable modes of obtaining knowledge, as is suggested by Western intellectual history. Traditional metaphysical habits of reduction and atomism, causality and linearity, are being exposed by some feminist analyses and shown to be misdirected and ill-fitting. We must remember that plastics and chemicals, advances of 20th-century technology, may not be the best, much less the only, building materials. In fact, without careful inspection of their properties, they may be quite caustic and harmful. Alternative building materials—wood, stone, natural fibers, and ecologically safe energy sources—should be given equal consideration.

Similarly, white upper-middle-class European and American males were the theorists and writers in 19th- and early 20th-century intellectual history. Their views of the world and of human nature were limited by their own experiences. Fantasies of grand designs, which elevate the supremacy of reason (rationalism), or mechanistic blueprints that focus on the functioning of elements known only through the material senses (empirism) are no longer adequate models. These intellectual models served to justify the dominance and authority of the privileged classes within the nationalistic and colonial empires of Germany, England, and the United States in the 19th and early 20th centuries.

The chapters in Part I each seek to unearth the underlying assumptive views of human nature and the particular characteristics centralized and valued within personality theories developed through traditional intellectual models. In so doing, the chapters excavate foundational views of human nature too limited, from a feminist perspective, to support the constructions needed in the latter 20th century. The building of theory in this era requires a vision of human nature that is diverse and inclusive of the experiences and knowledge of nondominant groups, that is, non-male, non-European-American, non-upper-middle-class, non-white peoples. Contemporary views of human nature will require a valuing of different but equally important characteristics, phenomena, and worldviews. Conceptualizations of human nature and its development and functioning must attend to interactive influences of social/political/ economic/cultural forces with and upon old-model individual psychology. Also, the narrow focus in psychology on the de-contextualized individual, so foundational to the hierarchical power relations and political-control mechanisms of the 19th and early 20th centuries, must be replaced according to feminist critiques with an attention to relational and interactive models. New "building codes" demand contextual centers, placing importance upon the numerous levels of interactive, extraindividual forces and the individual factors of race, class, gender, ethnicity. These are the principal requirements of new-theory construction, as proposed by the feminist analyses in this volume.

Feminist analysis is political, in that it is essentially an identification and assessment of power relations located centrally in gender. Feminist analysis contains an important focus on the social, economic, cultural, and institutional contexts that form and define individuals' lives, values, cognitions, emotions, motivations, and work and kinship patterns. The chapters in Part I each use aspects of feminist analysis to evaluate traditional personality theories, raising a number of points central to the feminist perspective. Okun's chapter discusses assumptions about gender in human characteristics, relationships, and life patterns as they are embedded in object relations theory. Romaniello's chapter points out the rigid dichotomous thinking and differential evaluation of human characteristics as either male and female contained within Jungian theory. Lerman's critique of humanistic psychologies calls attention to the power of gendered external forces in the context and structures of individuals' lives, as they shape and interact with internal psychological phenomena. Kantrowitz and Ballou's chapter on cognitive–behavioral theory articulates the problems with exclusive use of a single human function and a single intellectual mode, concluding that neither cognition/behavior nor empiricism allow for the multiple aspects of human nature and modes of knowing. Espin and Gawelek's chapter is striking in its discussion of the need for personality theories to understand and respond to the multiple and interactive contexts of peoples' lives. These, and other points made throughout the chapters, are strong illustrations of feminist analysis applied to theories of human development.

The chapters in this Part raise serious questions about whether the traditional personality theories can simply be redesigned. Certainly phallic towers can be rounded, but modification, gained through a change in assumptions regarding gender, will not suffice. The challenges inherent in these critiques require fundamental change in contextual and structural metaphysics, as well as epistemologic expansion. Environmental, ecological, and interactive systems perspectives would seem to require new excavation and the laying of a new foundation, not merely repair on the traditional personality theories. Indeed, feminist personality theory, as Espin and Gawelek suggest, may require a new paradigm setting forth essentially different specifications of personality theory building codes.

These feminist critiques lay the groundwork for the development of new theories of personality that would more adequately describe human nature, normal development, and the sociocultural factors integral to them both. Such new theory will draw from, and take seriously, the feminist critiques of cultural, class-based, racial, political, and philosophic biases held by the current conceptualizations that are institutionalized within mainstream personality theories.

CHAPTER ONE

The Limits of Phenomenology: A Feminist Critique of the Humanistic Personality Theories

HANNAH LERMAN

The humanist personality theorists in psychology emphasized the wholeness of human experience in their postulates and expressed the view that human choice, intentionality, and awareness fundamentally influence our actions. This is contrary to the view that our behavior is always determined by unconscious conflicts and/or behavioral conditioning. The humanist personality theorists stated their precepts in contradiction to what they saw as the "mechanomorphism and sterility of academic and behavioristic psychology" (Bugental, 1966, p. 223). In labeling this group the "third force," Maslow (1968) contrasted its thinking directly with psychoanalysis and behaviorism, the other two forces in psychological thinking. In general, theorists in the humanist group focused on personal experience and perceptions as primary determinants of human action.

When our present wave of feminism began in the late 1960s, the humanistic psychology movement was at its peak. The *zeitgeist* of the time created a context in which the emphasis of these theories on individual awareness and personal responsibility was very compatible with social movements that emphasized caring and expression of feelings. Feminists and protofeminists[1] in the social sciences found

1. This term is meant to describe those people (mostly women) who were groping toward an awareness of the social oppression of women, but who had not yet found the framework through which to express their discomfort and distress with the patriarchal status quo.

much that was compatible in humanistic views, most particularly a positive view of human nature, support for a more egalitarian view of therapy, as well as a focus on starting with individual experience as the basis for explanations of behavior. All of these aspects were essentially absent in the other personality theories then available. Sturdivant (1980) and Greenspan (1983) remind us that, during the first groundswell of feminist thinking in psychology, the humanistic theories were not criticized and critiqued as were other theories. Psychoanalytic theory, for example, was an easy target for criticism because it was so clearly patriarchal in form and structure (Lerman, 1986).

Feminist humanists were interested in extending the humanistic view to include women more specifically and engaged in a "positive reevaluation of the female value system so that some attributes and qualities traditionally assigned to women and thus devalued as trivial, unimportant, or undesirable for 'human beings,' become valuable and valued traits" (Sturdivant, 1980, p. 89). The humanistic perspective fostered immediacy, egalitarianism, and respect for the other, all of which fit the feminist consciousness. Feminist therapy did not have (and to some extent still does not have) a well-developed theoretical basis. Insofar as we initially borrowed from humanistic theory, we were indeed often all but indistinguishable from the humanists within the behavioral sciences, except that we focused primarily on women.

What was not immediately recognized was that the humanistic theories downplay and neglect external reality factors in both personality development and therapy. Ballou and Gabalac (1985) point out:

> [Women and other oppressed groups] are denied inclusion in the rewards and necessary conditions for growth. The third force's neglect of these dynamics is a tragic flaw, one which not only does not account for external forces in its conception, but which incorrectly places the total responsibility and obligation on the individual for her growth and development. (p. 74)

Much of the work of the past 15 years in the realm of feminist psychology has demonstrated that personality structure and development are very complexly related to the world in which we live. We have learned that the reality of women's oppression at all levels, from the early sexual and physical through the psychological, not only affects what is externally possible for women in our world but also indelibly marks how women view themselves and what they can become as persons (Miller, 1976).

The aspects of humanistic personality theory that we feminists originally found congenial remain so, although the lack of emphasis given to environmental constraints achieves increasing prominence in our thinking as we begin to develop our own models more fully. For the most part, however, feminists have not tried to address our concerns within the terms of the theories that are presently available. It is worth examining the degree to which humanistic theories could provide us with a theoretical base. This chapter will explore the special issue of the theorists' perspectives on internal/external reality and examine how the theories relate, in general, to feminist concerns.[2]

A BRIEF REVIEW OF THREE HUMANISTIC THEORIES

Carl Rogers' viewpoint is basically phenomenological. His theory of personality grew out of his clinical work with individuals. He is primarily identified with the method of psychotherapy he developed, which is called *nondirective* or *client-centered.* He came to view the therapeutic process as an instance of all optimal interpersonal relationships and movement in therapy as the paradigm for normal personality development.

According to Rogers, the organism is the locus of all experience. The person's phenomenal field is made up of conscious (symbolized) and unconscious (unsymbolized) experiences. People test their subjective hypotheses against other sources of information. The self is gradually differentiated out of a portion of the phenomenal field. Rogers (1951) states: "The organism has one basic tendency and striving—to actualize, maintain and enhance the experiencing organism" (p. 491). It only operates, however, when the choices are clearly perceived and adequately symbolized. "Behavior is basically the goal-directed attempt of the organism to satisfy its needs as experienced, in the field as perceived" (p. 491).

Frederick (more familiarly known as Fritz) Perls also developed his theory of personality primarily out of his clinical work. Most of his books, and books about him, deal more with his therapy than with his theory. Only in his earliest book (Perls, Hefferline, & Goodman, 1951) is his theory discussed in any consistent fashion. His basic concept is that the only concrete subject matter is always an organism–environment field. This is the *gestalt* from which his gestalt

2. Although there are many different theories available in the humanist group, I will focus on the work of Carl Rogers, Fritz Perls, and Abraham Maslow in my attempts to discuss the relevance of humanistic theories for feminist psychologists.

therapy gets its name. The field is seen as always tending to complete itself, albeit in ever-changing conditions. Perls indicates that an organism preserves itself only by growing. The self may be regarded as the boundary of the organism, but it is not isolated from the environment; it is always in contact with the environment. The view is that the present is a passage out of the past and toward the future, as the self contacts the actuality. The past is unchanging and unchangeable but can dissolve into many possibilities in the present, as a new figure continually emerges into the future.

Abraham Maslow, unlike the other humanist theorists, based his views upon investigations of healthy and creative persons. People, he believed, have an inborn nature that is essentially good or at least neutral. As personality unfolds through maturation in a benign environment and by the active efforts of the person to realize his or her essential nature, the creative powers of humans are seen to manifest themselves ever more clearly. Humans are miserable or neurotic because the environment has made them so through ignorance or social pathology or because of distortions in their thinking. *Basic* needs are differentiated from *meta* needs. The basic needs—hunger, affection, security, self-esteem, etc.—are deficiency needs, while the meta needs are growth needs. These include justice, goodness, beauty, order, unity, etc. The meta needs are as instinctive in humans as the basic needs, and a person becomes sick when they are not fulfilled (Hall & Lindzey, 1978).

INTERNAL/EXTERNAL REALITY

There are differences among humanist theorists in their relationship to external reality. Rogers, for example, pays almost no attention to the so-called "real world" or "reality," concepts he frequently puts into quotation marks. He has some difficulty when he deals with the needs of persons to test their perceptions externally, and he essentially sidesteps this dilemma. One of Rogers' (1951) fundamental proposition: "The organism reacts to the field as it is experienced and perceived. This perceptual field is, for the individual, 'reality' " (p. 484). He uses an example of two men to illustrate this point:

> [They are] driving at night on a western road. An object looms up in the middle of the road ahead. One of the men sees a large boulder, and reacts with fright. The other, a native of the country, sees a tumbleweed and reacts with nonchalance. Each reacts to the reality as perceived. (p. 484)

In his anecdote, Rogers does not indicate what the external object was, although he implies that the local man was correct. He also fails to point out that the outcome of the incident would be different if the object turned out to be a large boulder instead of a tumbleweed, regardless of what it was perceived to be—or whether it was perceived at all—by the two men. This example clearly illustrates the limits of the phenomenological approach to human experience. Reality is not wholly determined internally. Contact with a boulder will hurt no matter how it is perceived.

Fritz Perls is not as extreme as Rogers in his view of external reality. He, for example, speaks of the environment and of the outside world, although he does so mainly in terms of how external factors affect our awareness (Perls, 1969). He puts his emphasis, however, on our internal perceptions. He follows Freud's early differentiation between the traumatic neuroses and the psychoneuroses (Perls, 1973, p. 31), which leads him to acknowledge that the external environment has a role in behavior. He does not, however, consider traumatic circumstances to be a major or common factor in determining behavior and, like Freud, focuses primarily on the psychoneuroses. Almost parenthetically and without really focusing on the implications, he accepts the concept of a need hierarchy such as Maslow's.

Maslow is clear in his depiction of the role of external reality. As a fundamental part of his theory, he postulates a pyramid that begins with the physical needs. When these are satisfied, the individual can move into the associated social and interpersonal needs, and then, as each level is satisfied, move up to the needs that come into play when the deficiency needs have been met. Maslow (1968) indicates that, unless the more basic physical, physiological, basic security, and belongingness needs are satisfied, the growth or actualization needs do not come into play. Although Maslow does not elaborate on this, there would seem to be enough room in his conceptualization for interweaving with it a feminist analysis of the external world and people's well-being. Although he acknowledged the external world in a potentially useful fashion, Maslow did not give his greatest emphasis and attention to the role of basic needs. Neither did he show how the environment (physical and human) operates in denying the satisfaction of basic needs to women and other oppressed persons.

Maslow did not suggest any differentiation between the development of women and men in terms of the need hierarchy itself or in how deficiency needs are customarily responded to. We can see potential merit in the use of the need hierarchy Maslow postulated to define what is often absent in women's development and, therefore, in their lives. The potential integration of Maslow's views and feminist models has never been elaborated, however. Maslow was himself both inconsistent and ambivalent in his discussions about women in relationship to their social roles, often seeing femininity in highly stereotypic fashion (Kasten, 1972).

From a feminist viewpoint, we can see that there is a basic defect in the humanistic personality theories. To a greater or lesser extent, all of the theorists in this group have narrowed their focus almost exclusively to the phenomenological position. Since this emphasis is almost totally absent in the official theories of the other two forces, psychoanalysis and behaviorism, it was initially a useful corrective in the then-prevailing psychological climate. But the humanistic theories did not go for enough. They failed to recognize that no person constructs their own reality without external influences. The theories did not take into account exactly how influential external forces really are.

Feminist psychologists and sociologists, in their studies of the real lives of women, have demonstrated that patriarchal institutions limit and severely constrict the possibilities for women—regardless of whether the women involved believe themselves to be oppressed or not. An early study pointing out the difference between perceived discrimination and objectively measured sexual inequality on the job was done by Levitin, Quinn, and Staines (1971). Carrying this further, it is clear that believing that one has the legal right to leave a battering relationship does not, in and of itself, guarantee that any particular woman can succeed in leaving, that she will be safe after she does leave, or that she has the economic wherewithal to support herself and her children if she does. Neither does the fact that a woman feels secure in her own home, or trusts her dating partner, guarantee that she will not be raped. Examples can be multiplied ad infinitum.

Thus, women's lives, when they are examined in terms of realistic appraisals of the external environment, whether physical or psychological, do not permit us to say that, if we actualize our psychological selves, the result will be either personal serenity or the absence of physical or psychological hardships. This is the point upon which the protofeminists, who initially had felt an affinity for the humanistic position, deviated to become the feminists who focused on their own conceptualization of the complex interaction of the internal and the external.

OTHER FEMINIST CONCERNS

How do the humanistic theorists measure up on other fundamental feminist points? Based on the values of feminist psychology, I have developed a set of metatheoretical markers by which to evaluate a theory of personality. Briefly, the markers are: (1) whether a particular theoretical viewpoint has clinical usefulness for women's issues, (2) whether the theory in question encompasses the diversity and complexity of women and their lives, (3) whether the theory views women positively and centrally, (4) whether it arises from women's experience, (5) whether the theory remains close to the data of experience, (6) whether the theory recognizes that the internal world is inextricably intertwined with the external world, (7) whether concepts are confounded by particularistic terminology or the terminology of other theories, and (8) whether the theory supports feminist (or at minimum nonsexist) modes of psychotherapy. Most of these points are self-evident to any reasonably knowledgeable feminist psychologist or therapist, but the reader is referred to Lerman (1986) for more detailed information about them. Going through the points in order we find:

Clinical Usefulness

Clinical usefulness is a very fluid and elusive concept (Lerman, 1986). What is clinically useful for one is not for another. Rogers and Perls each have fully developed theories of therapy that have demonstrated clinical usefulness to their followers. Rogers' nondirective or client-centered therapy today has less of the flavor of a separate school of therapy, and many of his therapeutic concepts and techniques have been incorporated into other approaches. Perls' work remains separate, however, to a large extent.

Both approaches have apparently worked well with a great many individuals. There is little material available, however, about how these approaches work with women or other individuals who have suffered battering, assault, rape, incest, or other such massive traumas, which are all-too-common factors in women's physical and psychological lives. Also, without the addition of a feminist perspective on women's daily lives, it is difficult to ascertain whether these theories supply therapists with any understanding and conceptualization of women's specific daily difficulties in a patriarchal world.

As Greenspan (1983) and Ballou and Gabalac (1985) suggest, it is all too easy, from the phenomenological position that the humanistic theories espouse, to insist—especially in the absence of any awareness of the presence and effects of external oppression—that all a woman has to do is to change her perception of herself. To imply that such an internal change would eliminate all cultural, economic, legal, and interpersonal obstacles to a woman's physical and psychological actualization is absurd. The degree to which this attitude exists varies among those applying the theories, but it is certainly implied within humanistic theory (in general) and is an aspect of humanistic therapy to which feminists need to be alert.

Maslow's work is not directly applicable to psychotherapeutic practice. There are, however, aspects of his need hierarchy, as mentioned above, that could usefully inform our thinking about personality change and could be used to point up more systematically where the problems exist for all women, especially environmentally severely traumatized women and other oppressed groups.

Encompassing the Diversity and Complexity of Women and Their Lives

None of the theorists that we have been discussing has any differentiation at all in their theoretical structures between the personality development of males and females, nor, generally speaking, do other humanist theorists. Unlike psychoanalytic theory, however, none of the humanistic theories contain theoretical structures that actively discount women and women's issues. Although little work has been done in the area, it is not unlikely that enterprising feminist practitioners of Rogers' and Perls' viewpoints and adherents of Maslow could extend these theories beyond what was envisioned by their originators. There is, in fact, a recent report by a British feminist who is attempting to reinterpret and utilize Maslow's need hierarchy in her clinical work (Taylor, 1989).

It must be recognized, however, if we do extend our feminist analysis in an effort to reinterpret and use what is appropriate within the humanistic theories, that the basic concepts of the humanistic theories are directly compatible with the values of the U.S. middle class in the late 20th century. All theories bear some relationship to the time and place of their origins, so this should not be surprising to us. Concepts like actualization, individuation, autonomy, and the like and the psychotherapeutic concepts based on them are not likely to be directly applicable either to other segments of the U.S. society or to persons who are members of or who identify with other cultures in which these aspects of development are neither fostered nor appreciated. In effect, this becomes another way in which the external world, here identified as "culture," is not recognized in the form and structure of humanistic theories. By failing to identify the political and social implications of the focus on extreme individuality, these theories imply that their stance is apolitical while, in actuality, they serve a highly political function—in service of the continued acceptance of the specifically patriarchal status quo of present society in the United States.

All of the humanistic theories predate the growing awareness of cultural diversity that is building in psychology, especially feminist psychology. Because of their lack of awareness, the humanistic theories are not by themselves capable of encompassing the diversity and complexity of women and their lives. Because of their focus on individuality, so well-attuned to dominant groups in our society, it may also be extremely difficult for the theories to encompass the values of societies where group, family, or common good is more highly valued.

Viewing Women Positively and Centrally

This is closely related to the preceding criterion. Although it is true that none of the three theorists view women in a fundamentally negative way, none of them view women positively and centrally, and some aspects of the theories are tainted with the almost casual expression of the sexism of their era (see Kasten, 1972).

Arising from Women's Experience

It is not possible to say that any of the humanistic theories arise from women's experience. Like most traditional theories, they were developed by men and reflect the theorists' lives and their experiences of themselves and their culture. The theories were formulated without awareness that the male theorists' perspectives were not as universal as they seemed to be. On the other hand, there do not seem to be any intrinsic structures in the humanistic theories that preclude the incorporation of women's experience into their perspectives.

Remaining Close to the Data of Experience

One very positive aspect of the humanistic theories is that they do remain close to the data of experience, even if it is not primarily women's experience, in formulating their concepts. Although not explicitly stated in any listing of humanistic postulates, this aspect—of remaining close to the data of experience—does seem to characterize the humanistic point of view. It is obviously one of the aspects of humanistic theory that feminists initially found appealing, especially when contrasted with the elaborate structure of abstract concepts that makes up psychoanalytic theory.

Internal/External Worlds

That the phenomenological position cannot include the real factors of the external world, nor can it explain how they interact with one's internal perception, is already abundantly clear. (See earlier discussion, pp. 11–13.) Addressing this deficiency is fundamental to a feminist viewpoint on humanistic theory.

Particularistic Terminology

The use of particularistic language is less of a problem in dealing with humanistic theory than it is, for example, with psychoanalytic theory, and is an only barely relevant consideration for this group of theorists. In the humanistic arena, each theorist uses his own, rarely generalized language, although theorists may occasionally borrow concepts from one another. It is true, however, that sexist conceptualization and language remain to be worked out of many of the theories in the third force, as has been already pointed out.

Supporting Feminist Therapy

There is little in the humanistic theories that is inherently unsupportive of feminist or nonsexist psychotherapy. In general, the theories were formulated before the present growth of feminist psychology and neither support nor preclude our concepts.

TOWARD A FEMINIST PERSONALITY THEORY

Within feminist psychology, we still argue about whether it is possible to use and modify the already developed masculine and male-oriented theories that exist, or whether it is necessary to begin development of our own models from our own theoretical bases. The most promising developments here have surprisingly arisen from the outskirts of the psychoanalytic school, especially the *self-in-relationship* work of Jean Baker Miller and her associates (Miller, 1984). The humanistic theories, although congenial to many feminist therapists and psychologists, have not been extended or modified at a theoretical level. Perhaps one reason might be that the theories already are very amorphous and general, and it is difficult to perceive what might derive commonly from them. The problem of the role of the external has been discussed in some detail. Apart from that issue—a very significant one—the humanistic theories generally seem to be potentially compatible with feminist views, although the actual formulation of a feminist model would entail extraneous sexism being eliminated and blind spots being carefully examined in each of the theories.

Allan Buss (1978) suggested that revolutions in psychological thought have been brought about by transforming the subject–object dichotomy. For example, he says that, when psychology shifted from structuralism to behaviorism, it changed its view that the person constructs reality to the view that reality constructs the person. He suggests, too, that psychoanalysis' view that human nature is irrational was a shift from the pre-Freudian view that human beings are rational—a move, in essence, from the personality constructing reality to reality constructing the person. He sees humanistic psychology as a shift from the view that reality constructs the person to the view that the person constructs reality. Buss called for a revolution to end all revolutions, a movement to end the subject–object dichotomy, by viewing the subject–object relation as two-dimensional rather than one-dimensional and thus emphasizing the reciprocal, interactive relationship between the person and reality, so that each may serve as both subject and object. A union of humanistic theory and the feminist perspective might possibly accomplish this revolutionary goal.

REFERENCES

Ballou, M. & Gabalac, N. W. (1985). *A feminist position on mental health.* Springfield, IL: Charles C. Thomas.

Bugental, J. F. T. (1966). Humanistic psychology and the clinician. In L. E. Abt & B. F. Reese (Eds.), *Progress in clinical psychology* (Vol. 7, pp. 223–239). New York: Grune and Stratton.

Buss, A. R. (1978). The structure of psychological revolutions. *Journal of the History of the Behavioral Sciences, 14,* 57–64.

Greenspan, M. (1983). *A new approach to women and therapy.* New York: McGraw-Hill.

Hall, C. S., & Lindzey, G. (1978). *Theories of personality* (3rd ed.). New York: Wiley.

Kasten, K. (1972). Toward a psychology of being: A masculine mystique. *Journal of Humanistic Psychology, 12*(2), 23–43.

Lerman, H. (1986). *A mote in Freud's eye: From psychoanalysis to the psychology of women*. New York: Springer.

Levitin, T., Quinn, R. P., & Staines, G. L. (1971). Sex discrimination against the American working woman. *American Behavioral Scientist, 15,* 237–254.

Maslow, A. H. (1968). *Toward a psychology of being* (2nd ed.). Princeton, NJ: Van Nostrand.

Miller, J. B. (1976). *Toward a new psychology of women*. Boston: Beacon Press.

Miller, J. B. (1984). *The development of women's sense of self* (Work in Progress, No. 12). Wellesley, MA: Stone Center.

Perls, F. S. (1969). *Gestalt therapy verbatim*. Lafayette, CA: Real People Press.

Perls, F. S. (1973). *The gestalt approach and eye witness to therapy*. Ben Lomand, CA: Science and Behavior Books.

Perls, F. S., Hefferline, R. F., and Goodman, P. (1951). *Gestalt therapy: Excitement and growth in the human personality*. New York: Dell.

Rogers, C. R. (1951). *Client-centered therapy: Its current practice, implications, and theory*. Boston: Houghton Mifflin.

Sturdivant, S. (1980). *Therapy with women: A feminist philosophy of treatment*. New York: Springer.

Taylor, M. (1989). Fantasy or reality? The problem with psychoanalytic interpretation in psychotherapy with women. In Erica Burman (Ed.), *Feminists and psychological practice* (pp. 104–118). London: Sage.

CHAPTER TWO

Object Relations and Self Psychology: Overview and Feminist Perspective

BARBARA F. OKUN

In recent decades, object relations and self psychology theories have evolved into major models of contemporary psychoanalysis. Although there are variations among object relations and self psychology theorists, particularly with regard to their foci and the degree of their retention of Freudian concepts, the theorists share some basic philosophical and theoretical concepts: (1) They all emphasize interpersonal relationships rather than innate biological drives as the basis of personality development. (2) They focus on preoedipal development during the first 3 years of life rather than later (age 3–5 years) oedipal conflicts, viewing developmental stages in terms of relationships with objects (e.g., people) rather than development of erotogenital zones. (3) They view pathology as resulting from early developmental arrests or deficits deriving from primary family relationship experiences, where the mother is viewed as the primary caretaker, rather than from intrapsychic conflict between the id, ego, and superego. (4) They view aggression as a response or reaction to frustrating interpersonal relationships rather than as an instinct. (5) They disregard the id and highlight the energetic primacy of the ego in terms of personality development.

With regard to therapy, object relations and self psychology emphasize the role of relationships, stressing the importance of an empathic therapeutic relationship that allows the client to experience and integrate into his or her adult personality the fragmented aspects of the self (along with the accompanying chaotic feelings) defensively split off from the ego in early childhood. Therapy focuses on how present relationships have been distorted and influenced by early primary relationship experiences and interpretations. Emphasis is on environmental influences rather than innate biological factors, on how one develops a self through relationships within one's family of origin and how this self determines the way one relates toward others in adulthood. The empathic therapeutic relationship becomes the single most curative variable in treatment. It provides the necessary context in which repressed parts of the ego or self and repressed unbearably painful feelings can surface, become understood, and integrated with the help of the therapist's supportive interpretation.

The purposes of this chapter are to: (1) present an overview of the theoretical development of object relations and self psychology theory, and (2) consider this model from a contemporaneous feminist perspective. Before beginning the views of representative object relations and self psychology theorists, it is necessary to clarify some basic terms.

DEFINITION OF BASIC TERMS

A fundamental premise of all psychoanalytic models of personality development (classical and contemporary) is that object relations, regardless of the definition and conceptualization of the term *object*, have been and are the central core of psychoanalytic thinking and treatment. The word "object" has different implications for classical and contemporary psychoanalysts. Because it is used so freely as part of professional jargon, it is important to clarify these different implications.

For Freud, "object" referred to the aim or target of the aggressive and libidinal instincts: that which satisfies a need. The object, therefore, may be a thing, a person or a part of a person, or a goal. Since the Freudian view is that the purpose of interpersonal relationships is to release tension from sexual and aggressive instincts, it follows that Freudian thinking did not include the notion of object-seeking drives. The Freudian focus is on the instinctual roots of object relations rather than on the object relations themselves. Object relations in the Freudian sense include relationships between people, between individuals and things, between individuals and goals. These relationships develop in order to satisfy sexual and aggressive needs. Thus, for Freud, constant object relations, the capacity to feel and use the psychological presence of the primary love object even when this object is not present or not approving, can occur only if an integration of libidinal and aggressive instincts and the development of erotogenic zones into genital primacy have been achieved.

For object relations theorists (such as Balint, 1952, 1965, 1968; Fairbairn, 1952, 1954, 1963; Guntrip, 1971; Klein, 1975a, 1975b; Mahler, 1968, 1975; and Winnicott, 1958, 1965, 1971, 1975), objects are defined as other people, both external and internal, both real and imagined. The term *object relations* refers, in general, to the relationship between an individual's internal and external object (person) worlds. The external object is the real person and the internal object is the internalized mental representation—the internal image—of the person, which may or may not resemble the real person. More specifically, the term *mental representation* refers to one's internal images of others based on one's experiences and interpretations of relationships with real, external people. It is important to remember that these mental representations may or may not resemble the actual, observable, external people; they may be distorted and skewed versions of the real objects.

While the definition of object relations differs somewhat among object relations theorists according to their specific conceptualizations, the generic definition given applies broadly to the various theoretical positions. Thus, object relations theories focus on studying the relationships between an individual and real, observable, external people; an individual and his or her psychic internalization or mental representation of these real, external people; and the relationship between internalized residues of an individual's early significant relationships and his or her later interpersonal relationships.

In addition to internal mental representations of external objects, the individual also develops internal representations or images of his or her self, called *self representation*. This internal self-image is also based on actual relationship experiences and is a critical factor in how one later relates to others and the environment. Thus, object relations theory and treatment focuses on how one's present-day relationships are influenced by the internal mental representations of external objects and the internal representation of self, which are residuals from the earliest formation, development, and differentiation of inner images of the self and of the primary caretaking other, the object. One's perceptions of self and others and one's relationships with self and others are derived from the residues of these crucial early relationships with primary caregivers, in particular the mothering person.

Heinz Kohut's self psychology, an American offshoot of object relations theory, emphasizes the influence of earliest primary relationships on the development of self—"the center of the individual's psychological universe," (Kohut, 1977, p. 99)—rather than on the development of the ego or internalized self representations. He focuses on the relation of self to *self object*. Self object refers to the function or service provided by a significant person (not yet differentiated from the child) in the child's environment that the child takes into himself or herself as part of his or her self. This self object becomes part of the self by a process called *transmuting internalization*, which allows the child to form a cohesive self with esteem and a sense of well-being. Transmuting internalization then refers to the process by which the child internalizes the functions and services of significant persons in the environment. These functions and services become part of the child's self structure and functions. An example of a self object might involve the infant's hearing the mother's approaching footsteps and feeling soothed. As the child becomes and older more secure, he or she is able to take over the self-soothing function and tolerate the frustration of not having his or her needs always met by the mother. This capacity to soothe oneself has been transmuted and becomes part of the self. Self objects are necessary throughout life, although they are ultimately symbolized. One might symbolize the mother's earlier soothing capacity by feeling calmed in adulthood when listening to a certain type of music. The goal of maturity is to develop the capacity to cue the self object to one's needs, to be able to engage in dialogue with the self object in order to develop the capacity for engaging in mutually empathic relationships.

Four important defensive processes of object relations and self psychology theory are: *splitting*, whereby one separates parts and processes of objects and feelings, usually separating them into separate good and bad aspects; *projection*, whereby one splits and disowns parts of one's self or feelings and attributes them to another person, believing that the other person owns the parts or feelings that actually belong to the projector; *projective identification*, more primitive than projection, whereby one splits off part of oneself and attributes it to the other person, who unconsciously accepts it and responds as the projector intends; and *introjection*, the fantasy process of taking something perceived in the external world into one's internal world, where it becomes an active, real part of the self and partially reflects the external world.

THEORETICAL DEVELOPMENT

In the early 1900s, several theoretical splinter groups, such as those led by Jung and Adler, had already broken off from Freud. Throughout this century, different schools of psychoanalytic thinking have continued to emerge and develop. Two major developments began around the same time: the interpersonal movement (i.e., Sullivan, Fromm, and Thompson) in this country and the object relations movement in Great Britain. There is some question as to how much knowledge each of these groups had of each other and whether or not they influenced each other. Our brief review of the British school of object relations analysts begins with Melanie Klein, who provided the significant transitional movement away from the Freudian emphasis on innate biological instincts.

The British school of object relations began in the 1930s with Melanie Klein's reformulations of classical psychoanalytic theory based on her actual analytic work with young children. Klein was one of the first theorists to work directly with young children, and this work was the first systematic attempt to study children in the pre-oedipal period. (Freud's theories about childhood were based on the memories of his adult patients and focused on the later, oedipal period of development.)

Klein retained drive theory from Freud, but developed the notion of the child's fantasied representation of drives, calling attention to the critical importance of the early infant–mother relationship. For Klein (1975a; 1975b), instincts seek people as objects. This differs dramatically from the Freudian view that instincts seek pleasure as their aim. Another striking difference is Klein's view that drives are psychological forces using the body as a vehicle for their expression, whereas Freud viewed drives as physiological tensions with psychological manifestations.

The notion that objects are internal fantasies and not images of real people in the child's life is a critical concept developed by Klein and her followers. These internal objects are part of the heritage (both cognitive and constitutional) that the infant brings into the world along with instincts. Where an instinct arises, so does the internal image of an object to satisfy it. When an infant is hungry, he or she fantasizes the image of a nipple on a breast (part object) to provide food. Thus, real people are screens upon which the infant can project his or her internal fantasies. In later life, this is also so: Object relations are based on other people becoming a projection screen for the internal objects of one's psyche.

The child's experience of people in the real world either confirms or disconfirms the experiences of the child's internal object relations. This presumes that the infant is born with cognitive and fantasy capacities that allow him or her to deal with the ambivalent love and hate, libido (life) and aggression (death) instincts present from birth. The infant engages in an internal battle between these two instincts and the ego develops on this battleground. Thus, there are crucial battles within the developing psyche during normal infant development, and we see that Klein retains the Freudian concept of intrapsychic conflict struggle.

Whereas the central human struggle for Freud is between sexual and aggressive drive gratification and the demands of social reality, the central conflict for Klein is between love and hate, between the preservation of caring and the malicious destruction of others. From the beginning of life, the baby internalizes his or her "good" experiences at the mother's breast and projects the "bad" experiences onto the mother's breast. When the infant hates the mother's breast for not being immediately available, the infant projects this hatred onto the mother so that mother is experienced as "bad," as hating the infant, who then experiences *persecutory anxiety*. Thus, when experiencing the mother's breast and later, when the infant can experience the mothering person as a whole, this person becomes both a good and bad object. This paradigm was the first formulation of the infant's primitive anxieties about rejection and persecution and the resultant defenses of splitting and projective identification. These defenses weaken the ego and, if used excessively, can impair ego development. This splitting and projection—where the infant internalizes the "good" and projects onto the outside the "bad" or splits off parts of the self and projects these parts, usually the "bad," onto another person—involve identification with other people because one has attributed qualities of one's own to them. But relationships with external others are distorted due to excessive splitting and projecting, which blur the objective and subjective perceptions.

Klein (1975a) calls the first 6 months of the infant's life the *paranoid–schizoid phase*. During this first developmental phase, the infant realizes his or her total dependence on the mother and is overcome with rage, anxiety, and frustration when his or her needs are not satisfied (which cannot always be done). When good experiences with the mother predominate, the infant dreads losing her but can tolerate her absence, due to the internalization of good images and experiences and the splitting and projective identification of the frustrating (bad) images and experiences. The next developmental stage, the *depressive phase*, occurs between 6 and 9 months of age. During this phase, the infant learns to tolerate the possibility of loss, being sustained by his or her good internal images.

As the infant's ego develops, he or she learns to differentiate and integrate objects, so that bad internal objects and anxiety can be modified internally and transmitted back in a less malignant relationship form. Then the infant becomes able to tolerate frustration and aggression in order to achieve differentiation between self and object. When differentation is achieved, the child learns to tolerate ambivalence, to accept both good and bad in people and one's self, to both love and hate. This enables children to learn to differentiate between fantasy and reality.

Klein's critical contribution focused on the infant's mental image of the mother being distorted by the infant's oral, anal, and genital impulses toward her and by the fantasies aroused in the projection of these anxiety-provoking impulses onto the mother. For Klein, drives become relationships, and it is these relationships that dominate one's emotional life. As with Freud, the origins of psychopathology are internally derived in that the child's aggressive instincts, experienced by feelings of sexuality, guilt and anxiety, create harsh, punitive internal objects that are as influential as real external objects. A predominance of good internalized objects allow for a cohesive ego development, which will lead to satisfactory interactions with others throughout life. A predominance of bad internalized objects weakens the ego and impairs interactions with others throughout life.

Whereas Klein provided important descriptions of the fundamental organizations of object relations and emotional life based on the preoedipal relationship between the infant and mother, she also strove to adhere to the Freudian notion that all significant mental life variables are derived internally from the death instinct. Fairbairn's work carried this thinking further.

In the 1940s, in reaction to the libido-based theories of Freud and Klein, the Scottish psychologist Ronald Fairbairn (1952, 1954, 1963) developed an object relations theory of ego development that was based more on social relationships than on instincts. Fairbairn believed that the ego strives for relationship rather than to serve bodily impulses. This work completed the transition in psychoanalytic theory from Freud's drive–structure model to the object relations psychologists' relational–structural model.

Dismissing the notion of instincts as primary determinants in the formation of personality, Fairbairn postulated that individuals have a primary drive for human contact, for relationships. Pleasure is an outcome of these relationships, not an end in itself. Relationships with objects are essential for ego development, which begins at birth in real (not fantasied) relationship to the mother, the primary caregiver, and which develops gradually throughout infancy and early childhood. With this rejection of Freud's notion of drives, Fairbairn assigned the energy of the id to the ego.

If the infant's real relationship with the mothering person is unsatisfactory, the infant's developing ego sets up within the personality a variety of inner objects to compensate for bad external objects. Thus, Fairbairn believes that the ego is related to its object from birth, and he predicates an initially undivided ego that, by processes of splitting and introjection, controls the anxiety associated with maternal deprivation. The importance of the real mother–infant relationship for healthy personality development is highlighted in Fairbairn's writing. Whereas Klein theorized that the child internalizes and splits off images of its relation to its mother as bad and hateful due to an instinct of hatred, Fairbairn attributes the child's internalization and splitting off images to the mother's actual handling of the child.

Therefore, infantile dependence in the earliest period of life is the pivotal period in ego development. During this period of infantile dependence, the ego splits into three facets: (1) a *libidinal* (need-exciting) self, which retains the positive aspects of the object and provides enticement and excitement; (2) the *antilibidinal* (rejecting, frustrating) self which introjects the negative aspects of the object and provides pain and anger; and (3) the *central ego*, which represses the ambivalence and negative, rejecting experiences internalized as defense against intense pain and which can represent gratification. It is the central ego that is available for relations with real people. If the central ego is too weak because of poor relationship experiences, inner fantasies of relationships predominate over real relationships with real people.

In the course of ego development during infancy, the infant splits off the antilibidinal ego, the schizoid part, and represses it. This schizoid part is comprised of the intense anxiety and pain that accumulate from not having all infant needs met. The infant denies this intolerable pain and in so doing cuts off a part of him or herself from the outer world and relationships, burying this part into an inner world. It is this innermost, hidden, schizoid part that we keep private, that part of us that may seem somewhat inauthentic later in adulthood, that we can only let emerge within the context of intimate, safe relationships.

The core human conflict, according to Fairbairn, involves the developmental urge toward relational dependence. Development begins with the infant's utter dependence on and fusion with the mother and leads to mature dependence on a separate, differentiated object. The goal of healthy development is the capacity for intimate mutual relations with others. Pathology arises when this capacity is impossible due to the excessive splitting and internalization of bad objects, which resulted from deprivation in the mother–infant relationship. Thus, maternal deprivation is the root of psychopathology and suffering. This contrasts with Klein's view that bad objects derive from the child's own inherent death instinct, from the child's inner world, not from real relationships with external objects. Another difference is Fairbairn's view of aggression, thought to be manifested in the form of frustration and pain that results from early maternal deprivation; it is not a primary instinct as it was for Freud and Klein.

Fairbairn (1954) elaborates his concept of fantasy, which represents one's withdrawal and retreat from the basic motivational push towards establishing and maintaining relations with other people, in contrast to Klein's view of fantasy as a basic activity of the mind. For Fairbairn, fantasy and internal objects substitute for unsatisfactory relations with real people and are neither primary nor inevitable.

An important developmental concept of Fairbairn's is the presence of a transitional stage between the infantile dependence stage and the mature adult dependence stage. This transitional stage consists of less repression and more reliance on good objects and leads to the mature, adult dependence stage (the desired goal of development), when one can tolerate frustration with objects and utilize mature love to meet dependency needs.

D. W. Winnicott was a popular British pediatrician during the 1940s and later became a psychoanalyst. Like Fairbairn, Winnicott (1958, 1965, 1971, 1975) believed that the infant is initially psychically merged with the mothering person. Likewise, at first the *good enough mother* (one who is able to gratify the physical and psychological needs of the infant) experiences herself as psychically merged with her baby. So the psychic fusion between mothering person and child is mutual. "There is no such thing as an infant, meaning, of course, that whenever one finds an infant one finds maternal care and without maternal care there would be no infant" (Winnicott, 1975, pp. 52–55). This psychic merging is termed "primary maternal preoccupation" and requires the baby's needs to be foremost for the mothering person. It is this relationship between the mothering person and infant based totally on the baby's needs, as opposed to the mothering person's needs, that allows the baby to develop into a separate, differentiated person. The identification of the mothering person with the infant, the mothering person's capacity to empathize and to provide a psychic umbilical cord that nourishes the developing ego, allows *ego relatedness* to develop. Ego relatedness is the capacity of the ego to develop a sense of security within the self and the environment through good-enough mothering.

As a result of good enough mothering, the baby constructs an internalized image of the mothering person that it can hold in its mind when the mothering person is absent. As the baby begins to recognize and tolerate the mothering person's occasional absence, the baby learns to appreciate both the mothering person's and its own separateness, and the baby's self can develop. Shortcomings or failures in early maternal nurturance lead to splits in the ego. This occurs when mothering persons are "not able to become preoccupied with their own infants to the exclusion of other interests" (Winnicott, 1958, p. 302), because they then fail to anticipate their baby's arising needs. In order for the baby to defend itself against this maternal deprivation, the ego splits into a *true self*, the capacity to relate to the self and others; and a *false self*, the accomodating, pleasing self that complies with the mothering person's needs and behind which hides the authentic true self. Thus, because of maternal deficiencies, the child's ego development is inhibited and the child's false self grows at the expense of the true self. Obviously genuine interpersonal relationships in later life would bear the brunt of this impaired ego development.

The *transitional object* is an important concept developed by Winnicott. This refers to something like a teddy bear, thumb, or blanket (symbolizing certain characteristics and functions originally provided by the mother) that the child uses for self-soothing and security as he or she moves from one level of development (fusion) to a higher level (differentiation). The transitional object becomes the vehicle for the gradual process of separation and individuation from the symbiotic maternal relationship. Throughout life, transitional objects can provide soothing by offering symbolic experiences of early pleasurable merging. Examples include activities like eating, smoking, listening to music, or working, each of which can alleviate anxieties and provide the soothing comfort once provided by the mothering person.

Another of Winnicott's (1958, pp. 29–36) important concepts is the *capacity to be alone*, when the internalization of the environment provides sufficient support and soothing for the ego that one does not have to develop objects for ego relatedness. In other words, maturity

involves the capacity for two people to be with each other interdependently, but retaining the capacity to be separate true selves:
There is balance rather than symbiotic fusion.

Winnicott's (1958) major view is that development cannot occur
without effective parenting. The mothering person, by virtue of her
caring and mirroring, provides a gratifying environment that adapts
to the infant's needs and fosters the emergence of a true rather than
false self. The mothering person's pervasive gratification of the infant's needs enhances the child's omnipotent fantasies ("hallucinations") and allows the infant to progress from absolute dependence to
relative dependence to independence—to an integrated ego. During
the relative dependence stage, the mothering person begins to provide optimal frustration so the infant can learn to differentiate self
and object and realistically modify the omnipotent fantasies. The
important point is that the infant needs to have experienced total
gratification and omnipotence in the early dependency stage in order
to tolerate the gradual separation that leads to independence.

Winnicott defines *psychosis* as environmental deficiency disease,
and all psychopathology is viewed as a result of parental deficiency
that impairs the self by burying the true self and emphasizing the
false self. This psychopathology is manifested in impaired interpersonal relationships—relationships based on false self are troubled—that are derived from primary parenting failure. When troubled, one regresses to that point in time when the parents, representing the environment, failed the child. The goal of therapy, then, is to
compensate for these early parental failures by providing a holding
environment that allows the client's true self to become unstuck and
grow to maturity.

Unlike Freud and Klein, Winnicott (1958) believed the child's
internal world to be an accurate reflection of an uncontradictory
external world. The mothering person is not a projection screen for
the baby's individual perceptions and experiences of gratification or
frustration; she is an actual "good" or "pathological" contributor to
the baby's ego development. Winnicott does not acknowledge differences between the individual's perceptions and actual experiences of
external reality.

Margaret Mahler, who came to New York in the 1940s via Vienna
and London, developed her theories about the psychological birth of
the individual based on her observational investigations. Her work is
conceptually related to Freud's instinct model and the British object
relations theorists, and she focuses on the psychological processes by
which the infant separates and individuates from the mothering
person in order to become an individual. This elaboration of early

developmental processes is a significant contribution to our understanding of infancy and early childhood. Mahler (1968; Mahler, Pine & Bergman, 1975) postulates three developmental phases.

The first phase is the *normal autistic phase*, which occurs in the first month of infancy. This first phase is objectless in that there is no sense of another person and, like Freud's conceptualization, is a period of absolute primary narcissism during which the major task is for the infant to gain some sense of equilibrium outside the womb. The next phase is *normal symbiosis*, which lasts for 5 months. During this phase, the infant is fused with the mothering person and experiences a sense of omnipotence as a result of this psychological fusion. The infant gradually begins to differentiate between good and bad experiences, between pleasure and pain, and ego development commences. The mothering person is experienced as a unitary, omnipotent system and this attachment phase becomes a crucial determinant of later intimate relationships, of the capacity to merge and form attachments. If the infant has a favorable experience of this symbiotic union with the mothering person, then the infant can move on to the third phase, *separation and individuation*, which is necessary to attain a more realistic sense of self and separateness. The processes of separation (involving psychological differentiation, distancing, and formation of boundary from the mothering person) and individuation (involving the development of intrapsychic autonomy) enable the infant to become aware of being a self separate from the mothering person, to develop an original sense of self and of the reality of the external world.

The processes of mother–child interactions critical to ego development are elaborated in Mahler's (Mahler et al., 1975) subphases. These processes include: hatching (shifting from inward-directedness to outward-directedness), which occurs in the first subphase called *differentiation and body image;* practicing (attempting to physically move away from the mothering person while holding on), which occurs in the second subphase called *practicing* or *refueling* (returning to the mothering person for reassurance while practicing separation); shadowing and darting (returning to the mothering person for periodic comfort about separation anxiety after having achieved some physical separation and autonomy) during the third subphase, *rapprochements;* and attaining some degree of object constance and individuality in the fourth subphase, *object constance and individuality.* These subphases occur during the first 3 years of life.

Appropriate timing of these subphases and maternal reactions to them determine their success or failure. Developmental disturbance and borderline and narcissistic disorders can occur if the child's ego development is impaired by inadequate or inappropriate timing of these developmental processes caused by ineffective mothering (Mahler et al., 1975). Thus, object relations in later life (interpersonal relationships) depend on the early mother–child symbiosis and merger as well as the child's successful differentiation and separation. In later intimate relationships, one is looking for some replication of this early gratifying symbiosis or merger with the mother. Mahler et al. (1975) found the practicing and rapprochement subphases that occur during the crucial separation–individuation process to be particularly vulnerable periods in the formation of the self. She postulates that narcissistic and borderline disorders may result from the developmental deficits and arrests occuring during these subphases.

Recent works by developmental psychologists (Kagan, 1984; Stern, 1985) suggest that Mahler's first stage of normal autism is inaccurate, that infants have the cognitive capacities to recognize others in their environment from birth. However, Mahler's delineation of the processes of attachment, separation, and differentiation provided the foundation for understanding both normal and pathological development and influenced the work of others, for example the American theorists Kleinberg and Kohut.

The work of Heinz Kohut (1971, 1977) focuses on the development of the self as an active structure within the context of relationships. His data is based on his analytic work with narcissistic personality disorder patients, and his greatest contribution relates to his development of an understanding of and a treatment for this type of patient. Kohut focuses on the relation of the self to self objects, on understanding human experience as being based on how the infant sought and cued surrounding caretakers to gratify his or her needs and how the infant developed a self from transmuted internalization of self objects. The infant starts with no self but does have innate potential, as well as his or her parents' hopes and projections.

Kohut proposes the concept of a coexisting bipolar self: the archaic *grandiose self* and the *idealized self*, which develop into a cohesive self capable of being connected empathically with others. There is an arc of tension between these two aspects, between the yearning to be admired and responded to *(mirroring needs)* on the one hand and the merging with the competence, wisdom, and calmness of an idealized figure *(idealizing needs)* on the other hand. In other words, there is a dynamic tension between the grandiose self and the idealized parental image continuums. The formation of a cohesive self within the first two or three years of life depends on: (1) the availability of a caretaker's mirroring responses to the grandiose self—the parent's gleam in their eye as they mirror, admire, and empathize with the child's natural exhibitionistic needs, so that the child can internalize others' approval and admiration to form positive self-esteem and a positive self concept; and (2) the capacity of the caretaker to provide strong, competent soothing and empathic conditions for limit setting so that the child can internalize values and ideals and develop an effective superego (Kohut, 1971). Thus, the caretaker's ability to provide optimal frustration and empathic sensitivity and responsiveness to the phase-specific needs of the infant are crucial in order for a cohesive self to develop. The way in which parents shape, guide, and influence the child determines if and how the self becomes integrated into a cohesive self, as opposed to polarized and arrested at the grandiose self pole or the idealizing self pole. Empathic parenting that recognizes the needs of the child as separate from the needs of the parent strengthens harmonious self development. Lack of mirroring, idealizing, and empathic parenting causes fragmentation of self, developmental arrest. These deficits become structured into self disorders, which are manifested in faulty self boundaries and failure to transform and integrate childhood grandiosity into energy, ambition, and self-esteem as well as failure to introject the idealized parent object into an idealized, standard-setting superego.

Thus, good enough mothering, in addition to constitutionally given qualities (i.e., temperament, genetic propensities), allows the child to experience grandiosity at an appropriate phase of development. Gradually, with realistic and empathic mirroring from parents, the grandiose self becomes tamed and merged into the more realistic cohesive self. The mothering person's values, ideals, and standard setting lay the foundation for the development of a superego, comprised of the internalized values and ideals of the self object (caretaker). These experiences allow the infant to develop empathic relationship skills leading to the consolidation of a cohesive self. Kohut (1971, 1977) believes that affect is innate and, with proper parenting, develops into feeling, cognitive awareness, and the mature capacity to feel with another person. Drives are subsumed within this developing cohesive self, and aggression and disintegration occur when the individual is not responded to empathically. Kohut viewed psychopathology as self disorder, emanating from deficits in either pole, in the mirroring or the idealizing self. Severe pathology, such as borderline and narcissistic personality disorders, results from weaknesses of both poles.

Thus, the primary factors contributing to the development of the self are the infant's innate potentials and the appropriate empathic relationship between parents and the child. The parents, responding empathically to the child's needs for mirroring and idealizing, enable the child to develop a self structure by transmuted internalization of their mirroring and idealized soothing into self objects. Self boundaries develop around the beginning of the second year of life and continue throughout life as the child continues to incorporate self objects into one's self.

Kohut's elaboration of empathic relationships in both parenting and therapy emphasizes five transference needs subsumed under mirroring, idealizing, and twinship partnering needs: These include the need to be admired, to have one's dreams, hopes and fantasies recognized; the need to be favored or preferred; the need to be comforted, to have somebody listen and respond empathically; the need to be stimulated and to be attended to; and the need to be forgiven. Kohut's work focusing on people in relation and its implications have contributed significantly to our understanding of both the parenting and healing processes.

SUMMARY OF OBJECT RELATIONS AND SELF PSYCHOLOGY: BASIC TENETS

As we have seen, object relations and self psychology theories focus on the primacy of relationships over innate instinctual drives. More specifically, the initial mother/infant relationship is the single most significant factor affecting the development of the child into a healthy, relating adult. The emphasis of this approach is on the early formation and differentiation of psychological structures that comprise the inner images of the self and others. These inner images, based on actual relationship experiences, particularly with the mothering person, and the infant's interpretations of these relationship experiences, form the basis of later actual interpersonal relationships. The images may be distorted versions of actual persons.

The earliest attachment and separation processes are crucial determinants of later interpersonal relationships, of one's capacity to develop an integrated, individuated self and to form, tolerate, and maintain intimate relationships. Both attachment and separation are necessary developmental processes.

Critical personality development, then, occurs within the first 3 years of life during the preoedipal phase. This development includes the earliest hallucinatory, omnipotent fusion between the mothering person and infant, the oscillations of the separation process, and the achievement of an accepted differentiation and eventual consolidation of self. If all goes well, the child develops the capacity for empathy, for concern, to love and hate simultaneously, and to feel guilt—which serves as a standard-setting guide. If all does not go well, the sense of self is faulty or underdeveloped. Primitive defenses of splitting, projection, and projective identification then predominate and result in ego deficits and fragmentation that cause developmental arrest. This state precludes the possibility of forming, developing, and maintaining the necessary healthy interpersonal relationships that, in turn, provide a context for work and family functioning.

Treatment from this perspective focuses on understanding present interpersonal relationships in terms of past ones, on creating a safe, collaborative empathic relationship (with the characteristics of good enough mothering, mirroring, and idealizing) as a context in which repressed split-off pieces can be brought into consciousness, experienced, and reintegrated into the ego. The focus is on the inner life, the residual internal images of object and self, both conscious and unconsious.

IMPACT OF OBJECT RELATIONS
AND SELF PSYCHOLOGY

Theories must be considered within their context. Given the *zeitgeist* of the 1930s and 1940s, when classical psychoanalytic thinking reigned supreme in the western mental health field and conventional sex-role stereotypes and family styles were unchallenged, object relations and self psychology theories were innovative, courageous paths taken by men and women who had been trained by Freud or his disciples. It is important to remember that our early professional socialization experiences are as crucial to the development of our professional identity as are early family socialization experiences to our personal identity. The revisionist theorists were subject to the disapproval and alientation that accompanies questioning and straying from conventional, mainstream views.

Object relations and self psychology theories represented the first step away from the notion that personality develops solely from innate biological drives. The theorists began to consider the influence of the environment (in the person of the mother) as determining personality development and to develop concepts to explain the interactional relationship between external and internal realities.

The impact of object relations and self psychology theory has been increasing steadily in recent years both within the psychoanalytic movement and within other movements such as family systems theory (Kantor & Okun, 1989; Luepnitz, 1988). The theories provide a comprehensive conceptual understanding of the individual's contribution to relationships that integrates well with the more general contextual contributions to relationships promulgated by systems theories. While there is still tension between the classical and neoanalytical sectors within the psychoanalytic movement, object relations and self psychology have drawn attention to environmental and social factors in the form of the primary caretakers by focusing on relationships. They have also drawn attention to the importance of mental representations, how one's idiosyncratic inner life is based on one's interpretation of reality, and why there are discrepancies between what one experiences in one's inner and external worlds. The notion of the reciprocal influences of internal processing and external reality are pivotal.

The delineation of infant and early child development and preoedipal personality formation and the importance of the influence of early life on later life is another significant contribution. By specifically examining the developmental proccesses of attachment, differentiation, and separation, these theorists have influenced childrearing practices, addressing the qualitative aspects of parenting. Kohut's self psychology, in particular, elaborates the empathic awareness required of parents and their mirroring, confirming, and guiding functions. There is little argument among child developmentalists about the importance of bonding, attachment, and separation in infancy; the argument is over who can provide these processes to the infant and how.

More importantly, object relations and self psychology theories have provided a jumping off point for careful consideration of female development (Chodorow, 1978; Dinnerstein, 1976; Eichenbaum & Orbach, 1983; Miller, 1976). Whereas the original object relations and self psychology theorists did not postulate different gender development, their focus on the mother as the necessary primary parent enabled the above writers to consider the differences of same-gender and opposite-gender primary parenting. They conclude that males and females are socialized differently because of their same-gender or opposite-gender relationship to mother, the primary caretaker. Males and females experience relatedness and separateness differently. Males are taught to separate from mother, the opposite-gender parent, whereas females are taught to remain attached to mother, the same-gender parent. This results in females defining their self in relation and males defining their self in separation. Therefore, males and females experience different vulnerabilities and strengths in the process of maturation and development, and these differences profoundly affect their self concepts as well as their life styles.

Because of gendered differences in attachment and separation experiences with mother, males and females develop different values and capacities for relationships and achievement. For example, there is sufficient research, summarized by Kanfield (1985), to support the notion that women unconsciously fear success because of their anxiety about arousing others' envy and mother's in particular. If they achieve, they may face isolation, loss of connectedness in relationship, as well as loss of their "feminine" identity. The devaluation of females and relationships by our culture and the impact of this devaluation on their gender identity and development has been highlighted by current feminist writers. There is continued dissension over gender-linked values assigned to attachment and separation: Are they equally weighted in value and importance for healthy development for both males and females? Kohut's self psychology focuses on the importance of both individuation and relationship for everyone, on the importance of mutual empathy, twinship partnering, and mirroring in both therapeutic, parenting, and other intimate relationships.

Self psychology theory has also provided insight into the characterology and treatment of severe personality disorders, which seem to be more characteristic of and prevalent in our current culture than the type of hysterical neuroses seen during Freud's day. The theory continues to gain consideration because of its temporal and cultural relevance.

The emphasis on an empathic, more collaborative therapeutic relationship has been highlighted by object relations and self psychology theorists, in reaction to the more distant, authoritative, interpretive therapeutic relationship fostered by Freud. More careful attention to the use of the therapist as a vehicle of change through person-to-person relating, as opposed to interpretive and strategic technique, has resulted.

FEMINIST PERSPECTIVE

When the philosophical and theoretical assumptions of object relations and self psychology theory are considered in the current *zeitgeist*, there are glaring deficiencies. The two major issues that will be discussed are: (1) notions pertaining to gender roles and parenting, and (2) lack of attention to larger sociocultural systems. There are also some methodological weaknesses that must be mentioned.

Like classical psychoanalysis, object relations and self psychology are too dependent on inference and confuse data with interpretation. Therefore, there is a lack of systematic empirical documentation, despite the careful investigation and observation of infants and children. Importance is given to subjective relationship processes that cannot be observed or measured. Infants and babies cannot talk, and we can only infer their feelings based on their behaviors. Furthermore, there is some confusion between normal and pathological development—the development and nature of attachment and separation—and the overlap is unclear.

Another methodological deficiency is that development from age 3 onward is not really attended to by these theories, implying that the first 3 years are the only important developmental period. No consideration is given to the influences of parents on child development after age 3. Some of the early infant concepts have been disproven by current research, which shows that neonates and infants have cognitive capacities and activities heretofore unknown (Kagan, 1984; Stern, 1985).

Gender Roles

Object relations and self psychology theories' focus on mothering as the primary determinant of the child's development represents the most blatantly restrictive account of women's role in our culture and contributes to the already devastating cultural devaluation of women, mother-blaming, and perpetuation of patriarchal society. The basic assumption is that women possess an innate psychological endowment that enables them to merge and subordinate their needs and interests to others, and that this capacity translates into a prevailing maternal instinct. Thus, women who attempt to behave autonomously and self-sufficiently, the norm for male behavior, are viewed as being sick and dangerous to the developing child. Stereotypical norms then predominate, putting women who exhibit active, instrumental, autonomous behaviors and men who exhibit passive, expressive, dependent behaviors into the "pathological" category. Gender norms become polarized and similarities and overlaps between genders, as well as individual differences within genders, are ignored. Furthermore, an implication of this theory is that mothers working outside the home or women who choose not to have children are psychologically disturbed and disturbing, by not adhering to their natural roles.

The theory assumes that the mother–child relationship is both inevitable and necessary and that the father's role is peripheral. This has resulted in the encouragement of gender-unequal child care, which perpetuates imbalances in family relationships and leads to the simultaneous contradictory state of mother-blaming and mother-idealization. In infancy, the mother is experienced by both males and females as an omnipotent object, whose inexhaustible power and resources can both inflict and relieve pain and fear. It is this fear that causes the lifelong aftereffects of the child's rage and fear about his or her early total dependency on the mother in childhood (Dinnerstein, 1976). This fear and the subsequent defensive devaluation of women underlies later adults' struggles to form balanced intimate relationships with others. Men may be unable to risk merger and rejection (similar to what they experienced when their mothers encouraged their separation) and need to retain their control over women in their lives. Women may overcomply to others' needs, fearing their own autonomy (in response to their mothers encouraging them to remain attached) and achievement, as well as their anger and aggressive impulses.

The object relations theoretical account of child development pathologizes those women who do not adapt well enough to the baby's needs and, therefore, mothers are blamed for the baby's ego splits and later pathology. There is no acknowledgment of the sociocultural influences on the mother–infant relationship, such as the changing roles and positions of women, and of the fact that splits are inevitable because there are always ambivalences and contradictions in social interactions and relationships.

Our sociocultural values influence the devaluation of women and mothering. Both men and women reinforce these sociocultural values. Chodorow (1978) and Dinnerstein (1976) show us how stereotypes of mothers become perpetuated over generations as women continue to be reared to view themselves as the primary parent. Mothers, then, become the overwhelming targets of love and hate for both male and female offspring, seen as powerfully rejecting or engulfing throughout life. The object relations and self psychology theories do not address gender characteristics relating to parenting, how the realities of structural power relations ascribe unequal dominant economic, social, and political power to the father, leaving the mother to exercise her limited power—relational power—in her relationships with her children. Her identity becomes tied to her children and their successes and failures become hers. Her children are taught to adopt these gendered roles and carry them on as adults into their own families. Females fear their own aggressive, competitive strivings, and males are equally fearful of acknowledging their own passive, dependent yearnings.

Lerner (1984) addresses the cultural devaluation of women by commenting on the object relations theorists' emphasis of the mother's breast in early infancy. Fairbairn (1954, p. 121) states "the breast is the earliest source of gratification and frustration, of love and hate as well as the first vehicle of intimate social contact." Klein (1975a, pp. 5–6) writes that "the breast in its good aspect is the prototype of maternal goodness, inexhaustible patience and generosity as well as of creativeness." For Klein, the desire to internalize and possess the breast is the infant's way of internalizing power and magic. This early matriarchy is a threat to both male and female infants, who spend the rest of their lives attempting to defend themselves by comfortably adopting to the larger patriarchal society or by risking anxiety and alienation by not conforming to social mores.

Another point to consider is the heightened ambivalence of mother–daughter relationships that is an outcome of these socialized gendered developments. The mutual identification of mother and daughter results in a mutual dependency and lifelong struggle. This complicates the girls' struggle for autonomy. She receives a very powerful mixed message, which gets perpetuated through the generations, from her mother, who tends to experience her as an extension: "Achieve what I have been unable or not allowed to do, but do not grow up and leave me." Thus, anxiety and guilt accompany autonomy, and females grow up feeling totally responsible for others. This puts them at psychological risk, because this scripting leads them to fuse with others, depending on others for their identity and sense of worth yet unable to control others and actively determine their own fate. This results from the socialized gendered developments elaborated by Chodorow (1978) and Eichenbaum and Orbach (1983).

Just as Klein's focus on internal reality ignored the extent of external social reality conditioning and Winnicott's theory overlooked contradictions between external reality and the child's interpretation, there is no understanding in object relations or self psychology theories of how the unequal power of mothers and the cultural devaluation of women shape the mother's psychology, as well as the psychology of male and female offspring.

There is no attention given to how infants influence mothers' attitudes and behaviors. Bassoff (1987) asserts that, with few exceptions, research emphasizes the effects of the mother's behavior on the child to the exclusion of the effects of the child's behavior on the mother. Certainly the mother/child relationship is interactive and reciprocal, just as there is a reciprocal influence among subsystems, between subsystems and the larger family system, and between the family system and other social systems. In object relations and self psychology theories, there is no attention paid to different styles and varieties of family organization and of childrearing practices. In fact, there is little attention to the effects of ethnicity, socioeconomic class, or race on parenting and family styles as well as on development, both normal and pathological.

A feminist analysis would raise questions that include: How are women who themselves did not receive "good enough mothering" supposed to supply it to their offspring? What about the influence of the marriage relationship and the different types and styles of couple and family systems on parenting? What are the benefits and hazards of maternal attachment and how does it affect the father's relationship to the children? Are attachment and separation equally valued and weighted for both males and females?

The theorists seem to have defined "good enough mothering" but have not defined "good enough fathering." Fathering is not really explored by the theories, although the implication is that the father will help the children to separate from the mother. Yet, recent research on attachment by Lamb (1981) and Pruett (1983) indicates that when fathers or others are involved with infants, attachments are formed, suggesting that both male and female parents have the capacity to form caretaking attachments. Parents' styles may be different, and there is often an undermining power struggle between the genders within the family to define and control parenting styles and functions. This power struggle has resulted from gender polarization, from the fact that womens' power has been confined to the private sphere, the family, whereas men have exercised power in the public sphere, outside the family (Okun, 1989).

Children do have attachment needs, and our devaluation of parenting on a society level has adverse effects on society's responsibilities to help parents, both male and female, attend to these needs. Brazleton (1987) refers to the detrimental effects of the isolation of the mother–child dyad from wider social factors, particularly within single-parent families. This may be particularly true with middle- and upper-class single-parent families; lower-class single-parent families tend to be embedded in larger extended families. Brazleton also suggests a massive reorganization of our occupational system with full societal support to achieve shared parenting that allows parental preoccupation for the first 4 months of an infant's life. Whereas equally shared parenting as suggested by many feminist writers might be the ideal objective, the realities of our current occupational organization and the increase of single-parent families suggest that interim alternative solutions be supported.

Systems

Like classical psychoanalysis, object relations and self psychology ignore the sociocultural context of internal conflicts. True, the theories do focus on the mother's powerful influence, but the mother's role and functioning are not considered within a larger sociocultural context. Likewise, since pathology is thought to emanate strictly from internal conflicts, the implication follows that the use of primitive defenses such as projection, splitting, and projective identification is a sign of pathology. This scheme of thought underestimates the power of contextual events to undermine even the most well-integrated among us. Object relations and self psychology theories replicate the medical model focus on intrapsychic conflicts as the only source of pathology, ignoring the possibility of a different type of dysfunction emanating from contextual events or the possibility of a synergistic effect of both internal and external sources of conflict. In other words, they do not consider how pathology may reflect conflict between the individual and society, between stereotypical and alternative sex roles or life styles.

It becomes clear that gender differences, while biologically influenced, are primarily a result of social dominance. These theories pay no attention, however, to the social, political, historical, and economic determinants of family systems and to the concept of social dominance. There are many influences and determinants of family life that originate outside the family. Likewise, within the family, inadequate attention is given to the realities of unequal power structures and to the low priority of parenting activities. Certainly this low priority results in social and economic dependence, which furthers the imbalance within the structure of the family and affects the quality of family relationships. For example, family and larger sociocultural systems exert powerful pressures to ensure conformity to systems rules and mores. The alienation and anxiety that one experiences by not conforming are well documented.

In addition, these theories have ignored social learning theory, which focuses on imitation, modeling, and social reinforcement; and cognitive development, which focuses on the capacities of the infant to interpret and organize behaviors. The fact that the nature of the mother/infant attachment differs for male and female infants may be influenced by the behavioral cues, responses, and reinforcements of the relationship, as well as by the infant's capacities for cognitive processing. The research by Mahler et al., (1975) and Stoller (1976, 1977), which shows that girls emerge from their preoedipal separation and individuation struggle (between 18 months and 3 years) with a core feminine identity, suggests that parental sex role assignment and cultural and social child-rearing attitudes are more important than biological and hormonal factors (the predominance of which would suggest that infants are born with gender identity). The child's socialization experience as male or female shapes his or her cognitive schema (Bem, 1981), which are comprised of the content, form, and process of perceptions and thinking. Cognitive schema determine the beliefs (views of self and the world) that impact behaviors.

There is a danger of polarization, of overbiasing ourselves in an overly reactive fashion to mainstream thinking. We then can become just as doctrinaire as the theorists we react against. We need to attend carefully to androgynous needs of both males and females—how men sense themselves as relational and how women sense themselves as separate or individuated, how males and females share the same aspirations for relation and mastery. While we need to incorporate a sociocultural and systems viewpoint in order to actively empower clients to examine their internal and external realities in relationship to each other and to actively and politically impact these realities, we also need to acknowledge and attend to the powerful influences of early family life and rich internal fantasy.

The emphasis on separation–individuation by object relations and self psychology theories has been criticized by Miller (1976, 1989) and her colleagues at the Stone Center. These theorists believe that womens' development is primarily relational, that the self can only develop within the context of connectedness and, therefore, that the object relations and self psychology goal of autonomy does not apply to women. Their focus is not only on the mother–daughter relationship, but also on the marital, familial, and larger sociocultural contexts of what they consider to be primary relationships ignored by the traditional theories.

Object relations and self psychology theories can be useful in helping us to bring to consciousness social as well as intrapsychic conflict and contradictions. As Sayers (1986) points out, psychoanalysis stops when individuals become conscious of their realities, of the conflicts between individual needs and society's oppressions. Feminist therapy begins with this recognition and works to bring about the changes in society necessary to fully meet the needs of clients. In a stunning argument for object relations psychoanalytic theory as a conceptual source for feminist psychotherapy, Luepnitz (1988, p. 169) states that "psychoanalytic theory, for all its errors and anachronisms, continues to be a most subtle and powerful means of understanding patriarchy . . . feminism is necessary to bring psychoanalysis to its full radical potential." The personal is political and the political is personal.

REFERENCES

Balint, M. (1952). *Primary love and psycho-analytic technique.* London: Tavistock.

Balint, M. (1965). *Primary love and psychoanalytic technique.* New York: Liveright.

Balint, M. (1968). *The basic fault: Therapeutic aspects of regression.* London: Tavistock.

Bassoff, E. S. (1987). Mothering adolescent daughters: A psychodynamic approach. *Journal of Counseling & Development, 65*(9), 471–474.

Bem, S. (1981). Gender scheme theory: A cognitive account of sex-typing. *Psychological Review, 88*(4), 354–364.

Brazleton, T. B. (1987, March 27). *Changing perceptions: Child development and child care.* Presented at the annual meeting of the American Orthopsychiatric Association, Washington, D.C.

Chodorow, N. (1978). *The reproduction of mothering: Psychoanalysis and the sociology of gender.* Berkeley: University of California Press.

Dinnerstein, D. (1976). *The mermaid and the minotaur.* New York: Harper & Row.

Eichenbaum, L., & Orbach, S. (1983). *Understanding women: A feminist psychoanalytic view.* New York: Basic Books.

Fairbairn, W. R. (1952). Endopsychic structure considered in terms of object relationships. *Psycological studies of the personality.* London: Tavistock.

Fairbairn, W. R. (1954). *An object-relations theory of the personality.* New York: Basic Books.

Fairbairn, W. R. (1963)., Synopsis of an object-relations theory of the personality. *International Journal of Psychoanalysis, 44,* 224–225.

Guntrip, H. (1971). *Psychoanalytic theory, therapy, and the self.* New York: Basic Books.

Kagan, J. (1984). *The nature of the child.* New York: Basic Books.

Kanfield, L. (1985). Psychoanalytic construction of female development and women's conflicts about achievement. *Journal of the American Academy of Psychoanalysis, 13*(20), 229–246.

Kantor, D., & Okun, B. F. (Eds.) (1989). *Intimate environments: Intimacy, sex and gender in families.* New York: Guilford.

Klein, M. (Ed.) (1975a). *Envy and gratitude and other works: 1946–1963.* New York: Delacorte Press.

Klein, M. (1975b). *Love, guilt and reparation and other works: 1921–1945.* London: Hogarth Press.

Kohut, H. (1971). *The analysis of self.* New York: International Universities Press.

Kohut, H. (1977). *The restoration of the self.* New York: International Universities Press.

Lamb, M. (Ed.). (1981). *The role of the father in child development* (2nd ed.). New York: Wiley.

Lerner, H. G. (1984). Early origins of envy and devaluation of women. In P. R. Reiker & E. H. Carmen (Eds.). *The gender gap in psychotherapy: Social realities and psychological processes.* (pp. 111–124). New York: Plenum Press.

Luepnitz, D. A. (1988). *The family interpreted: Feminist theory in clinical practice.* New York: Basic Books.

Mahler, M. (1968). *On human symbiosis and the vicissitudes of individuation.* New York: International Universities Press.

Mahler, M., Pine, F., & Bergman, A. (1975). *The psychological birth of the human infant: Symbiosis and individuation.* New York: Basic Books.

Miller, J. B. (1976). *Toward a new psychology of women.* Boston: Beacon Press.

Miller, J. B. (1989, June). *Self in relation theory.* Panel discussion at the 1989 Conference on Women, Harvard Medical School, Cambridge, MA.

Okun, B. F. (1989). Therapists' blind spots related to gender socialization. In D. Kantor & B. F. Okun (Eds.). *Intimate environments: Sex, intimacy and gender in families.* (pp. 129–163). New York: Guilford.

Pruett, K. D. (1983). Infants of primary nurturing fathers. *Psychoanalytic Study of the Child, 38,* 257–277.

Sayers, J. (1986). *Sexual contradictions: Psychology, psychoanalysis and feminism.* London: Tavistock.

Stern, D. N. (1985). *The interpersonal world of the infant: A view from psychoanalysis and developmental psychology.* New York: Basic Books.

Stoller, R. (1976). *Sex and gender: Vol. 2. The transsexual experiment.* New York: Jason Aronson.

Stoller, R. (1977). Primary femininity. In H. P. Blum (Ed.). *Female psychology: Contemporary psychoanalytic views.* New York: International Universities Press.

Winnicott, D. W. (1958). *The maturational processes and the facilitating environment.* New York: International Universities Press.

Winnicott, D. W. (1965). *The family and individual development.* New York: Basic Books.

Winnicott, D. W. (1971). *Playing and reality.* London: Tavistock.

Winnicott, D. W. (1975). *Collected papers: Through paediatrics to psychoanalysis.* London: Hogarth Press.

CHAPTER THREE

Beyond Archetypes: A Feminist Perspective on Jungian Theory

JO ROMANIELLO

The conceptualizations, writings, and theories of Carl Gustave Jung have had a wide, but not always acknowledged, impact on the world of modern personality psychology. Jung's unique deviations from the prevalent psychoanalytic theory of his day did much to advance our understanding of psychology. His attempts to deal with "feminine" principles have resulted in some of the contemporary appeal of his work:

> For nonfeminist Jungian women, Jung's validation of the "feminine" has great appeal. They find permission in his psychology to be "feminine," as well as to actualize their "masculine" side. In a world where women now compete on male terms, Jungian women (many of whom are successful in the "outer" world) feel vindicated in relying on what Jung would call their "feminine instinct." (Wehr, 1987, p. 6)

For many women who are Jungian analysts and authors, Jung's psychology describes their own personal experience and that of women in general. His separation of "masculine" and "feminine" in the very structure of his theory opened possibilities for the understanding of women's psychology. The work of these Jungian women has contributed much to the process of understanding Jung from a woman's perspective. Although their work does not necessarily embody a feminist perspective, it deserves comment and will be touched upon in this chapter.

The appeal of Jung's work to women has also called forth feminist scrutiny and criticism. To that end, many prominent feminists such as Mary Daly and Naomi Goldenberg have condemned the work of Jung, as well as that of the female Jungians. These feminists, not bound to Jung's theories as a point of departure, have raised significant questions regarding the underlying assumptions about women embedded in Jungian psychology. Despite its potential, Jung's apparent validation of the "feminine" was anchored in androcentrism. Although appealing, Jungian theory must be examined from a perspective that honors women's understanding of their own ways of knowing, psychology, and context.

There have been those who have attempted to synthesize the seemingly conflicting ideologies of Jungian psychology and feminism. For example, Polly Young-Eisendrath, a self-identified feminist Jungian analyst, notes:

> Despite the androcentrism of some Jungian concepts, Jung's theories and methods provide unique means for understanding symbolic expressions and for transcending personal loss. A feminist approach to therapy using Jungian psychology is easily accessible and is consistent with Jung's theory of psychic development . . . (Young-Eisendrath, 1984, p. 24)

Others, like Linda Leonard, Brinton Perera, and Jean Shinoda Bolen, have also applied Jungian theory in ways that seek to incorporate feminist principles. Like the nonfeminist Jungian women, their efforts at synthesis have contributed to an expanded understanding of women's psychology in specific ways.

This chapter attempts to clarify some of the controversy surrounding Jung's theories in relation to feminism and contains appreciations of the work done by both nonfeminist and feminist Jungian women. However, this chapter also contends that the new psychology of women demands that we, as women, must go beyond the constructs and constraints of traditional theory. A feminist analysis of Jung's work is an essential step in that process.

Jung's work is extensive and complex; it is not easily distilled or summarized. This chapter focuses on selected aspects of his work. It reviews concepts most relevant to a feminist discussion, and does not provide an in-depth assessment of Jungian theory. The critique that follows gives a feminist analysis of selected theoretical points. There is a general focus on Jung, his views of women, and the relationship of his viewpoints to the structure of his theory. Specific attention is given to the archetype, because it is both a concept central to Jungian theory and to a feminist analysis of Jungian thought. The work of selected feminist and nonfeminist Jungians is briefly examined before the final summary and recommendations.

OVERVIEW

For Jung, the total personality is the *psyche*. It is comprised of several interacting systems: *ego, personal unconscious, collective unconscious,* various *complexes, persona,* and the *archetypes*—such as the *anima–animus, shadow,* and *mother.* The *self,* another archetype, is the center or unifying midpoint of the personality.

Initially, Jung conceptualized the self as the totality of the psyche. As he continued to study symbolism and the racial foundations of personality, he described the self as the energetic center of the psyche, around which all other systems revolve:

> This centre is not felt or thought of as the ego but, if one may so express it, as the *self.* Although the centre is represented by an innermost point, it is surrounded by a periphery containing everything that belongs to the self—the paired opposites that make up the total personality. This totality comprises consciousness first of all, then the personal unconscious, and finally an indefinitely large segment of the collective unconscious whose archetypes are common to all mankind. (Jung, 1959, p. 357)

For Jung, the center is not immediately accessible to consciousness or ego-experience, but rather is something that is glimpsed. As an individual attains greater psychic integration, these glimpses of the self become more frequent.

The ego is the conscious mind, primarily comprised of a general awareness of one's body and existence. Secondarily, it is constituted of memory (Jung, 1968). The self exists in delicate balance with the ego. Jung believed that the self contains a great deal of unconscious material that exerts considerable influence on the ego. It is important, then, to fix clear boundaries, lest the ego be overpowered by the unconscious contents. In the reverse, if the self is assimilated into the ego, its image of wholeness can be rendered inaccessible. The ego is also closely related to the persona, or the role assigned to individuals by society. When the ego identifies with this public personality, individuals become more concerned with their social role than with their true feelings, and a sense of personal alienation can set in.

The unconscious is divided into two regions, the personal unconscious and the collective unconscious. The personal unconscious adjoins the ego and consists of experiences that were once conscious, such as those now forgotten, repressed, or ignored. These contents are accessible to the ego. Also within the personal unconscious are organized groups of thoughts, feelings, memories, and perceptions that revolve around a thematic center or nucleus—the complexes.

These complexes can take control of the personality when the associations from the normally unconscious nucleus and related elements intrude into consciousness. An example, in Jungian terms, is the individual with a mother-complex, who is dominated by feelings, thoughts, ideas, and childhood memories about the mother.

The collective unconscious is a deeper layer of unconsciousness. Unlike the personal unconsciousness, it does not contain once-conscious experiences. Rather, the contents of the collective unconscious include material and modes of behavior common to all individuals. There is a "common psychic substrate of a suprapersonal nature which is present in every one of us" (Jung, 1959, p. 4). The collective unconscious is viewed as a reservoir of imagery. Jung believes that the primordial imagery in the collective unconscious is inherited from a past that includes human, prehuman, and animal ancestry. It is not a conscious inheritance; rather, these images are predispositions for experiencing the world in ways similar to that of our ancestors. For example, humans are likely to fear snakes due to an inherited tendency built into the psyche by past ancestral experiences. Such a predisposition might then be strengthened by an actual experience with snakes in the present. The tendency to fear snakes is already in the collective unconscious, predisposing the individual to a frightening experience in the present.

The contents of the collective unconscious are instincts and archetypes. Instincts are physiological urges that can be perceived by the senses. Jung theorizes that, when instincts manifest themselves in fantasy or through symbolism, they are archetypes (Jung, 1964b). This archetypal "stuff" of the collective unconscious consists of primordial images that have existed since the dawn of time. There are many archetypes, such as those of death, energy, power, unity, the hero, the old wise man, the earth mother, God, and the demon. Archetypes contain a large element of emotion; as such they drive human beings to repeat and elaborate on their past experiences.

For example, the archetype of energy drives people to search for new energy sources. The manifestations of this archetype can be seen in the scientist's obsession to split the atom. Jung found confirmation for the existence of archetypes in the content of dreams, in fantasies produced by deliberate concentration, and in the delusions of psychotic individuals. Motifs of archetypal imagery not consciously known nevertheless show up in these forms of expression. In Jung's theory building, the repetition and commonality of the archetypal imagery across generations and cultures renders them timeless and universal. This important concept will be critically examined later.

The images of the unconscious archetypes become accessible to the conscious mind through *projection*. "Projection is an unconscious, automatic process whereby a content that is unconscious to the subject transfers itself to an object, so that it seems to belong to that object" (Jung, 1959, p. 60). The archetypes can be mirrored in the events of nature or when the individual resists the archetype within, only to discover it projected onto another person. Jung believes that a person is well-adjusted only when the realities of the external world are balanced with the demands of the collective unconscious.

The shadow, anima–animus, and mother archetypes are particularly significant to Jungian theory and feminist thought. The shadow archetype is comprised of human's inherited animal instincts. Therefore, the shadow typifies the animal side of human nature. It is that part of us responsible for the presence in conciousness of socially reprehensible behavior, thoughts, or feelings. It is our dark and private side:

> The shadow is a moral problem that challenges the whole ego-personality, for no one can become conscious of the shadow without considerable moral effort. To become conscious of it involves recognizing the dark aspects of the personality as present and real. This act is the essential condition for any kind of self-knowledge, and it therefore, as a rule, meets with considerable resistance. (Jung, 1959, p. 8)

Jung recognized the shadow as having a distinctly emotional nature. As such, it can have an autonomous, possessive quality. Resistance to aspects of the shadow can easily be bound up in projection. The intense emotion that is characteristic of the shadow makes the recognition of these projections extremely difficult. The lack of recognition intensifies the unconscious projection-making mechanism. Consequently, "the effect of the projection is to isolate the subject from his environment, since instead of a real relation to it there is now only an illusory one, the projection changes the world into the replica of one's own unknown face" (Jung, 1959, p. 9). An important distinction must be made about the shadow: It is a motif that represents both an aspect of personal unconscious and an archetype. Self-criticism allows us to break through the personal nature of the shadow, or see one's own dark side, but when the archetype of the shadow dominates, we are faced with the terrifying possibilities of the dark side of humankind.

Jung's concept of duality in human nature, as represented by the shadow, is again seen in the manifestation of the archetypes of anima–animus. The anima and animus represent the contrasexual contents within the female and male, respectively. Jung believed that a man has a primarily masculine consciousness and a feminine unconsciousness, while the opposite is true for a woman. These archetypes influence and inform our understanding of and response to members of the opposite sex. However, because the images of the anima or animus often take on a personified form, they, like the shadow, can initiate misunderstanding. The anima or animus can become projection-making factors that show little regard for the real nature of one's partner. For example, love at first sight is often the result of the projection of one's anima (or animus) onto the beloved. In a man, according to Jung, the beloved becomes the carrier of the ageless images and outstanding characteristics of the feminine being. When a man is under the influence of this unconscious projection, he is unable to recognize the real nature of the actual woman. The corresponding mechanism is true for women. Frequently, it is the man's anima that meets and falls in love with the woman's animus. Note the profound impact Jung ascribes to this archetype:

> The anima is a factor of the utmost importance in the psychology of man wherever emotions and affects are at work. She intensifies, exaggerates, falsifies, and mythologizes all emotional relations with his work and with other people of both sexes. The resultant fantasies and entanglements are all her doing. When the anima is strongly constellated, she softens the man's character and makes him touchy, irritable, moody, jealous, vain, and unadjusted. (Jung, 1959, p. 70)

The force of the animus is equally important for a woman. However, it is already obvious that Jung has some very definite conceptions about the characteristics of feminine and masculine beings. From a feminist perspective, the content of these archetypes is of particular interest and will be dealt with in greater depth later.

The archetype of mother, like that of the anima–animus, rests in a prehistoric reservoir of imagery. The mother-image is also a projection-making factor in relationships. As a result of his study in history and mythology, Jung ascribed to the mother archetype numerous aspects ranging from actual mother and grandmother roles to highly symbolic imagery such as the moon, cornucopia, or ploughed field. The qualities of this feminine archetype are:

> Maternal solicitude and sympathy; the magic authority of the female; the wisdom and spiritual exaltation that transcend reason; any helpful instinct or impulse; all that is benign, all that cherishes and sustains, that fosters growth and fertility. The place of magic transformation and rebirth, together with the underworld and its inhabitants, are presided

over by the mother. On the negative side the mother archetype may connote anything secret, hidden, dark; the abyss, the world of the dead, anything that devours, seduces, and poisons, that is terrifying and inescapable like fate. (Jung, 1959, p. 82)

This archetype forms a base for the mother-complex discussed earlier. Jung believed that this complex is different for a son or daughter. The expression of this complex in the son is made difficult by issues of sexuality and his projected anima archetype onto the mother. In the daughter, the complex is clear and uninvolved, having to do with "an overdevelopment of feminine instincts indirectly caused by the mother, or with a weakening of them to the point of complete extinction" (Jung, 1959, p. 86). As with the anima–animus, the mother archetype, which plays an important part in the development of the personality, needs to be questioned in terms of its underlying assumptions about women. For example, what exactly are "feminine instincts"?

Before exploring these issues in the critique, it is important to touch upon Jung's views of *individuation*. In his analytic psychology, Jung postulated a developmental approach. Humans progress toward a more complete stage of development characterized by the increasing ability to realize themselves as distinct from other humans around them (i.e., to differentiate). The goal of human development is individuation (or self-realization), which means the harmonious blending of all aspects of the psyche. According to Jung, when the psyche is individuated, the ego can make fine distinctions in its perceptions of the world and the substance of the personal and collective unconscious can express itself in more subtle ways. For Jung, the process of individuation is a compelling drive, with each individual developing from an undifferentiated state of wholeness into a differentiated, individual, balanced personality. "During individuation, theoretically the ego comes to realize that its feeling of supremecy is false, as its "centrality" is replaced by an increasing governance of the archetype of the self" (Wehr, 1987, p. 100).

JUNGIAN PSYCHOLOGY AND FEMINISM

By 1910, Jung had deviated enough from Freudian theory to preside over his own institution, the International Psychoanalytic Association. His appeal was mainly to an upper-middle-class intellectual audience. Like Freud, Jung lived in a time when women were bound by sex-role constraints. Women did not enjoy the public life that men did. They were expected to be compliant in their roles as daughter, wife, sister, and mother. They held less-than-powerful positions in the various male-dominated societal systems—the state, church, and family. Therefore, Jung's theories must be assessed with a recognition of the culture-bound influences on his life and work.

Jung's *Women in Europe* (1964), written in the latter part of his life, provides insight into the evolutional process of his thoughts on the subject of women. In this work, he attempts to recognize the changes in social structure that allowed women to "take up masculine professions, become active in politics, to sit on committees . . ." (p. 117). While Jung recognizes this change toward social independence as a courageous, self-sacrificing economic necessity, he goes on to say, "But no one can get round the fact that by taking up a masculine profession, studying and working like a man, woman is doing something not wholly in accord with, if not directly injurious to, her feminine nature" (p. 117). The injury Jung alludes to would presumably be both physiological and psychic. Jung's opinion is that, since a predominant characteristic of woman is to do "anything for the love of a man," it is uncharacteristic for her to do anything for the love of a "thing" (p. 118). He clearly states "a man should live as a man, and a woman as a woman" (p. 118). Jean Shinoda Bolen (1984) notes that:

> Although Jung did not see women as inherently defective, he did see them as inherently less creative and less able to be objective or take action than men. In general, Jung tended to see women as they served or related to men, rather than as having independent needs of their own. (p. 41)

Jung's attitudes about women are fused with his theories, both in terms of structure and content. His works, in many ways, foster traditional sex roles and demonstrate his expectations for and denigration of women.

It can be argued that the later Jungians, especially women who consider themselves Jungians, seek to transcend the androcentrism in Jungian theory. However, it is important to acknowledge how difficult that task is:

> Androcentrism drowns or silences women's voices and perceptions by the continual pouring-out of male perceptions into the world. It conveys the messge of women's inferiority to them on a subtler, deeper level than does simple negative treatment or belittlement. (Wehr, 1987, p. 16)

Such androcentrism is subtle and pervasive throughout Jungian psychological theory. Ann Belford Ulanov, a Jungian who wrote extensively about the feminine in Jungian psychology, explains her attraction to his particular theories: "Because Jung focuses on the feminine in an original way that consistently respects the unique qualities of the feminine, I have chosen him to represent the psychological point of view" (Ulanov, 1978, p. 3). This statement both evidences Ulanov's admiration of Jung and gives striking contrast to his opinions of women as quoted previously. The contrast points out just how difficult it is to separate inherent sexism from value in Jungian theory.

In her work on Jung and feminism, Demaris Wehr (1987) clearly identifies the cause of ambivalence when assessing Jung's views:

> I will focus instead on a particular aspect of patriarchy's wounding of women's self-esteem; internalized oppression and how it can be fostered by Jungian psychology as it stands. "Internalized oppression" refers to the process by which women internalize patriarchal society's definition of themselves. This definition is oppressive, negative and inferior in many ways, although it is also often compensatory and romantically "exalted." (p. 10–11)

It is precisely such internalized oppression that makes unbiased assessment of Jungian psychology so difficult. Can Jungian theory, built on such a foundation of cultural and gender bias, be in any way adequate to describe women's psychology? Is there even enough room to start the conceptual process? Feminist theologian Mary Daly is emphatic in her opinion: "C. G. Jung, whose theories are pernicious traps which often stop women in the initial stages of mind-journeying . . ." (Daly, 1978, p. 253). If, as Ulanov and many others suggest, the strength of Jung's psychology is in his "original" focus on the feminine, then we must be critically attuned to the origin of that focus, lest we find ourselves stopped or, more dangerously, oppressed on our journey.

In addition to cultural bias and androcentrism, Jung's work is further marked by his training. As a psychiatrist, he was instructed in a medical approach:

> Jung was a physician and despite his challenge to the medical model on such issues as whether diagnosis is useful, he continued to describe analytic work in the terminology of the medical profession, for example, "doctor," "psychotherapy," and "healing." (Matoon, 1981, p. 234)

The medical model seeks to identify and heal symptoms and disease: to fix, change, or somehow intervene to help human beings to achieve health. It requires an "expert" to make the necessary assessments and implement the required healing. The relationship between doctor and patient is hierarchical by nature. The power imbalance engendered in such a relationship, left unquestioned, can have critical negative impact:

> Feminists believe that non-hierarchical egalitarian relationships should exist in human interaction and in institutional settings. They hold that oppressive (non-egalitarian) social structures and relationships have delimited and shaped women's status and often self-deliniation. . . . feminists contend that the accumulation of knowledge has been controlled by a male hierarchy and the shaping of knowledge has occurred in accordance with male criteria of achievement, performance and so on . . . (Ballou & Gabalac, 1985, p. 23)

The quotation points out how Jung is once again trapped by his perspective. There exists in Jungian theory the underlying assumption that the psyche starts out as somehow imperfect, needing remediation and adjustment of some kind. The goal of this adjustment is predicated on an understanding of what is healthy. Secure in his professional training and outlook, Jung formulated a model that defines health. The danger with such a model, especially one implemented in the context of a hierarchical relationship, is that the underlying assumptions in the definition of health go unchallenged. In contrast to Jungian analysis, "feminist therapy does not impose any model of health but rather seeks to assist women in evolving and developing their own critique, analysis, skills, options, and criteria" (Ballon & Gabalac, 1985, p. 66).

Indeed, many (female) Jungians, while building therapeutic methodologies on the foundation of Jungian psychological theory, often add qualifiers when discussing their applications of that theory to women:

> If we seek from Jung a precise definition of the feminine, we will still seek in vain. . . . To gather the full wisdom of Jungian psychology of the feminine, therefore, it is necessary to piece together a mosaic of quotation and paraphrase from Jung and his followers. (Ulanov, 1971, p. 154)

> Jungian methods fill out these basic strategies (for change) in ways which are quite compatible with feminist therapy, provided we clarify the use of certain theoretical concepts as they impinge on technique. . . . As a feminist and a Jungian, I focus on four particular contributions made by Jung in the work I do in analysis and psychotherapy. (Young-Eisendrath, 1984, p. 27)

The implications of this creative adaptation of Jungian theory will be addressed later. The theoretical construct of Jungian theory will be explored next.

The focus of Jungian theory is clearly intrapsychic. From a feminist perspective, rather than confining our understanding of the personality to a single phenomenon of intrapsychic forces, we must take a pluralistic view and recognize the interaction of many phenomena: "social forces, family dynamics, class, sex, race, institutionalized patterns, and so on, all shape personality" (Ballou & Gabalac, 1985, p. 62). Feminism holds that external forces, such as discrimination and economics, must be acknowledged as being causative of pathology. In many ways the core of the conflict between Jungian theory and feminism is ideological orientation. Feminism, a decidedly more sociological approach, clashes with the internal focus of Jung's depth psychology. It is interesting to note that Jung's concept of the collective unconscious could relate to this conflict, because it does set a context. Such context analysis is an essential ingredient of the sociological perspective. However, Jung's context fails to articulate the influence of external structures, and hence remains individualistic. Further, the presumptiveness of many Jungian concepts makes a more sociological interpretation of his theory elusive at best.

Jungian theory postulates that the psychic entity must move from undifferentiated wholeness into a differentiated, more balanced state. This is a developmental process, and as such, it assumes an initial state of fragmentation. Consequently, individuation is something to strive for. We must question, though, if such "individuation" is necessarily something women must strive for. Again the a priori nature of Jung's theory holds that this goal is relevant to women's development. But, are women actually undifferentiated, as Jung assumes?

In Jungian theory, the developmental process so essential to individuation centers on balancing the contrasexual parts of oneself:

> Jung maintained that the task of development in middle life lies in counterbalancing the onesidedness of one's earlier life. For men this usually involves the need to integrate into personal identity the "repressed feminine" aspects of their own personality, called the anima. Women generally need to integrate the "repressed masculine" or animus. (Young-Eisendrath, 1984, p. 20)

First, feminism would question the implied notion of fragmented parts that become integrated, for some, only in middle age. Feminists would shift the emphasis from well-defined component parts to an

interrelated personality structure that *begins* by operating as a in-
terconnected whole. How valid is the notion of the "repressed masculine" in women? It is equally possible that these "masculine" characteristics have been oppressed in women, just as the "feminine"
aspects may have been devalued in men.

Second, as feminist theory begins to describe women's experience, it becomes clearer that Jung's notion of individuation may not
be relevant to women's development. To adequately describe
women's developmental process, the existence of different value
systems must first be acknowledged. For example, Carol Gilligan
discusses an aspect of women's definition of themselves:

> Thus women not only define themselves in a context of human relation-
> ship but also judge themselves in terms of their ability to care. Women's
> place in man's life cycle has been that of nurturer, caretaker, and help-
> mate, the weaver of those networks of relationsips on which she in turn
> relies. But while women have thus taken care of men, men have in their
> theories of psychological development, as in their economic arrange-
> ments, tended to assume or devalue that care. (Gilligan, 1982, p. 17)

Jean Baker Miller, in defining women's psychology, notes that it
may be entirely inappropriate to impose traditional psychoanalytic
definitions of ego onto women: "Women have different organizing
principles around which their psyches are structured" (Miller, 1976,
p. 62). The understanding of women's ego and, most importantly,
the process by which that ego is established, must be considered from
the perspective of women's organizing principles. Wehr notes that a
key part of the individuation process is "annihilating the ego," and
that such a process is inappropriate:

> For many women, however, Jung advocates by this process their "an-
> nihilating" something they may not even have. Or if they have it, it may
> be so wounded as to need building-up, not "annihilation." While Jung
> by no means intended to encourage feminine pathology, in fact was not
> even aware of that possibility in his individuation process, his term
> "annihilation" comes close to reinforcing the self-abnegation in which
> women already engage, to their detriment. (Wehr, 1987, p. 102)

The process of individuation lends itself all too easily to being a form
of oppression, because Jung failed to differentiate men's and
women's "conciousness into the individuation process" (Wehr, 1987,
p. 102).

Much of Jung's experience of the feminine psyche is related to
images in the collective unconscious. It is here that "feminine" is

defined and redefined through the often unchallenged mythological imagery of archetypes. According to Jung, the archetypes populating the collective unconscious serve as cornerstones for the psychic evolution of humankind and, thus, for the process of analysis. Jung sees all archetypes as somehow advantageous to the race and to individuals because they are, in his estimation, so much a part of human nature. This is dangerous circular reasoning, which offers women a very limited structure for understanding their psyches, and attributes to the psyche an even less favorable content.

> The collective unconscious is nonindividual, universal, suprapersonal. We experience it, therefore, as other than ourselves, as objective, acting upon us quite independently of our conscious volition, intentions, or ideas, as if it were an autonomous authority. (Ulanov, 1971, p. 35)

The concept of the autonomous authority of the collective unconscious must be shattered. If Jungian theory, as Ulanov suggests, defines the collective unconscious in this way, where then does the definition leave either the personal unconscious or the conscious psyche? Most importantly, where does such an explanation leave women? Women's unique ways of knowing must be acknowledged and validated. A study about this subject, *Women's Ways of Knowing* (Belenky et al., 1986), illustrates the necessity of women defining their own mechanisms for self-discovery. For example, the authors asked the question, "How would you describe yourself to yourself?"

> [The women in the study] described themselves in terms of their own movements in and around the geographic space that surrounded them. . . . When these women attempt to describe the self, they remain standing in their own shoes, describing only what they see gazing outward from their own eyes. They find no vantage point outside of the self that enables them to look backward, bringing the whole self into view. (p. 32)

For such women, a concrete, subjective, present-oriented construct is needed to describe and validate their intrapsychic experience. Other women in the study displayed a kind of "connected knowing":

> Connected knowing builds on the subjectivists' conviction that the most trustworthy knowledge comes from personal experience rather than pronouncements of authorities. . . . Connected knowers develop procedures for gaining access to other people's knowledge. At the heart of these procedures is the capacity for empathy. Since knowledge comes from experience, the only way they can hope to understand another person's ideas is to try to share the experience that has led the person to form the idea. (p. 113)

Both examples argue for a very different way of describing the structure and content of women's psyches. From this standpoint, the model of the collective unconscious and its archetypal content seems inadequate, even inappropriate. The archetype, as a central conceptualization in Jungian theory, warrants closer specific feminist analysis. As mentioned above, the very concept of "archetype" is itself problematic. It connotes a fixed reality, established in generations past, that continues essentially unchanged into the present and future. For the Jungian, the reality of archetypes goes undisputed: To discuss it is to discuss an almost natural law. However, in actuality it is not a scientific law whose evidence is public—a law that can be challenged and changed. Since archetypes, in truth, are more myth than scientific law, their regulation and evaluation relies at base on beliefs. As articles of belief, archetypes are not open to rational argument or empiric evidence. Archetypes like the "earth mother," the "virgin," the "witch," the "wise-old man," the "hero," and the "god," tend to perpetuate male-dominated definitions and opinions of women's roles. If we are convinced that such archetypes are necessities of the human race, then we could be all too easily convinced that women's roles should be fixed.

It may be argued that Jung did not invent specific archetypes, he merely recorded them. However, we must continually remind ourselves that what Jung discovered, and how his discoveries were incorporated into his views of women's psychology, was weighted by his biases. In short, successful Jungian analysis risks reinforcing the status quo by accepting traditional stereotypic images of femininity. Again, the very appropriateness of applying archetypal theory to women must be challenged:

> If a prostitute were to come to a Jungian analyst's office the analyst's goal would be to free her from an identification with the unadapted aspect of the hetaira [courtesan] archetypal image. The question I raise is, why archetypalize the experience of such a person in the first place? Doing so always gives a cosmic dimension to social arrangements. Unlocking, seeing-through, the linking of sexist arrangements and the sacred could be truly healing, demystifying the distortions of the patriarchal perspective writ large in social reality. (Wehr, 1987, p. 116)

Why indeed, as Wehr questions, is such a construct superimposed on women? This deflection denies the pluralistic concerns deemed a necessity from a feminist perspective. Nonetheless, in uncriticized Jungian theory, the actual existence of archetypes is assumed, and interpretive discussion about their application proceeds from there.

This attitude discourages further investigation of a broader understanding of archetypes, one that includes their cultural context.

Human intellectual processes, whether they are components of rational, scientific, or belief systems, occur in cultural context. However, in myth, cultural beliefs, assumptions, and traditions are less open to change. Once an archetype is held to be true and is asserted to explain images, feelings, and thoughts in and out of awareness, little can be done to alter that belief structure. We might disagree with the superimposition of a particular archetype on our life circumstance, but according to Jung, the archetype itself is indisputable. It becomes determined and functions as an a priori truth. Despite the fact that archetypes are not open to scientific, rational intellectual correction, they are asserted in their complexity as articles of faith that shape assumptive reality. They become basic structures for processing information and shaping reality.

Jung, a product of 19-century, Western, industrialized culture, had a propensity for thinking in terms of a "grand design." Expressing the arrogance of his privileged class as well as his ideas about women, he made grand intellectual assertions about archetypes. Archetypes are problematic in their status as articles of belief, being inacessible to corrective reason. Their cultural embeddedness and insensitivity to fundamental changes in the human construction of reality lock them into a particular historic period. By themselves, the Jungian archetypes are incapable of dealing with gender role changes. Those female Jungians and feminists that persist in working within the confines of archetypal psychology must first bridge the chasm of inaccessibility, and, in turn, reinterpret the original mythological material.

Jung structured his understanding and interpretations of mythological material in very particular ways. As discussed in the Overview, Jung's concept of duality in human nature is clearly evidenced in the dichotomous thinking of his differential evaluation of archetypes. The same structural form used to describe the psyche is again employed to characterize different archetypes. Consequently, many archetypes are split into oppositional forces. For example, the nurturing mother–engulfing mother, the virgin–whore, anima–animus, eros–logos. As with the fragmentation of the psyche, the structural implications of Jungian theory usually are ignored when the content of archetypes is discussed. The very form of such dichotomous conceptualization can be a vehicle for the oppression of women:

> the greatest danger in dichotomization is in the belief that such traits must be held exclusively, that there is a need for difference, separation

and tension. This belief insists that for him to be strong, she must be weak; for him to be a man of intellect, she must be a woman of emotion; for him to be brave, she must be cowardly. Dichotomization declares that the world is either/or, separation and differences. (Ballou & Gabalac, 1985, p. 87)

Many stereotypical assumptions about gender are contained in Jung's differential evaluation of archetypes. As suggested above, oppositional thinking forces the design of a model of human nature in which women are defined in relation to men. Hence, the ideas used to describe the female psyche are simply oppositional derivations of the ideas used to explain the personality of man. A masculine/ feminine polarity is created, and specific "masculine" or "feminine" qualities are attributed to each pole. These attributes were influenced by Jung's own culture-boundedness. The archetypes of shadow and anima–animus clearly illustrate this point:

The animus corresponds to the paternal Logos just as the anima corre- sponds to the maternal Eros. . . . I use Eros and Logos merely as conceptual aids to describe the fact that woman's consciousness is char- acterized more by the connective quality of Eros than by the discrimina- tion and cognition associated with Logos. In men, Eros, the function of relationship, is usually less developed than Logos. In women, on the other hand, Eros is an expression of their true nature, while their Logos is often only a regrettable accident. (Jung, 1959, p. 14)

Jung is highly subjective in his understanding and explanation of these "archetypes." There is confusion as he distinguishes between women themselves and what he believed to be their "true" nature as embodied in the anima archetype. Wehr, using Jung's own psycho- logical system, offers an explanation for this confusion:

He often states specifically that he is going to discuss the anima—an aspect of male psychology—and then launches into a discussion of the psychology of women. Jung's declared agenda, then, is to discuss this "contrasexual other" (anima) in the lives and psyches of men, but the unintentional agenda covers the psychology of women. . . . But Jung does not follow these two agendas in logical sequence. Instead, he projects his own anima willy-nilly into the discussion of women's psy- chology. (Wehr, 1987, p. 104)

This confusion is highly damaging. The anima–animus archetype is intrinsic to an understanding of human relationship in the Jungian theoretical model. However, it is counterproductive to an understanding of women. The Jungian notion of anima does not characterize the essential nature of women; rather, it demonstrates a male interpretation of the nature of women. Giving this interpretation status as an explanation of truth about women's nature represents a serious imposition on women. Further, to arrive at such an explanation of women's psyche, Jungian theory draws upon mythological and historical data. It then postulates that, since there is a feminine nature to man, there must be a corresponding masculine nature to women. Dichotomous and oppositional thinking lead to women being evaluated in terms of standards derived from and pertinent to men. Against the standard of a male-based principle (e.g., logos), women are judged deficient.

From our contemporary perspective, it is possible to wonder why Jung felt compelled to characterize different kinds of energy in gender terms. Certainly, different kinds and qualities of energy do exist. Perhaps Jung's cultural bias was simply too fused with his fascination with mythological material. Williams (1978) suggests that "man has always felt the need to explain and codify women, to come to terms with her presence on earth and to accommodate her within his rational system" (p. 222). She cites man's need to explain woman as the motivating force behind the creation of myths and stereotypes. Stories are used to explain women as a group and to infer basic truths about feminine nature. Mythologically, this is expressed in figures like the "old maid," "virgin," and "whore," which are held to embody essential truths. Jung certainly generalizes in this way, and by associating anima–animus with logos–eros, he further extends gender confusion. Gender attachment reflects sexism and oppositional thinking in the structure of the archetype, as is clearly demonstrated in Jung's (1959) description of the anima-possessed man relating to the animus-possessed woman, "when the animus and anima meet, the animus draws his sword of power and the anima ejects her poison of illusion and seduction" (p. 15). Further, by assigning the anima to man's unconscious, Jung traps himself into naming the "positive" and "negative" qualities of women. It is the "worst" of women's qualities that populate the man's shadow-side:

> Because the fantasy of opposites keep the anima in a social tandem with either the persona or the shadow and in a gender tandem with masculinity, we neglect her phenomenology per se and so find it difficult to understand her except in distinction to these other notions (masculinity, shadow, animus, persona). (Hillman, 1985, p. 15)

Through his emphasis on archetypes that reinforce both cultural stereotypes of women and oppressive social systems, Jung does more to confound than clarify understanding about the nature of women or women's psychology. The assessment of "animus" in women is no less problematic or damaging than its contrasexual opposite. Its overriding derivative quality lends itself easily to the attribution of misconceptions about women and women's psychology. For example, Wehr (1987) notes Jung's belief about the soul (or lack thereof) in women:

> Jung felt that men's images of the soul were feminine and projected onto women. He found corroboration for his theory in religious art from all ages and from his own experience and of his patients. In contrast, Jung translates animus as "spirit," Logos, power of the word. Since he observed that men lack Eros (relatedness, or what he called "soul") and women lack Logos (access to the spirit, the intellect), both anima and animus compensate for what is lacking to consciousness. Because anima means "soul" and because woman have an animus, not an anima, Jung frequently repeated the old Church conundrum as to whether or not women have souls. (p. 64)

It is important to again inquire how, in Jungian theory, a woman is supposed to "know" her animus. It is heralded as an essential part of her self, that contrasexual part that must be integrated in the individuation process. Jung himself noted that women often had difficulty understanding this "essential" archetype. Jung derived the existence of the animus from that of the anima. Wehr (1987) suggests that its derivative nature puts it beyond women's experience (p. 65). Indeed, as discussed previously, women base an important part of their "knowing" on experience. It is no wonder that the animus remains somewhat enigmatic from a woman's standpoint. It is ironic that Jung's own perspective leaves the process of women's knowing no less puzzling to him.

Jung's (1959) treatment of the mother archetype is yet another example of his presumptive assignment of qualities to women. "Evil symbols are the witch, the dragon (or any devouring and entwining animal, such as a large fish or a serpent), the grave, the sarcophagus, deep water, death, nightmares and bogies" (p. 82). The positive qualities are ". . . maternal solicitude and sympathy; the magic authority of the female; the wisdom and spiritual exaltation that transcend reason; any helpful instinct or impulse; all that is benign, all that cherishes and sustains, that fosters growth and fertility" (p. 82). Jung goes on to explain a daughter's mother-complex in terms of the over- or underdevelopment of the "feminine instinct" of eros. Once again, Jung's assumptions about women's nature are embedded in his elucidation of archetypal truths.

The content and structure of archetypes within Jungian theory are then both sexist in their treatment of women and classist in their elevation of intellect and achievement. Naomi Goldenberg (1976) articulately summarizes the challenge that feminists must make to the concept of archetypes:

> Feminist scholars must examine the very idea of archetype in Jungian thought if sexism is ever to be confronted at its base. Indeed, if feminists do not change the assumptions of archetype or redefine the concept, there are only two options: either (1) to accept the patriarchal ideas of feminine as ultimate and unchanging and work within those or (2) indulge in a rival search to find female archetypes, ones which can support feminist conclusions. (p. 448)

The beginning steps in the second option Goldenberg describes have already been taken by Jungian women and Jungian feminists. Their work seeks to make Jungian theory their own. For example, Jean Shinoda Bolen (1984) prefaces her work on the archetype of the Great Goddess:

> Only my Jungian colleagues were aware that I was (and am) advancing new ideas about feminine psychology that differ from some of Jung's concepts, as well as integrating feminist perspectives with archetypal psychology. Although this book is written for a general audience, the sophisticated Jungian reader might note that a psychology of women based on feminine archetypes challenges the general applicability of Jung's anima–animus theory . . . (pp. 9–10)

Bolen's work focuses on the examination of seven goddess archetypes, which she divides into three categories: virgin, vulnerable, and alchemical. She contends that "goddesses representing all three categories need expression somewhere in a woman's life—in order for her to love deeply, work meaningfully, and be sensual and creative (p. 16).

Bolen (1984) acknowledges that the "female psychology I develop within these pages comes from more than just a professional experience. Much of what I know is derived from being a woman in women's roles. . . ." (p. 3). Obviously Bolen's starting point (personal experience) for understanding mythological material makes sense from a feminist perspective, since it provides for a much wider range of interpretation and more diverse conceptualization. However,

Bolen is a Jungian analyst, and in the final analysis believes that: "The individuation journey—the psychological quest for wholeness—ends in the union of opposites; in the inner marriage of 'masculine' and 'feminine' aspects of the personality . . ." (p. 294).

Sylvia Brinton Perera (1981) also searches the goddess archetypes for appropriate answers. She notes the co-opting of goddess mythology: "We need to return to and redeem what the patriarchy has often seen only as a dangerous threat and called terrible mother, dragon, or witch" (p. 7). Perera offers a striking image in describing the injurious process of androcentrism:

> For what has been valued in the West has too often been defined only in relation to the masculine: the good, nurturant mother and wife; the sweet, docile, agreeable daughter; the gently supportive or bright, achieving partner. As many feminist writers have stated through the ages, this collective model (and the behavior it leads to) is inadequate for life; we mutilate, depotentiate, silence, and enrage ourselves trying to compress our souls into it, just as surely as our grandmothers deformed their fully breathing bodies with corsets for the sake of an ideal. (p. 12)

Despite her strong feminist perspective, as a Jungian analyst Perera returns to the structure of her theoretical underpinning and is, at times, trapped by her induction into that system.

> The Inanna mythologems of descent and return reintroduce two great goddesses, primal feminine energy patterns and their partners, and the possibility of an individual human response to bring them into incarnated, personal life. The story presents a model for health and for healing the split between above and below, between the collective ideal and the powerful bipolar, transformative, processual reality underlying the feminine wholeness pattern. (Perera, 1981, p. 94)

Perera is bound to Jung's polarities, dichotomous understanding of women, and the concomitant definitions of what is "healthy."

Linda Schierse Leonard comes closer to making Jungian theory her own by adapting the idea of the archetype to the relationship between fathers and daughters. She draws heavily on personal experience in defining her journey through archetypes. Leonard (1982) states:

> I feel now the time has come for women to wear their own clothing and to speak out of their feminine wisdom and strength. The feminine—what is it? I don't think we can define it. But we can experience it and out of

> that experience try to express it via symbols and images, art forms through which we can be in the mystery of that experience and yet somehow articulate it too. (p. 170)

Ultimately, her journey leads her to aim at healing the relationship between the masculine and the feminine:

> When women begin to feel confident and to express the values of their own way of being, then they will enable the healing of the masculine. The masculine in women, in men themselves and in the culture is wounded in its poor relationship to the feminine. (p. 171)

Others, like Polly Young-Eisendrath, have sought to directly fuse Jungian concepts with feminist theory. Young-Eisendrath (1984) is still tied to oppositional framing, but openly challenges the gender assumptions in archetypes:

> I do not assume that women and men represent these archetypal domains through their gender identities. Rather, I have come to see both domains as potentially available to each gender for both identity and action purposes. (p. 12)

In her writing, Young-Eisendrath clearly defines herself as both a Jungian and a feminist.

The women quoted above, as well as many others, have made strong first steps in challenging Jungian theory. Significant and valuable contributors to women's psychology have come out of their work. A process has begun.

SUMMARY AND CONCLUSIONS

Jung's influence on the evolution of psychodynamic accounts of personality and therapy is profound, yet often unacknowledged. Although the lack of acknowledgement is perhaps unfair, it lends an insidious quality to Jung's influence. The impact of his theories becomes hidden, difficult to uncover and to examine. This is particularly problematic with regard to the inequitable treatment of women. Jungian assumptions about women's nature, role, and appropriate function are sexist, and they have essentially gone unchallenged. The very construction of Jungian theory, through, for example, its primarily intrapsychic focus, fragmented definition of the personality, historical determinism of archetypes, dichotomous constructs, and gender-related evaluations of personality characteristics, creates a system that is counterposed to a feminist understanding of reality. Feminism calls for a theoretical structure built on principles of the perception and validation of wholes, interrelationships, pluralism, liberation from cultural and gender constraints, and an awareness of contextual influences. Jung's influence must be uncovered and understood for what it is, not what it appears to be.

The initial appeal of Jungian theory to some feminists of the 1970s was based on its recognition of specific gender-related capacities in each sex and on the historical integration occurring in archetypes. Hence, Jungian theory offers an understanding of personality that does not hide gender. That appeal, however, is superficial. To feminists, Jung and his theoretical views are initially worthy of attention, but further consideration reveals a set of beliefs that are detrimental to women and to the ways feminists think about human nature. While Jung appears to open vistas by postulating a "feminine principle," his underlying assumptions limit, constrain, and distort our understanding of women's personality and experience.

Those women who have attempted to adapt, build on, and otherwise transform Jungian psychological theory have laid a foundation. They have taken an initial step in a process. They have created a "relationship" with Jungian theory that also honors themselves as women. However, they have not gone far enough. Their continued attachment to Jung's theoretical framework needs to be questioned. It may be helpful to utilize the imagery of myth to describe and articulate women's experiences but the limits of this must be recognized. The creation of a system of dichotomous splits that then must be healed to achieve wholeness and health suggests that the system itself is inadequate. To truly understand woman's psychology, it will be necessary to go well beyond the confines of Jungian archetypal theory.

It may be that the next debate in the development of woman's psychological theory will reflect a general conflict between the revision of existing theories and the development of the new. The very notion that there exists an overriding psychology applicable to all individuals is an outdated, 19th-century concept of theory building. New theories must contend with and encompass diverse realities based on culture, race, age, class, and gender. How women come to know things must also be respected. It is my position that a woman's psychology not in any way derived from traditional androcentric theory is in order. Women's psychological theory must be built, possibly on its own, entirely separate foundation. Carol Gilligan, Jean Baker Miller, Janet L. Surrey, Judith Jordan, Alexandra Kaplan, and many others have begun that next step in theory building from a woman's perspective. It is here that the psychology of women will be discussed and defined, it is here that Goddesses may be invented or redesigned, it is here that women's images may be born.

REFERENCES

Belenky, M. F., Clinchy, B. V., Goldberger, N. R., & Tarule, J. M. (1986). *Women's ways of knowing: The development of self, voice, and mind.* New York: Basic Books.

Ballou, M. & Gabalac, N. W. (1985). *A feminist position on mental health.* Springfield, IL: Charles C. Thomas.

Bolen, J. S. (1984). *Goddesses in everywoman.* San Francisco: Harper and Row.

Daly, M. (1978). *Gyn/ecology, The metaethics of radical feminism.* Boston: Beacon Press.

Donelson, E. & Gullahorn, J. E. (1977). *Women, a psychological perspective.* New York: Wiley.

Gilligan, C. (1982). *In a different voice.* Cambridge, MA: Harvard University Press.

Goldenberg, N. R. (1976, Winter), *A feminist critique of Jung. Signs: Journal of Women in Culture and Society,* 2(2), 443–449.

Hall, C. S., and Nordby, V. J. (1973). *A primer of Jungian psychology.* New York: Taplinger.

Hillman, J. (1985). *Anima, An anatomy of a personified notion.* Dallas, TX: Spring.

Jung, C. G. (1953). In G. Adler et al. (Eds.), *Collected works of C. G. Jung* (2nd ed., Vol. 5). Princeton, NJ: Princeton University Press.

Jung, C. G. (1959). In G. Adler et al. (Eds.), *Collected works* (2nd ed., Vol. 5). Princeton, NJ: Princeton University Press.

Jung, C. G. (1964a). In Read et al. (Eds.), *Collected works* (Vol. 10). New York: Bollinger Press.

Jung, C. G. (1964b). *Man and his symbols.* New York: Dell.

Jung, C. G. (1968). *Analytical psychology: Its theory and practice.* New York: Vintage.

Kaufmann, Y. (1984). Analytical psychotherapy. In R. J. Corsini (Ed.), *Current psychotherapies.* Itasca, IL: Peacock.

Leonard, L. S. (1985). *The wounded woman: Healing the father–daughter relationship.* Boston: Shambhala.

Matoon, M. A. (1981). *Jungian psychology in perspective.* New York: Free Press.

Miller, J. B. (1984). *The development of women's sense of self* (Work in Progress, No. 12). Wellesley, MA: Stone Center.

Miller, J. B. (1986). *Toward a new psychology of women* (2nd ed.). Boston: Beacon Press.

Perera, S. B. (1981). *Descent to the goddess, A way of invitation for women.* Toronto: Inner City Books.

Samuels, A. (1985). *Jung and the post-Jungians*. London: Routledge and Kegan Paul.

Sturdivant, S. (1980). *Therapy with women—A feminist philosophy of treatment*. New York: Springer.

Ulanov, A. B. (1978). *The feminine in Jungian psychology and in Christian theology*. Evanston, IL: Northwestern University Press.

Wehr, D. S. (1987). *Jung and feminism, liberating archetypes*. Boston: Beacon Press.

Williams, J. H. (1978, May/June). *Woman: Myth and stereotype*. International *Journal of Womens Studies*, 1(3), 221–247.

Young-Eisendrath, P. (1984). *Hags and heroes, A feminist approach to Jungian psychotherapy with couples*. Toronto, Canada: Inner City Books.

CHAPTER FOUR

A Feminist Critique of Cognitive–Behavioral Therapy

RICKI E. KANTROWITZ
MARY BALLOU

Learning principles, the foundation of behaviorism, have their roots in Pavlov's research and Watson's applications of that research in the 1900s. During the 1950s and '60s, behavioral principles were rapidly developed and popularized. More recently, some of the basic learning constructs have been expanded and modified. Behavior theory, which derived its identity from an emphasis on the observable, measurable aspects of behavior, has been reconceptualized by many to include cognitive theory, with its emphasis on internal, cognitive processes. Cognitive constructivism, one emerging branch of cognitive theory, is currently examining the direct impact of emotional processing on behavior. As a result of these ongoing revisions and expansions, behavioral and cognitive approaches have gone beyond a narrow focus on overt behavior. In consequence, these theories have become more theoretically responsive to constructions of personality and psychopathology.

Much has been written describing and evaluating cognitive and behavioral techniques and applications. The goal of this chapter is to refocus our attention on the theoretical bases of these approaches and to critique the assumptions of these perspectives from a feminist vantage point. In order to provide a foundation for this discussion, it will be necessary to examine the historical and conceptual development of these theories, since the theory of personality associated with them is largely implicit.

HISTORICAL AND CONCEPTUAL DEVELOPMENT

Contemporary behavioral theory is based on the learning principles discovered and popularized by such figures in psychology as Ivan Pavlov, John Watson, and B. F. Skinner. Pavlov's experiments with dogs in the early 1900s led to the development of the theory of respondent conditioning—learning that takes place through paired association. It was discovered that a neutral stimulus (bell) could become a conditioned stimulus for the salivation response by being paired with an unconditioned stimulus (food). Salivation (conditioned response) could to be elicited by the bell alone. Watson—considered to be the founder of behaviorism—and Rayner (1920) demonstrated and helped popularize this principle of conditioning for humans in their well-known experiment with little Albert and the rat. Behaviorists' current understanding of respondent conditioning goes beyond the pairing of a single conditioned stimulus with a single unconditioned stimulus and recognizes that learning can take place due to either correlational or contingent relationships between conditioned and unconditioned stimuli (Wilson, 1989). Through the years, these Pavlovian concepts have been analyzed primarily to further an understanding of principles of learning, rather than to explain personality development (Pervin, 1989). Yet implicit within the work are presumptions of Locke's *tabula rasa,* the notion that personality is what one learns through paired associations.

Skinner made a major contribution to learning theory with his exclusive focus on overt behavior and his development of the principles of operant conditioning (Wilson, 1989). Behavior was understood by Skinner to be a function of its consequences. Whether a behavior has positive or negative results will affect whether a person (or animal) repeats the behavior. All behavior is learned, determined by the environment, and shaped by its consequences. There is no free will, so people respond in specific ways to stimuli depending on past experiences with the stimuli, in concert with their genetic endowment. What is learned can be unlearned. Therefore behavior that is considered undesirable or maladaptive can be extinguished and new, more desirable behaviors learned. Internal variables are not considered, and affect is viewed as involuntary behavior. According to Skinner's radical behaviorism, personality per se is an irrelevant concept. Individual differences are also not considered to be important. A person becomes who he or she is, depending upon general laws of learning. Since personality was defined exclusively as behavior and was not related to internal factors, behaviorists moved away from an examination of theories of personality (Staats, 1986).

Yet even here, in Skinner's denial of internal processes, implicit assumptions and overt statements about human nature and human functioning are persistent. Skinner assumes several positions, and implicit within his stance are several more notions related to the questions of personality and psychopathology. Foremost is the insistence on overt behavior, a position that stems from and is supported by logical positivism. Logical positivism is a philosophic position with a long history in academic psychology. It asserts that all meaningful ideas must be reduced to observable, measurable sensory experience. Skinner was working from a worldview that asserts that anything not observable and measurable through sensory experience is metaphysical nonsense, neither real nor knowable. This particular philosophic position, while very powerful in the development of academic psychology, has serious limits when applied to personality. It not only reduces the complexity of personality, but also restricts the allowable dimensions of consideration; and finally claims that any aspect outside its constructions are unreal. Hence, such phenomena germane to personality as compassion, trauma, cultural or gender beliefs, or moral, cognitive, and affective development amount to nonsense in Skinner's construction of personality.

Regarding psychopathology, Skinner's usage of the terms "adaptive" and "maladaptive" behavior reveal implicit notions about normative criteria. Normative criteria are those standards used to judge the rightness, or in clinical contexts, health, of behaviors. Unlike other philosophical positions, empiricism, of which logical positivism is a part, has a difficult problem. Questions of right must be settled by the norms dominant at the time, for there is no other authority. Hence right is relative. Yet the behaviorists neglect the implications of this problem. It is problematic to define health and illness on the basis of shared expectations of groups holding power at a given time. The normative standard of a dominant culture, gender, or worldview is not an adequate criterion for judgments of health. Unhappily, it is precisely such a standard that underlies the notions of adaptive and maladaptive. Skinner clearly assumes a logical positivist frame of reference. He also uses a normative standard of the dominant culture, implicit within the terms "adaptive" and "maladaptive" behaviors.

In the early years of behavior therapy, the principles of classical and operant conditioning were used in the development of psychotherapeutic techniques. Skinner practiced behavior modification, applying operant conditioning principles such as reinforcement, punishment, and shaping, as early as the late 1940s. Wolpe's development, in the 1950s, of systematic desensitization by reciprocal inhibition was the first major psychotherapeutic application of respondent conditioning (Wilson, 1989).

Other principles are now considered by some to be important extensions of traditional behavior theory. In the 1960s, Bandura's social learning theory (now called social cognitive theory), with its emphasis on cognitive mediational processes and learning through observation and imitation, provided new ways to think about behavior and behavior change, as well as new treatment strategies (Pervin, 1989). Personality development in Bandura's framework is based on direct learning, as well as imitation and vicarious learning, within a reciprocally determined model (environment and person). Behavior, whether maladjusted or adjusted, is a function of the environment, both in terms of external stimulus events and external reinforcers, and the person's internal cognitive processes (e.g., thoughts, self-efficacy beliefs, goals) (Wilson, 1989). In this interactional view, people both respond to external events and actively regulate and influence situations. Thoughts, feelings, and actions are also seen as interacting with one another (Pervin, 1989). A person's behavior in a given situation is likely mediated by the expectation of some kind of reinforcer (internal or external), self-perceptions of efficacy, and various cognitive processes. Reinforcements are understood as being more important in the performance and maintenance of a behavior than in the learning of the behavior. Individual differences are a result of a number of variables, including the situation itself, cognitive processes such as expectancies of consequences and knowledge of rules, and the behavior assessed. This view challenges traditional psychodynamic beliefs that consistent personality traits or structures exist (Staats, 1986) and that behavior is fixed as a result of early developmental stages. Rather, behavior depends upon what is happening in the present, not what happened in the past. Development is seen to occur in particular areas of behavior, such as aggression and self-regulation. In contrast to the behavioral approaches discussed earlier, the person is viewed as active, having the capacity to grow and develop and bring about change within his or her biological limits. These developments once again open the door to a consideration of a behavioral personality theory, if in somewhat redefined terms.

In the 1960s and '70s, Ellis, Beck, and Meichenbaum developed cognitive–behavioral approaches, which expanded the field of behavior therapy by allowing for the examination and restructuring of cognitive (internal) processes such as thoughts, attributions, self-statements, and images (Wilson, 1989). Although cognitive processes are not directly observable, cognitions are understood to be learned responses, influenced by the same principles of learning as overt behavior. In brief, cognitions, which give personal definition to life events, are seen as impacting on human motivation, affect, and behavior independently of the events themselves. Personality is shaped by central values or schemas, which develop early in life and then help to form other values, attitudes, and beliefs (Beck & Weishaar, 1989). Changing a person's thinking, from "irrational" to "rational," can change his or her maladaptive emotions and behaviors (Burns, 1980). However, it must be noted that this explanation of cognitive theory is too simplistic.

Mahoney and Lyddon (1988) have identified twenty different contemporary cognitive theorists. They differentiate two main clusters, rationalists and constructivists. Rationalists, including Ellis and Beck, view thinking as primary, determining emotion and behavior. Constructivists, such as Guidano and Liotti (1983) and Mahoney (1988) question whether thought can be meaningfully separated from feeling and action. They believe, for example, that emotion can influence and initiate behavior in the same way that thinking can. The cognitive theories are also differentiated by how they incorporate attachment theory, social learning theory, and developmental and systemic issues (Mahoney, 1988). It is clear that current developments in cognitive and cognitive–behavioral theory have expanded variables for consideration beyond overt behavior. Current views allow for the existence of a number of human functions within their constructions of personality.

It is beyond the scope of this chapter to discuss the many theorists identified by Mahoney and Lyddon (1988). However, to further clarify the differences between the rationalists and the constructivists, Ellis's Rational Emotive Therapy (RET) and some of the constructivists' views will be presented in more detail below.

RET theory views people as being biologically and culturally predisposed to be both irrational (stemming from false beliefs) as well as rational (logically and rationally based) in their thinking, and to have the capacity for self-harm as well as for self-growth. Although Ellis views thinking, perceiving, behaving, and feeling as simultaneous processes, he believes that cognitions are primary. He demonstrated this in his A-B-C theory, which defines A as the Activating event, B as the Belief system and C as the emotional Consequence. According to Ellis, although many believe that C is caused by A, it is actually caused by B, the person's belief system. Maladaptive emotions and responses are created by irrational and unrealistic beliefs and statements. According to Ellis (1989, p. 199), "the 'real' cause of upsets, therefore, is (people) themselves and not what happens to them (even though the experiences obviously have some influence over what they think and feel)."

Irrational beliefs include thinking that certain things should, ought, or must be a particular way and that what others think determines one's self worth. Children are especially vulnerable to cultural and familial influences and irrational thinking. Children and adults become more and more irrational as they incorporate the irrational belief systems of the environment into their own belief systems (Okun, 1990). These irrational beliefs can be disputed, and with technical instruction from the therapist and much practice and hard work on the part of the client, rational thinking can be learned and maladaptive consequences can be minimized or even eliminated.

In the constructivist approach, emotion, behavior, and cognition are examined from an interactive information-processing model. The person is seen as "an active constructive information processor who explores and adapts to the environment, organizing information about self and world into increasingly more complex views" (Greenberg, 1988, p. 235). Thinking is not considered to be the single valid source in information and organization. Personality development is conceptualized as a more complex process than in some of the reductionistic behavioral and cognitive approaches. "When viewed within the context of the developmental process of a single human knowing system, the interplay of cognitive growth, emotional differentiation, attachment processes, and family patterns of interaction all become vital subprocesses in the construction of a coherent and integrated personal identity" (Mahoney & Lyddon, 1988, p. 211). Maladaptive emotions and behaviors, such as anxiety, depression, and resistance, are viewed as normal, healthy parts of the developmental process that tend to precede cognitive reorganization and transformation (Kruglanski, 1988). Psychopathology is seen as the discrepancy between environmental challenges and the adaptive capacities of the individual. Human change is nonlinear, developmental, and process-focused.

Definitions of psychopathology have also changed in accord with expansions of views of personality. Psychopathology is currently defined in a more complex manner: It is thought to be a poorness of fit between environmental demands and adaptive capacities and can be manifested as beliefs, organizing schema, or expectancies. Yet, while definitions of psychopathology have become more complex and abstracted, earlier behaviorist views on the judgment of right and health continue to be problematic. The normative standard of the dominant cultural group continues to be a defining criterion, since the prescription for healthy capacities is individual conformance with institutionalized expectations of the dominant (most powerful), controlling social group. The relativity of this criterion is as problematic for the cognitivists as it was for Skinner. For not only do cognitive theorists ignore the relativity of the standard adaptive functioning (standard of health) but they collude with the institutionalization of a particular monolithic normative criterion. While the cognitivists have broadened the factors associated with psychopathology (e.g., thoughts, expectations, family, culture), they as behaviorists still hold the individual deviant. Cognitive and behavior theorists do not question the environment (factors external to the individual) as a cause of or interactive influence on individuals' capacities. Instead, even for individuals of different cultures, classes, ethnicities, and genders, they judge the individual by the environment.

In summary, there is not a unified view of personality development in the behavioral, cognitive, or cognitive–behavioral approaches. Watson, Skinner, and other behaviorists criticized many earlier formulations about personality. Variables such as traits, needs, and motives were seen by them as ambiguous and unverifiable. Yet, these same theorists have been criticized for their inattention to personality theory (Wilson, 1989). According to their critics, the deterministic view that environmental variables control people and that humans are passive respondents to external events loses sight of individual differences and the complexity of persons. Discrepancies between laboratory findings and therapeutic interventions have also led some to question the empirical findings that form the foundation of behavior therapy (Mahoney, 1989; Mahoney & Lyddon, 1988).

Social cognitive theory focuses on interactions between person variables and environmental variables. Individual differences are accounted for by examining, for example, the specifics of the situation, how one perceives and interprets the situation, and expectancies of reinforcement. As cognitive and cognitive–behavioral theories have developed, the person variable that has been highlighted is cognition. The focus on cognitive processes, although inferential, and their interactions with environmental factors has added to an understanding of human behavior. However, personality development has largely been studied by looking at parts of behavior, rather than seen as a process over time and the result of the complex interaction of internal and external variables. Developmental processes have largely been ignored. Greenberg (1988, p. 235) has stated that early cognitive and cognitive behavioral therapy . . . treated cognition more as internal behavior to be modified rather than as meaning and hence failed to provide us with models of cognitive functioning that were sufficiently rich and differentiated to provide a satisfying account of human functioning.

With the further development of social cognitive theory and constructivism, such factors as attachment, maturation, motivation, and emotion are beginning to be examined in depth. There appears to be great interest in the study of personal agency (Mahoney, 1989). There is movement away from a linear associationism to a more complex, multifacted view of human development and change. With the many revisions and changes through the years, it is not surprising that there is no consensus as to how the behavioral and cognitive–behavioral approaches define personality. There appear to be, however, some unifying assumptions within behavioral, cognitive, and cognitive–behavioral theories. The first is that the scientific method is the way to generate and validate knowledge. Strict logical positivism has evolved to a subtler and more complex empiricism. Reduction to a single variable—behavior—has been replaced with reduction to interactive internal processes. A second unifying assumption is that external (environmental) forces do exist and are varied (culture, family). The individual, however, is the primary focus of these theories and must adapt to these forces.

Obviously, behavioral and cognitive–behavioral theories are still in transition. Much has been learned, modified, and challenged in the decades since Pavlov first performed his experiments. The 1980s alone have brought about an increased awareness of several factors, including the impact of emotion, the complex interactions of affect, behavior, and cognition, and the importance of biological factors (Wilson, 1989). With these kinds of theoretical changes in such a relatively short time frame, who knows what the 1990s will bring? It is an opportune time for feminists to make further inroads, developing cognitive–behavioral theories and strategies compatible with a feminist philosophy.

FEMINIST CRITIQUE

Cognitive–behavioral approaches are currently very popular with many psychotherapists. Feminist therapists, too, have made use of a number of cognitive–behavioral techniques in their work with clients (e.g., math anxiety, imposter phenomenon, agoraphobia, assertion; see Brody, 1984). This section will employ a feminist perspective to examine the strengths and weaknesses of the behavioral, cognitive, and cognitive–behavioral models.

The behavioral view that what an individual learns is largely determined by the environment (external events, conditioning, social pressures, etc.) as well as the social cognitive and cognitive–behavioral concepts of reciprocal determinism and the impact of cognitive processing were met with initial enthusiasm by feminists.

> Much of the initial appeal of CBT in addressing women's issues in the mid-1970s was based on the assumption that by focusing on cognitions as well as teaching new behaviors it was possible for women to transcend the constraints of their own prior socialization experience and to become the agents of their own change. (Fodor, 1988, p. 96)

These theories implied a shift from intrapsychic, person-centered interpretations, which seemed to place blame squarely on individual development, to a context-relevant model of socialization. With reinforcement as a central concept of socialization theory (Fodor, 1988), a variety of gender-role–related behaviors seemed to be explained. Change could come about by altering the environment, the women, or both. However, in spite of this perceived potential, much of the enthusiasm has diminished over time, as feminists have recognized that there are many shortcomings in this theory and its applications.

One of the basic assumptions of a learning model of human behavior is that maladaptive behavior is learned, and therefore can be unlearned. The premise is simple and sounds value-free. Yet, by conceptualizing people as learning principles, rather than as human beings with richness and diversity, much is lost. Complex human processes are reduced to that which is measurable or observable and broken down into such small segments that the "big picture," the specific individual living within a certain context, gets overlooked. Behaviorists' reductionistic view has been mostly replaced by an interest in studying mediating variables. Yet, even as social cognitive theorists, constructivists, and others have begun to more closely study the complexities of the individual, key issues are still being ignored. Environmental stimuli can be altered and maladaptive behavior can be changed, but what is health in this model? Who defines what is adaptive and what is maladaptive behavior? How are decisions made about which interventions are used? Who and what has to change? Are cognitive–behavioral techniques being used to encourage clients to conform to normative standards? Are cultural norms appropriate for a specific client? Is society doing all that it can do? The theory behind the clinical applications does not address these and many other important issues and, therefore, biases such as culture-bound and male-dominant assumptions can emerge as easily (if not more easily since therapists are also members of and conditioned by society) in the guise of value-neutral assumptions. A model of human functioning and change that does not allow for diversity and difference, that uses white, middle-class, masculine norms as the standard for healthy development, is not compatible with a feminist philosophy.

One key issue in a feminist critique of the cognitive–behavioral model is the criterion question. These theories implicitly support the uncritically examined standards of a dominant social group, which have become institutionalized in American culture. The unacknowledged relativity (discussed earlier with Skinner) of "right" judgments about behavior continues. Dominant social standards are the normative criterion for the cognitive–behavioral models. Another key issue is the essential failure of these theories to consider and challenge the environmental stimuli to which people are subjected. Instead, individuals are expected to improve their adaptive capacities to meet the environmental conditions, which serves to reinforce the dominant social standards. These theories with their abstract language (contingencies, expectancies, mediating variables, reinforcement), and their cloak of value-neutral science have not escaped politics. That is, the power of dominant groups is carried out, if implicitly, in these theories.

The support of the dominant group's values and a lack of consideration of external factors (environmental factors) are illustrated by the example of prescribing assertiveness training for a woman who has been sexually harrassed in the workplace. Certainly, there is nothing wrong with improving assertiveness skills, and empirically supported interventions do exist. However, by focusing on the woman's skill development and schema change, neither the external factors—aggressive sexuality and boundary violation—nor the dominant social norm of women's duty to protect themselves are articulated and questioned.

At first glance, the emphasis on empirical support for learning principles and the "scientifically" supported effectiveness of many cognitive and behavioral interventions with a wide range of clients seems entirely positive, to those trained in a scientist–practioner model. More research has been conducted by adherents of these approaches than those of other models (Okun, 1990). However, too often those using science and experimental methods assume that their findings represent the "truth." In fact, any theory is fraught with bias, and these biases need to be identified (Dutton-Douglas & Walker, 1988; McHugh, Koeske, & Frieze, 1986). Another limitation with the use of empirical methods is that they tend to be linear, reductionistic, and cause-and-effect related. It may be that the complex processes of human nature, based upon the interdependence of a number of phenomena, cannot be adequately defined and measured using these methods.

Questions about the method, values, and exclusive appropriateness of science are being asked by a number of contemporary thinkers, feminists among them. Harding (1987), Ballou (1990), and Unger (1984), for example, each raise questions about scientific method that are as yet unaddressed by cognitive–behavioral theories. Harding raises demanding epistemological issues about logical positivism. Ballou calls for judging information as knowledge only when multiple methods yield the same information. Unger suggests the critical need for deconstruction of hidden assumptions in both psychological theory and research. Each of these feminists provide analyses suggesting important limits to the scientific method. Epistemological vulnerabilities, hidden assumptions, and multiple-method confirmations are serious challenges to the cognitive–behavioral theories, because they build their theoretical foundations on empirical finding.

Furthermore, the emphasis upon behavior, "rational" thinking, and science within behavioral and cognitive personality theories fits very well with the preferred and valued functions, processes, and structures of white, male European-Americans. It, however, may neither fit nor be responsive to diverse ways of knowing and to the preferred processes and alternative world views of non-whites, non-males, or non-Europeans. Those studying the cognitive–behavioral theories have overlooked the fact that many people have a style of cognitive processing that differs from white, middle-class, masculine norms. Some women's cognitive processing styles may, for example, be nonlinear, circular, and related to the interpersonal context (Dutton-Douglas & Walker, 1988; Belenly et al., 1986). Other ways of knowing that may be more associated with some female orientations, such as intuition, spirituality, consciousness, and connection, are ignored or devalued in these models. Jackson (1987) noted the existence of a distinct African-American cognitive style that differs in many ways from a European-American style. For example, "Afro-Americans tended to prefer inferential reasoning, based upon contextual, interpersonal, and historical factors; and Euro-Americans preferred either inductive or deductive reasoning, based upon a belief in the permanency of the stimuli" (p. 233). Jackson believes that this Afrocentric cognitive style is often perceived by persons trained in a traditional European-American counseling model as negative or ineffective; they therefore may attempt to change it to more closely resemble their own European-American cognitive style.

The cornerstone of cognitive-therapy theory has been the concept that thinking is primary and determines one's feelings and behaviors. Therefore, for change to occur, one's beliefs and thoughts must be challenged. However, challenging beliefs and thoughts may not fit well with many cultural and gender socialization patterns. Asians, for example, have been taught to create emotional harmony and avoid conflict in accordance with their cultural norms. Traditionally, women's perceptions, views, and thoughts have been minimized and misunderstood (Piasecki & Hollon, 1987). Cognitive theory's emphasis on cognition often leads to the systematic confrontation and change of the individual's thoughts and beliefs. For— instead of articulating unique values, perceptions, and views— confrontive efforts to change cognitive schemata may reinforce a woman's belief that her thinking is inaccurate and that she needs to rely on others, including the therapist, to help her think. The theory does not adequately address individual differences and thereby ignores the importance of valuing one's own perceptions, diverse processes and structures of knowing, and relative and context-dependent judgments of appropriateness. Instead, cognitive–behavioral theory forces a more stereotypically masculine view and manner of interacting in the status quo world. Constructing views of personality based on cognition and behavior (thought and action) and structuring knowledge through empiricism support the dominant norms, but ignore nondominant norms and disallow value differences among individuals.

As noted earlier, behavioral and cognitive–behavioral theories have either tended to ignore the question of personality or have examined only parts of human functioning rather than the development of the whole person. No explanations are given, for example, for how mediating variables change over time and within individuals. How are 8-year-olds different from 40-year-olds? Stewart and Healy (1989) argue that the impact of social experiences depends upon a person's life stage, having "consequences for individuals' worldviews when they are experienced in childhood, for their identities when they are experienced in late adolescence and the transition to adulthood, and for their behavior when they are experienced in mature adulthood" (p. 40). An adequate model should take such factors as the stage of a person's life, the ability to control elements in his or her environment, and the level of abstract thought into consideration when trying to understand a person's problems. A theory that professes to recognize the interdependence of internal and external variables, but tends to focus on parts of personality/behavior and does not closely examine developmental and life stage differences, would not be acceptable to feminists. Theory, if it is to be adequate from a feminist perspective, must consider the context of individuals' lives, including society, culture, class, race, developmental status, and individual experiences.

Much attention in cognitive–behavioral models has been given to the development of skill-building programs and to the treatment of very specific problems such as anxiety, depression, assertion, and aggression. The emphasis on the teaching of specific skills is an example of the pragmatic, functional quality of cognitive–behavioral therapy (Okun, 1990). Since full theoretical development has not occurred in cognitive–behavioral models, implicit assumptions must be inferred from clinical usage. Models applied in clinical settings that focus on parts rather than wholes and contexts are problematic. "Maladaptive" behavior often seems to be changed or modified without examining the larger context. The goal of behavior change has typically been to produce individuals who are effective, functioning, and successful in the public domain, for example, by decreasing the agoraphobic's level of anxiety and getting her out of the house. "The paradox is that individuals are taught skills to succeed in competitive systems of relationships which are responsible for the person's situation in the first place" (Okun, 1990, p. 197). There is nothing in the theory that enhances sensitivity to gender, race, and class issues, such as the importance of relationships in many women's lives. Too often, the therapist's own values—typically society's norms—are used to define what is pathology and what is health.

Assertion training is an example of how the application of the supposedly value-free cognitive–behavioral theoretical model can be biased. Assertion training has its roots in behavior therapy and the women's liberation movement (Fodor & Epstein, 1983). From a learning theory model, nonassertion can be viewed as a socially conditioned feminine trait that is often maladaptive. Assertion training seeks to "remedy" stereotypic "feminine" behavior: to teach women assertiveness skills, such as how to express personal rights and power and meet their own needs without violating the rights of others. Fodor and Epstein (1983) have questioned many of the underlying assumptions of assertion training. A few of these points will be discussed below.

The model of assertion that has typically been taught in cognitive–behavioral programs uses a male assertive style. Individuals are taught skills for functioning in a competitive, male-dominated world. Yet individuals of various ethnic, class, and gender backgrounds have different ways of being assertive. What is effective, appropriate, assertive behavior for a particular individual dealing with specific interpersonal and environmental factors is not adequately understood and is not addressed in typical assertiveness programs. It is also a compelling example of cognitive–behavioral therapy's lack of pluralism, in that there is one adaptive assertive style, not many.

Although the medical model, with its emphasis on psychopathology, is not consistent with cognitive–behavioral therapy, there is often the sense that what the client needs to change when there is a problem in living is his or her own behavior and cognitive processing. The implicit standard used to determine what is in need of change is based primarily on white, middle-class, masculine values. For example, Casas (1988) believes that some of the underlying assumptions of the cognitive–behavioral approaches are that people are responsible for or greatly contribute to their own problems, and that they have the potential to and responsibility for change. He asserts that these beliefs may

> not be congruent with the life experiences of many racial/ethnic minority persons. More specifically, as a result of life experiences associated with racism, discrimination, and poverty, people may have developed a cognitive set (e.g. an external locus of control, an external locus responsibility, and learned helplessness) that . . . is antithetical to any self-control approaches. (pp. 109–110)

The lack of careful consideration of gender, class, race, and ethnic factors as well as contextual information, specific antecedents, and consequences of specific beliefs and behaviors is a problem in cognitive–behavioral conceptualizations of pathology. Also problematic is their attribution of responsibility, implied by their goal of changing the individual client.

Bandura (1989), in a recent article on human agency, states that "because judgments and actions are partly self-determined, people can effect change in themselves and their situations through their own efforts" (p. 1175). Although he uses the words "partly" and "some" in his discussion of self-direction and self-control, superficially acknowledging the impact and interaction of environmental variables, there is little discussion of socialization processes, oppression, or other noxious external structures, again putting the onus for change on the individual. It may be that what a client expresses is a result of reality-based discrimination and the sexist thinking of others and is not due to her own "irrational" cognitions. The focus of change implies issues of responsibility and blame that can validate or invalidate an individual's experience. Cognitive–behavioral theory must broaden its view beyond the rank ordering of individual processes to see external conditions as powerful factors in developing personality and psychopathology. While Bandura has implied external and structural causation through written words, meaningful cognitive shifts must follow. Additionally, the potent change techniques of cognitive–behavioral theories must aim toward changing noxious external conditions.

In summary, overreliance on empirical concepts; the focus on thinking as opposed to other processes; and the lack of consideration of individual differences caused by gender, ethnicity, class, worldview, values and life stage in cognitive–behavioral theory has resulted in a restricted European-American, androcentric view of human nature. The notion of personality derived from cognitive–behavioral theory is limited, since it focuses on ahistorical, emitted behaviors and internal variables without examining the cultural and interpersonal context (Okun, 1990). There is little recognition in the theory and its applications that individuals with gender, class, and racial differences may have differing experiences in societies and that these experiences can influence peoples' cognition, behavior, and emotion. Little attention has actually been given to the role of external forces, structures, processes, and differential social reinforcement in the development and maintenance of "maladaptive" behavior. The powerful and differing effects of environmental influences—social/ economic class, gender, ethnicity, political structures, and religion— so central in feminist theory are not present in cognitive–behavioral theory. Rather, they are merely environments to which individuals adapt.

Yet, cognitive–behavioral theories should not be dismissed by feminists. While it is true that a theory that focuses on parts of humans without an integrative theory of external forces, diverse peoples, and complex development is inadequate, the model is certainly neither rigid nor completed. Cognitive–behavioral theorists are continuing to examine, question, and revise basic tenets of the theory (Dobson, 1988; Mahoney & Lyddon, 1988). For example, ongoing debate and research about the role of emotion may bring about a new "cognitive revolution," altering our understanding of such factors as personality development, the mechanisms of change, and the client–

therapist relationship. Work in the area of behavioral medicine may increase our understanding of mind/body interactions. New ways of thinking about personality and human growth might emerge if measures that could examine the complexity of human functioning and could view causality in circular rather than linear fashion were developed. Alternative methods of change might also be created if a full range of personal styles were viewed as positive and enhancing, and external factors were viewed as influencing differentially across the gamut from beneficial to noxious.

However, some may question whether the theoretical model that would result, one that would integrate so many changes, would really still have a cognitive–behavioral foundation. For example, constructivists' view of the therapist–client relationship has represented a return to some aspects of the psychoanalytic position (Mahoney & Lyddon, 1988). Fodor (1987), a feminist trying to integrate cognitive–behavioral concepts into a feminist position, has recently written about moving beyond cognitive–behavioral therapy by adding gestalt therapy techniques and a more interpersonal focus. If a new integration produces a broader, more comprehensive model that addresses the restrictions of the cognitive–behavioral model, will it still be considered cognitive–behavioral?

In the meantime, many articles have been written and much research has been conducted to demonstrate the pragmatism and effectiveness of numerous cognitive–behavioral treatment strategies and skill-building techniques. There is no doubt that behavioral interventions can provide change within the existing setting, and equitable, quality treatment for men and women (Blechman, 1980). Many clients from diverse backgrounds have been helped by therapists using these short-term, pragmatic approaches. Yet, while cognitive and behavioral techniques can be important tools for feminist therapy, it is possible to use these techniques in rigid, sexist ways. Moreover, the adequacy of the theory, not the effectiveness and appropriate use of change strategies, is the focus here.

Feminists need to be aware of the weaknesses in cognitive–behavioral theory and the potential pitfalls in the derived applications—including the tendency to focus on the individual and her symptoms; to prioritize cognition, deemphasize affect, and ignore other dimensions; and to define adaptive, appropriate behavior based on the norms of the existing culture. Cognitive–behavioral theorists must begin to construct their theories with nonsuperficial understandings of the equally valid differences of people from diverse cultures, classes, races, and genders. They must also expand their individual foci and address issues of social/cultural forces and dominant/normative collusion. Cognitive–behavioral theory must also attend to and develop programs aimed at altering the natural setting instead of changing the individual. Only when human beings are understood in all their complexity—influencing and being influenced by internal processes and external forces, with multiple meanings and inclusive variables—will cognitive–behavioral theory be compatible with feminist frameworks.

REFERENCES

Ballou, M. (1990). Approaching a feminist-principled paradigm in the construction of personality theory. In L. S. Brown and M. D. Root (Eds.), *Diversity and complexity in feminist theory*. New York: Haworth.

Bandura, A. (1989). Human agency in social cognitive theory. *American Psychologist, 44*(9), 1175–1184.

Beck, A. T., & Weishaar, M. E. (1989). Cognitive therapy. In R. J. Corsini & D. Wedding (Eds.), *Current psychotherapies* (pp. 285–320). Itasca, IL: Peacock.

Belenky, M. F., Clinchy, B. M., Goldberger, N. R., & Tarule, J. M. (1986). *Women's ways of knowing*. New York: Basic.

Blechman, E. A. (1980). Behavior therapies. In A. M. Brodsky & R. T. Hare-Mustin (Eds.), *Women and psychotherapy: An assessment of research and practice* (pp. 217–244). New York: Guilford.

Brody, C. M. (Ed.). (1984). *Women therapists working with women*. New York: Springer.

Burns, D. D. (1980). *Feeling good: The new mood therapy*. New York: Signet.

Casas, J. M. (1988). Cognitive behavioral approaches: A minority perspective. *The Counseling Psychologist, 16*(1), 106–110.

Dobson, K. S. (1988). The present and future of the cognitive-behavioral therapies. In K. S. Dobson (Ed.), *Handbook of cognitive-behavioral therapies* (pp. 387–414). New York: Guilford.

Dutton-Douglas, M. A., & Walker, L. E. A. (1988). Introduction to feminist therapies. In M. A. Dutton-Douglas & L. E. A. Walker (Eds.), *Feminist psychotherapies: Integration of therapeutic and feminist systems* (pp. 3–11). Norwood, NJ: Ablex.

Ellis, A. (1989). Rational-emotive therapy. In R. J. Corsini & D. Wedding (Eds.), *Current psychotherapies* (pp. 197–238). Itasca, IL: Peacock.

Fodor, I. G. (1987). Moving beyond cognitive-behavior therapy: Integrating gestalt therapy to facilitate personal and interpersonal awareness. In N. S. Jacobson (Ed.), *Psychotherapists in clinical practice* (pp. 190–231). New York: Guilford.

Fodor, I. G. (1988). Cognitive behavior therapy: Evaluation of theory and practice for addressing women's issues. In M. A. Dutton-Douglas & L. E. Walker (Eds.), *Feminist psychotherapies: Integration of therapeutic and feminist systems* (pp. 91–117). Norwood, NJ: Ablex.

Fodor, I., & Epstein, R. C. (1983). Assertiveness training for women: Where are we failing? In E. B. Foa & P. M. G. Emmelkamp (Eds.), *Failures in behavior therapy* (pp. 137–158). New York: Wiley.

Greenberg, L. S. (1988). Constructive cognition: Cognitive therapy coming of age. *The Counseling Psychologist, 16*(2), 235–238.

Guidano, V. F., & Liotti, G. (1983). *Cognitive processes and emotional disorders.* New York: Guilford.

Harding, S. (Ed.). (1987). *Feminism and methodology.* Bloomington, IN: Indiana University Press.

Jackson, G. G. (1987). Cross-cultural counseling with Afro-Americans. In P. Pedersen (Ed.), *Handbook of cross-cultural counseling and therapy* (pp. 231–237). New York: Praeger.

Kruglanski, A. W. (1988). Psychological constructivism in therapy and counseling: Some unresolved issues. *The Counseling Psychologist, 16*(2), 245–248.

Mahoney, M. J. (1988). The cognitive sciences and psychotherapy: Patterns in a developing relationship. In K. S. Dobson (Ed.), *Handbook of cognitive-behavioral therapies* (pp. 357–386). New York: Guilford.

Mahoney, M. J. (1989). Scientific psychology and radical behaviorism: Important distinctions based in scientism and objectivism. *American Psychologists, 44*(11), 1372–1377.

Mahoney, M. J., & Lyddon, W. J. (1988). Recent developments in cognitive approaches to counseling and psychotherapy. *The Counseling Psychologist, 16*(2), 190–234.

McHugh, M. C., Koeske, R. D., & Frieze, I. H. (1986). Issues to consider in conducting non-sexist psychological research. *American Psychologist, 41*(8), 879–890.

Okun, B. (1990). *Seeking connections in psychotherapy.* San Francisco: Jossey-Bass.

Pervin, L. A. (1989). *Personality: Theory and research.* New York: Wiley.

Piasecki, J., & Hollon, S. D. (1987). Cognitive therapy for depression: Unexplicated schemata and scripts. In N. S. Jacobson (Ed.), *Psychotherapists in clinical practice* (pp. 121–152). New York: Guilford.

Staats, A. W. (1986). Behaviorism with a personality: The paradigmatic behavioral assessment approach. In R. O. Nelson & S. C. Hayes (Eds.), *Conceptual foundations of behavioral assessment* (pp. 242–294). New York: Guilford.

Stewart, A. J., & Healy, J. M., Jr. (1989). Linking individual development and social changes. *American Psychologist, 44*(1), 30–42.

Stolz, S. B. (1984). Dissemination of behavioral interventions with women: Needed—a technology. In E. A. Blechman (Ed.), *Behavior modification with women* (pp. 94–108). New York: Guilford.

Unger, R. (1984). Hidden assumptions in theory and research on women. In C. Brady (Ed.), *Women therapists working with women* (pp. 119–154). New York: Springer.

Watson, J. B., and Rayner, R. (1920). Conditioned emotional reactions. *Journal of Experimential Psychology, 3*, 1–14.

Wilson, G. T. (1989). Behavior therapy. In R. J. Corsini & D. Wedding (Eds.), *Current psychotherapies* (pp. 241–282). Itasca, IL: Peacock.

CHAPTER FIVE

Women's Diversity: Ethnicity, Race, Class, and Gender in Theories of Feminist Psychology

OLIVA M. ESPIN
MARY ANN GAWELEK

Theories of psychological development and psychopathology have been notorious for their neglect of cultural variability as well as gender issues. Most psychological theory is literally Anglo–Saxon in its perspectives and conceptions of human nature. Psychology's preoccupation with scientific objectivity has divorced it from an understanding or description of human experience in its fullness, and has circumscribed it to data that is mostly based on the experience of white Anglo–Saxon men. Data on white women or ethnic minority persons of both sexes have mostly either been excluded as "nuisance variables" or included only as "difference," and have frequently been understood as deficiencies. Robert Levine says that psychology, as we know it, is nothing but the "folk beliefs of the West" (1981, personal communication). One might add that it is really "the folk beliefs of white, middle-class, North American males."

This chapter discusses weaknesses in feminist psychological theory that are derived from its inception in Western psychological theory. We seek to make explicit the connections between white, middle-class culture in the United States and feminist psychological theory. We try to demonstrate that current feminist psychological theory is encumbered by a scientific paradigm of psychology, and try to present a case for a feminist theory in psychology that would truly emcompass the diversity of female experience. We conclude by describing how a critique of theories of personality development will benefit from incorporating ethnicity, race, and class, as well as gender, at the core of its understanding of human development.

Although some of the comments we make are relevant and applicable to other behavioral sciences and mental health disciplines, we are confining our discussion to psychology in order to keep the comments focused and, simply, because psychology is the discipline in which we were educated and in which we practice.

PSYCHOLOGY AND HUMAN VARIABILITY

Basically, psychology has understood human diversity from diametrically opposed perspectives: Either diversity is a reflection of abnormalities or deficiencies, in which case efforts should be made to change the individuals and make them healthy. Or, these differences are dictated by nature rather than a result of the sociocultural context, so there is no need for any intervention.

As noted by feminist scholars (Fine, 1989; Hare-Mustin & Marecek, 1987), because psychology is the discipline that studies individual differences in human nature, it does not know how to study human diversity except as "difference." And differences, even when created by societal power structures, are defined as inherently abnormal or innate.

An analysis of diversity based only on difference camouflages oppressive structures and "naturalizes" these differences without a recognition for the need to alter the social context (Fine, 1989). The fact that power differentials in society play a role in these differences is totally obscured.

The work of feminist theoreticians in psychology has also tended to naturalize psychological characteristics associated with gender differences. Most feminist psychological theory assumes that the psychological characteristics exhibited by white, middle-class women (e.g., connectedness, empathy, nurturance, affiliative orientation, emphasis on the value of human interaction) are core to the psychology of all women (Jordan, 1984; Miller, 1983; Surrey, 1983). This essentialist assumption is made with little consideration that these characteristics, in fact, may be the consequence of defense mechanisms developed by women to deal with oppression. Only if the social conditions that have determined most women's behavior could be removed, would we be able to assess whether the character-istics ascribed to women are in fact part of "women's nature" (Espin, Gawelek, Christian, & Nickerson, 1989).

This criticism does not deny the value of a feminist psychology of women as it has evolved in the last two decades or so. Rather, we celebrate the impressive development of feminist theory in psycholo-gy, while we give witness to and acknowledge the difficulty in actual-ly examining the effects of the broad range of culturally determined variables on all women.

IS FEMINIST THEORY FOR ALL WOMEN?

Other chapters of this book focus more specifically on the exclusion of a feminist analysis from major theories of personality development. Most of those chapters make references to women of color in their discussion of the specific theories. In this chapter, the emphasis is on developing a feminist psychological theory that encompasses women of all cultures, races, and social classes.

Elsewhere (Espin, 1977; Espin et al., 1979; Espin, Gawelek, & Rodriquez-Nogues, 1981), we have addressed the concern that what is currently published as women's psychology literature is actually reportage of research and practice on white, middle-class women, and we have offered some alternatives to deal with this bias. Here we discuss how feminist psychology has addressed or has failed to ad-dress the experiences of all women. It is obviously important to assess how a feminist perspective in psychology has been more or less successful in achieving the inclusion of all women. We must be prepared to undertake this assessment of how a feminist psycholog-ical theory includes other aspects of human variability besides gen-der, how it has or has not focused on feminist diversity.

Feminist scholars (e.g., Brown, 1990) have begun to express their distress with a database and theoretical perspective that equate "women" with white, middle-class women because "lack of data and lack of awareness go hand in hand to create trained-in insensitivity . . . and ignorance" (p. 5). An isolated chapter on black women in women's psychology books is not an adequate response to the ethnocentric perspective of most psychology of women.

This ethnocentric perspective is expressed through the focus on white women in the development of feminist theory in the United States, as well as by a disregard and lack of knowledge of feminist perspectives being developed in other areas of the world. While French feminists (who are white and European) are recognized by name by North American feminists and have been translated into English, perspectives and theories on the psychology of women being developed in Latin America (e.g., Burin, 1987; Coria, 1988; Lombardi, 1988) or in other parts of the world (e.g., Katoppo, 1979), or even some perspectives on feminism developed by African-American feminists in the United States (e.g., Hooks, 1981; 1987; Joseph & Lewis, 1981), remain either untranslated into English or largely unknown to most white, North American feminists.

White Privilege and Feminist Theory

There are several factors that contribute to the focus of feminist psychological theories on the experience of white, middle-class women. As much as feminist theoreticians and therapists are conscious of the fact that the power structures of society are the cause of women's oppression, we tend to disregard our own participation in this structure of power when we are its beneficiaries. White, middle-class women, by virtue of their being members of the dominant race, have greater opportunities than women of color to be in positions of power, to engage in research, to publish the results of that research, and to otherwise be involved in professional and academic institutions where such knowledge is generated and distributed. Even while decrying the lack of feminist theory development by nonwhite women, white feminists (e.g., Jaggar, 1983) ignore the lack of access to sources of power by women of color, while minimizing the fact of their own connections to the sources of power in society.

Privilege leads white women to make the assumption that their experiences are universal, normative, and representative of others' experiences, although well-motivated, white, middle-class feminist scholars have fallen into the trap of presenting the experiences of "mainstream" women as the yardsticks of women's experiences. Therefore, the impacts of racial, cultural, and class-based factors are ignored, not only for women of color, but also for white women. Most white women are unaware of the fact that their racial privilege is an important cultural influence/factor in their lives (McIntosh, 1988).

This is not to say that feminist theoreticians are not well-intentioned. It is only to note that they are constricted by the limitations of their own phenomenological context, that is, their existence as dominant cultural beings (McIntosh, 1988). Painfully, much of feminist theory has done to the experience of women of color what men have done to the experience of women: ignore and/or silence it.

Personality theory about all women will not be developed until nonwhite, non-middle-class women are shaping the questions to be asked and interpreting the results, thus creating the theory. Because "the personal is political" in feminist thinking, it is the lived experience of the women theorists that determines what is "political," in other words, what is considered essential and important for feminists to focus on. Thus it is not surprising that white feminists focus on their own experiences.

The main source of data for feminist theorizing is the lived experience of women. The political and social context in which a woman lives has importance as a force influencing her psychology. These are basic principles from which feminist psychology evolves. As such, we recognize that our own personal histories (as a white, Cuban, woman immigrant with English as a second language and a Polish-American, working-class woman) have informed our awareness of the limitations of current feminist personality theories and our vision of what they should be like.

Feminist Psychology as a Reflection of Female Diversity

If feminist personality theory is to reflect the diversity of womankind, we must look for data that reflects all women's experiences. Naturalistic sources of data (Espin, Stewart, & Gomez, 1990; Fine, 1989) such as women's letters, journals, and stories must be encouraged as rich sources of data. Feminist therapists working with women of color need to be collecting and reporting data from their clinical experiences.

We must begin by recognizing that gender may not be a salient organizing variable in the lives of all women (Brown, 1990). "Salient" is the key word. For women of color, race or class rather than gender may be a more centrally determining factor in their identity. This should not be taken to assume that gender does not play a determining role in these women's lives. In fact, gender is always one of the most powerful organizers of behavior and self-understanding for all human beings. In all cultures, the experience and developmental contexts of women are different from those of their male peers. As such, all women, despite their racial/ethnic or social-class background have their phenomenological experience dramatically molded by the variable of gender. But the culture or social-class context from which each woman comes will influence how gender is experienced.

Because of this interplay among factors, the relative conscious salience of gender varies across societies and among individuals. Conscious awareness and salience of a factor are not the same as its psychological impact. This is clearly illustrated by the fact that although white, middle-class women often fail to recognize the impact of white privilege on their lives, this does not mean that their lives are not powerfully determined by their white skin. The salience of gender is modified by the racial and class variables shaping a woman's life. If a woman is part of the dominant culture, the impact of her race and social class is usually not acknowledged, either by the woman herself or by most psychologists. In this case, her gender appears as the most salient differentiating characteristic. In contrast, for a woman raised in a context where social class and/or ethnic background place her in a subordinate societal position, the salience of the gender variable may be less conscious and may seem less important. The need to identify with one's ethnicity or class is strong, due to the common oppression experienced by all individuals in that group regardless of gender. Because she is a woman, a black, working-class woman does not necessarily have more in common with a white, upper-class woman than with a black, working-class male. However, she is most likely to have more in common with other women of color than with the black male.

Hurtado (1989) has developed an analysis of the experience of subordination for different groups of women based on the premise that "each oppressed group in the United States is positioned in a particular and distinct relationship to white men, and each form of subordination is shaped by this relational position" (p. 833). According to Hurtado, white women's oppression by white men takes the form of seduction, while the oppression of women of color takes the form of rejection. This difference in the subordinate position of white women and women of color determines profound differences on the subjective experience of womanhood, and thus accounts for differences in the phenomenological world of these two groups of women. Tensions between white feminists and feminists of color are "affected in both obvious and subtle ways by how each of these two groups of women relate to white men" (p. 834). Although the experiences of both groups are conditioned by the fact that they are women, being a woman means different things.

To recapitulate, the importance of gender as a variable that affects the development of personality is unquestionable. However, the effect of gender is modulated by other variables, such as social class, race, ethnicity, and culture, which always affect personality development in critical ways. Understanding how the experience of gender is shaped by one's social position of power will help us understand the wide range of female experience.

In addition, understanding gender as a static variable may be a fundamental misperception that leaves the researcher with a clearer research paradigm, but a lack of understanding of the depth of this concept. Unger (1989) speaks to this issue when she says that "gender is constantly altered by social context, by culture, by cross-personal interactions, and by the consciousness of the individuals themselves. It is an inconsistent and sometimes contradictory category" (p. 3).

Thus, the first challenge, in broadening the psychology of women to apply to all women, is to understand that gender is but one variable that shapes women's lives, and, secondarily, that female-ness—the notion of what it is to be a woman—changes, based on intrapsychic variables and the social context.

Ostrander (1984), Komarovsky (1987), and Rubin (1976) have demonstrated the pervasive differences in the lives of women due to social class. Stack (1974) and Sennett and Cobb (1972) have shown the important structural and emotional differences observed in individuals and families of diverse social and ethnic backgrounds. Watson-Franke (1988) addresses the differences in gender roles and values found in men and women raised in matrilineal societies. Earlier, Vygotsky (in Wertsch, 1985) and most recently Rogoff (1990) have built a powerful case for the social constructionist nature of cognitive skills. We can safely assume that those differences must impact the personality development of individuals raised in diverse social and cultural contexts.

Maria Root's chapter in this book, on the impact of trauma on personality, opens up another perspective in looking at the experiences of different groups of women. She expands the conventional notion of trauma to include not only direct trauma, but also indirect trauma and insidious trauma. She believes that women are more prone to suffer indirect trauma because of their tendency to empathize with others and others' suffering. Thus a woman of color is bound to feel empathy for the pain suffered by men of color due to discrimination in the world of work and to other forms of racism. This type of reaction may be seen by white feminists as a proof that women of color continue to be male-identified, thus failing to recognize the woman's empathy and identification with the trauma suffered by others.

The third type of trauma discussed by Root is insidious trauma, which includes but is not limited to emotional abuse, racism, anti-semitism, poverty, heterosexism, dislocation, and ageism. The effects of insidious trauma are cumulative and are often experienced over the course of a lifetime. Needless to say, women of color are subject to different degrees of insidious trauma throughout their lives. According to Root, exposure to insidious trauma activates survival behaviors that might be easily mistaken for pathological responses when their etiology is not understood. Misdiagnosis of pathology can be a consequence of a lack of understanding of the impact of insidious trauma on women who have lived their lives under the impact of racism, heterosexism, or class discrimination.

An additional effect of insidious trauma caused by negative social sterotypes is their self-fulfilling influence. The destructive behavioral consequences of negative, self-fulfilling prophecy affect the personality development of the stigmatized person in dramatic ways (Allport, 1958; Snyder, Decker-Tanke, & Berscheid, 1977).

SOCIAL CONSTRUCTION THEORY AS A BASIS FOR FEMINIST PSYCHOLOGY

The challenge raised by these notions leads one to a consideration of social construction theory as a viable alternative for interpreting the varieties of women's experiences. According to Gergen (1985), the assumptions of the social constructionist orientation include:

1. The view that what we know of the world is determined by the categories (linguistic and conceptual) that we possess to define it.
2. The terms by which the world is understood are social artifacts, products of historically situated interchanges among people.
3. The degree to which a particular form of understanding prevails across time is not fundamentally dependent on its empirical validity, but on the vagaries of social process.
4. Forms of negotiated understanding are of critical significance in social life.

Social constructionism clearly challenges established, accepted beliefs in Western psychology, as well as much of the work done within the psychology of women field. While this perspective has had increasing acceptance among feminist scholars, our research, theory, and practice are still conceived in the language and paradigm of mainstream psychology. Moreover, as we have stated earlier in this chapter, when we try to escape traditional psychology's descriptions of female psychology, we frequently fall into the trap of embracing an essentialist position (in which observed characteristics are assumed to represent the essential "nature of women," with its inherent biological deterministic ideology) or, worse, of confusing characteristics developed by women as strategies for survival in the midst of oppression as essential and intrinsic characteristics of being female (Espin et al., 1989; Lykes, 1989a, 1989b).

The social constructionist paradigm, which sees psychological characteristics as resulting from social and historical processes, not as natural, essential qualities of one or another group of people, is a much more productive approach for a psychology of women that aims to include the full diversity of the female experience.

The basic tenets of social constructionism—that one must challenge the objective basis of conventional knowledge, that knowledge is basically a social artifact, and that knowledge, no matter how empirically valid it may appear to be, is socially and historically constructed—have important implications for theory building in feminist psychology.

The assumptions of social construction theory are not new to feminist thinkers. Feminist psychologists have consistently acknowledged the importance of the social, external structure of a woman's life in influencing the development of her sense of self. Feminist thinkers have recognized the importance of the individual experience of women and of the interplay of individual development and social context—an interaction which is so deeply entwined that it is fair to say there is no definition of an individual without a definition of her social context. One factor fails to exist without the other. A social constructionist perspective would mandate an examination of each theoretical orientation to determine if the sociocultural context of an individual is included as a central factor in how the theory describes the development of personality.

A feminist theory built on the social construction model would also necessitate an emphasis on pluralism. In recognizing differences and valuing their uniqueness, the complex entwining of race, ethnicity, class, religion, and sexual orientation can be understood. This understanding must include an assessment of the impact of prejudice, privilege/subordination, and how one's social roles are valued or devalued.

Theories of the psychology of oppression and resistance to oppression help us understand the impact of the sociocultural context in the development of personality and in the psychotherapeutic context. For example, Freire (1970) has described the impact of internalized oppression in determining behaviors and aspirations that seem completely individually determined. Bulhan (1985) has studied the effect of internalized oppression on violent behavior and the expression of anger. Lykes (1985) has developed a theory of social individuality to describe the intricacies of a self developed within a social context, rather than the usual interpretation of the self as individualized and totally autonomous. She has extended the implications of her theory to her studies of Guatemalan Indian women (Lykes, 1989a) and to her analysis of caring and powerlessness (Lykes, 1989b). Harre and others (1986) have studied how a variety of deep-seated individual emotions are in fact socially constructed and determined by culture, history, and other factors.

The lack of realization that sociocultural factors continually shape the development of individual personality creates distortions of the human experience in most psychological theories, including feminist theories. Understanding the influence of these distortions is critical in understanding why personality theories are lacking in their ability to incorporate and describe the whole of human experience. Conversely, the incorporation of the sociocultural context as an essential variable in theory opens possibilities heretofore unexplored in our understanding of human beings.

> Social constructionism means that we must continually question ideology and methodology that may deny gender its broader cultural and systemic meaning. Some of the issues that extend cognitive mechanisms are: the many ways the different cultures negotiate issues of gender, the function of gender (as well as other race and class categories) as a social control mechanism, and the role of consciousness (in the sense of awareness of and reflection upon our own behavior) in mediating the effects of gender upon us all. (Unger, 1989, p. 89)

Identity Development as Social Construction

In the light of these reflections about the value of a social construction orientation for the psychology of women, let us consider the very process of identity development.

Atkinson, Morten, and Sue (1979) have developed a model of ethnic minority identity development, and Cass (1979) has developed a similar one related to homosexual identity formation. Both models describe a progression that starts at a "conformist" or "confused" stage (in which images of the self are mostly negative because they are derived from society's negative attitudes toward those who are different). Several intermediate states in both models describe a questioning of the negative images, more or less strong reactions of anger at the realization that one has been the victim of societal oppression that has become internalized. Finally, both models describe the achievement of a "synergetic articulation" (Atkinson, Morten, & Sue, 1979) or "identity synthesis" (Cass, 1979) characterized by more stable patterns involving higher self-esteem and commitment to combating the causes of the original negative identity.

> Although these two models are not identical, they describe a similar process that must be undertaken by people who must embrace negative or stigmatized identities. This process moves gradually from a rejected and denied self-image to the embracing of an identity that is finally accepted as positive. . . . The final stage for both models implies the acceptance of one's own identity, a committed attitude against oppression and an ability to synthetize the best values of both perspectives. (Espin, 1987b, p. 39)

For lesbians of all colors, as well as for all men and women of color, the development of identity is quite complex. The more a person deviates from those who represent the "ideal type" in society, namely heterosexual, white, middle-class males, the more identity development requires additional efforts to incorporate the differences. This developmental process will most likely mandate periods of conflict and separation as those who are "different" struggle to incorporate their experience of subordination to and rejection by the standards of society.

Bernal and her associates (1990) have done research on children's efforts to understand and incorporate awareness of their ethnicity. They have demonstrated that the development of cognitive abilities in children is intertwined with their capacity to incorporate self-awareness of their ethnicity. This effort to incorporate an understanding of ethnic difference and its implications for the self is an additional developmental task required of children of color that begins at an early age.

Language is also an important and much neglected variable in personality development and identity formation. It is very clear from the work of poststructuralists (e.g., Weedon, 1987) that the structure of reality is modified by the language used to describe it. Moreover, language is not simply "transparent and expressive, merely reflecting and describing (pre-existing) subjectivity and human experience of the world" (Gavey, 1987, p. 463), but is, rather, an active creator of that experience. Extensive discussion of the affective and cognitive implications of bilingualism and language use for personality development is beyond the scope of this chapter. However it is important to state that, for those women who speak more than one language, there is yet another component in the development of personality and the expression of psychopathology. From what can be gleaned in therapy with bilinguals, it is apparent that self-expression in areas such as sexuality is highly influenced by the use of one or the other language (Espin, 1984). The expression of pathological affect, strong emotional states, and the experience of the self are affected by the language used (Marcos, 1976, 1977). An important aspect of language usage for women of color is its connection with self-esteem and identity development. Languages and speech do not occur in a vacuum. In the United States, black English and bilingualism are associated with an inferior social status. The differential valuing of languages and accents has a profound impact on the development of self concept and identity. Bilingual skills are devalued and, with them, those parts of the self that have been developed in the context of another language (Espin, 1987a).

Yet another example is provided by matrilineal societies. "The importance of the matrilineal message is that it puts sex and sexuality in a different perspective. . . . In this context the absence or low incidence of rape as well as the extremely negative views toward rape reported for some matrilineal systems are of interest" (Watson-Franke, 1988, pp. 14–15).

The above examples illustrate how societal standards and expectations deeply affect the development of identity and other components of personality. They illustrate how a social construction perspective serves as a useful tool in understanding how personality comes to be. Through the preceding discussion of factors affecting the development of identity for women of color, we hope to have demonstrated the significance of a social construction perspective for the understanding of the experiences of all women, and thus for the psychology of women.

A BRIEF LOOK AT THEORIES FROM A FEMINIST/CROSS-CULTURAL PERSPECTIVE

We now turn to an evaluation of traditional theories of personality development in a context that recognizes the reciprocal impact of individual development and social structure on development and meaning-making in the internal structure of personality.

The sexist bias in *psychodynamic theories* has been the object of discussion among feminists of diverse theoretical persuasions from Karen Horney (1924/1967) to the present (Chodorow, 1978; Lerman, 1986). Most psychodynamic theories place great emphasis on the interaction between infant and mother. This emphasis, as well as the basic psychodynamic postulate of the existence of an unconscious with a life of its own, assume the separate existence of an internal, individual world that is shaped by interactions with the mother during infancy.

Our most important criticisms of psychodynamic theories is their inability to recognize the cultural relativity of child rearing. Deep-seated beliefs about the influence of mothers in object relations theory, for example, presuppose a certain form of family organization that is not only sexist, but also culturally and class biased. How are we to understand psychological development based on relation with an other (the object) if the role of this other and the relationship between the developing child and this other are significantly different in different cultures? What psychodynamic thinking has consistently assumed as universal is a heterosexual family structure where the mother is the primary caretaker. Although this might be the experience of many individuals raised in our society, it is certainly not a universal experience. Recent developments of psychoanalytic theory such as object relations theory and self psychology, although breaking with Freud and traditional psychoanalysis in many respects, still maintain this bias of considering the mother as the primary caretaker, with the mother/infant dyad as the source of the most serious psychological trauma or distress. Feminist discussions of object relations theories, in terms of their emphasis on mother and their potential for mother-hating, seldom question the sociocultural context in which the mother is immersed (Brown, 1990). Much less do they question aspects of that context that might be equally as influential as the mother in the psychological development of the child.

The importance of women's role in childbirth and caretaking is almost universal; however, different cultures assign different meanings to this role, and may limit the role in significant ways. The variance of child rearing practices, such as the use of wet nurses, the involvement of the extended family, the raising of children by siblings or grandmothers, the presence or absence of fathers, all dramatically affect the development of personality. In addition, how the culture makes meaning of these practices also impacts the development of the individual.

For example, in poor, urban, black and Latino families in the United States, young mothers frequently turn over the care of their children to their mothers, who by then are in their late 30s and more able to take care of children than when they were young and had their own. Matrilineal societies provide us with another example of alternative relationships between mothers and children. According to Watson-Franke (1990), matrilining creates a different valuing of mothers and women and different father and husband roles than those we are accustomed to. "In congruence with the centrality of women, matriliny creates strong female role models, with the mother playing the essentially significant part" (Watson-Franke, 1988, p. 4). While in patriarchal societies, matrifocal families are seen as less valid than male-headed households, in matrilineal societies, matrifocus represents the legitimate philosophy. Western theoreticians, raised within a patriarchal context, find it difficult to conceptualize as "healthy" a family context in which women are central. "The centrality of women in female headed families has no publicly acknowledged and supported structural force" (Watson-Franke, 1988, p. 14). The female-headed family of all races is still seen as deviant in most of the Western world. Because the model of "healthy family" derived from patriarchal society resists and rejects a central position for women, it describes many black and Latino families, as well as all lesbian families, as "dysfunctional."

What implications does this have for object relations theories? Clearly, the necessity of a nuclear family structure, as we know it in Western society, becomes questionable for healthy personality development. Moreover, the culture-boundedness of the theories developed within a patriarchal context becomes more obvious. It also makes explicit that psychodynamic theorists have not addressed the value-laden messages internalized by individuals concerning the societal assessment of being male or female, black or white. The theorists' basic understanding of the development of the unconscious appears to be questionable, since these societal messages have not been taken into account.

Within feminist theory, it has been pointed out that interpretations of psychoanalytic theories and their variations, such as Chodorow's (1978) work, have tended to disregard variability across racial and class lines (Spelman, 1988).

Early feminists heralded *behavioral theories* and therapy as helpful to women, since they recognized the importance of social variables on personality development. However, the recognition of how these variables affect the individual did not address how the social structure might be unhealthy or how the individual might internalize these messages. The most significant criticism of behavioral theories has been their lack of attention to the interplay between the internal and external factors in an individual's life. The advent of the "cognitive revolution" in psychology has modified this approach into the more accepted cognitive–behavioral perspective. Because cognitive–behavioral theories incorporate the tenets of social constructionism, their potential for addressing the experiences of all women seems to be greater. As such, cognitive–behavioral approaches to the psychology of women are already developing (Gergen, 1988; Unger, 1989; Crawford & Gentry, 1989). However, ethnic minority psychologists frequently take issue with the limitations created by research samples of exclusively white persons as the source for the development of this theory (e.g., Casas, 1988). From a feminist perspective, Ballou (in the introduction to Part I of this book) questions the validity of a "scientific" claim that focuses on adaptation without questioning who is to decide what is "adaptive." Ballou also questions the emphasis on individual change without enough attention being given to needed changes in the environment.

Given their emphasis on the phenomenological world of the person, *humanistic, person-centered theories* have been well received by feminists. Hearing and respecting a woman's experience as a person are upheld by this theoretical school. However, there are two basic premises of this person-centered philosophy that are quite problematic for feminist psychology theory. The first is that a person's "story" is reflected and accepted as told. While this may seem validating, it may also create the opposite effect. Since all women are victims of an oppressive society, simple acceptance and reflection may result in validation of the oppressive status quo, or in defining as pathological that which is a defensive reaction to an oppressive situation (e.g., the high percentage of depression in women). The second assumption of person-centered theory is that the locus of control lies within the individual. This assumption is simply untrue for women who experience multiple discrimination: By definition, the external world is a major source of controlling factors in the lives of women, as we have already discussed extensively. Humanistic, person-centered techniques can be helpful to women when they are contextualized within an understanding of the women's social experiences.

THE FUTURE OF FEMINIST THEORY

The question remains: How does one develop a feminist theory that will adequately address womanhood, as shaped by all sociocultural variables and one's critiques of established theories? How does one, in fact, transform all psychological theory of personality development and psychotherapy to include the experiences of all human beings? As such, in analyzing any theoretical conceptualizations generated in regard to the psychology of women, one must emphasize the subjectivity of knowledge and understand the fact that phenomenological understandings of women will never be complete if only a certain group of individuals (white, middle-class women) have their experiences described.

A feminist paradigm must be the basis from which old theories are critiqued and new theories developed. Lerman (1986) and Ballou (1990) have articulated the basic tenets of this paradigm, with Lerman placing greater emphasis on a paradigm that integrates theory into practice, and Ballou focusing more on basic theoretical points. Their assumptions are parallel to those of social construction theory. Following Lerman and Ballou, we believe that the primary factors to be considered in the development of a feminist personality theory are:

1. *All women's experiences must be heard, understood, and valued.* This premise has serious implications when evaluating any theory—first to assess whose experiences have been listened to as the basis for theoretical development; second, to assess whether the diverse experiences have been appreciated on their own merits or used only in comparison to existing cultural standards; and, lastly, to assess the level of respect afforded to the populations discussed.

2. *Attention to the contextual influences is essential.* The internal experience of a woman is always and ever mediated by her social context, and the social context shifts as people change internally. "Social context," however, includes more than gender. Variables such as race, class, and ethnicity are not merely descriptors of a woman's characteristics, but powerful, active forces determining who she is. Theoretical postulates must always be assessed for their cultural relativity. Issues of social power, valuing, and opportunity for individual change must be variables considered.

3. *The psychology of women must be pluralistic.* We must recognize the vast differences among women based on sociocultural variables. Not only must these differences be identified but one must develop an attitude in which differences are equally appreciated. "The demand of diversity is not merely gaining information about other races, cultures, classes, and ethnicities, to know them in 'our' terms. It is considering diversities through 'their' own realities and modes of knowing" (Ballou, 1990, p. 33). Thus theories must be continually challenged to consider whether they are truths or social artifacts in order to expand the range of cultural forms and structures.

4. *Egalitarian relationships must be at the base of the development of the theory.* Where power is shared between partners (i.e., researcher/ subject, theoretician/participant, therapist/client), the research participant or therapy client has to be perceived as the shaper of knowledge for the reality of subjective knowledge to be appreciated. Understanding how a theoretical frame allows for the sharing of information is critical in this respect. Otherwise, the "knowledge" included in the theory may be applicable to a limited group of women, similar in characteristics to the researcher or theoretician.

CONCLUDING REMARKS

To analyze and reinterpret psychological theories of personality development and psychopathology, a feminist point of view that recognizes the centrality of variables of race, class, ethnicity, and culture, as well as the centrality of gender, is essential. This is not an impossible process, but clearly a humbling one. The brief examples in this chapter serve to illustrate some of the tasks involved in theorizing about human psychological development with an inclusive perspective and within a social constructionist theoretical frame. It may be that our attempts to prove and justify psychology as a science within dominant academic structures have led us to miss the fact that all science is in fact constructed by human processes (Hubbard, 1988). Thus, in order for a feminist theory to be developed and articulated from this perspective, theorists must recognize their subjective stance. Most psychological theory is created and presented as if psychological reality were objectively definable, and as if that reality were represented by that of white women. According to the principles of social construction theory, reality—particularly psychological reality—is constantly being constructed, rather than discovered, by scientists.

In developing a theoretical approach to the psychology of women, it is clear that the experiences of women of color must be incorporated. But to "add women of color and stir" will not produce an integrated theory. Moreover, the endless groups of women and their experiences that would need to be "stirred in" would condemn this approach to failure. But if we rely on social construction principles, the psychological make-up of all women will be seen as determined by social forces. This approach will provide us with a context from which to look not only at the experiences of women who are "different," but at the experiences of all women. The psychological impact of either social privilege or oppression because of factors other than gender, the impact of insidious trauma, the processes involved in the development of ethnic identity, the emotional implications of language use, the variety of cultural messages concerning sexuality, and other factors will be incorporated into the theory as constituting the experiences of all women.

In the articulation and construction of feminist psychological theory, and of all psychological theory that includes women, the presence of theorists from a wide variety of backgrounds is essential. Otherwise, feminist theory would continue to express more or less directly the structures of power in society that it attempts to change.

The participation of theorists from a diversity of backgrounds will provide for the development of "feminist theory from margin to center" (Hooks, 1984).

In summary, feminist theory should be a working theory that is evolving and regenerated by the inclusion of the experience of all women, and it should become a ferment in the development of all theory. One way to put it is "Feminist theory is [or should be] . . . vision guided by experience and experience corrected by vision" (Morawski, 1988, p. 187). This vision will only be clear if it includes the experiences of all women.

REFERENCES

Allport, G. (1958). *The nature of prejudice.* Garden City, NJ: Doubleday Anchor.

Atkinson, D., Morten, G., & Sue, D. W. (Eds). (1979). *Counseling American minorities.* Dubuque, IA: William C. Brown.

Ballou, M. B. (1990). Approaching a feminist-principled paradigm in the construction of personality theory. In L. S. Brown & M. P. P. Root (Eds.), *Diversity and complexity in feminist theory* (pp. 23–40). New York: Haworth.

Bernal, M. E., Knight, G. P., Garja, C. E., Ocampo, K. A., & Cota, M. K. (1990). The development of ethnic identity in Mexican-American children. *Hispanic Journal of Behavioral Sciences, 12*(1), 3–24.

Brown, L. S. (1990). The meaning of multicultural perspective for theory building in feminist therapy. In L. S. Brown & M. P. P. Root (Eds.), *Diversity and complexity in feminist theory* (pp. 1–21). New York: Haworth.

Bulhan, H. A. (1985). *Franz Fannon and the psychology of oppression.* New York: Plenum Press.

Burin, M. (Ed.). (1987). *Estudios sobre la subjetividad femenina: Mujeres y salud mental.* Buenos Aires, Argentina: Grupo Editor Latinoamericano.

Casas, J. M. (1988). Cognitive-behavioral approaches: A minority perspective. *The Counseling Psychologist, 16*(1), 106–110.

Cass, V. C. (1979). Homosexual identity formation: A theoretical model. *Journal of Homosexuality, 4,* 219–235.

Coria, C. (1988). *El sexo oculto del dinero: Formas de la dependencia femenina* (3rd. ed.). Buenos Aires, Argentina: Grupo Editor Latinoamericano.

Crawford, M., & Gentry, M. (Eds.). (1989). *Gender and thought.* New York: Springer.

Espin, O. M. (1977, March). *Women cross-culturally: The counselor and the stereotype.* Paper presented at the annual convention of the American Personnel and Guidance Association, Dallas, TX.

Espin, O. M. (1984). Cultural and historical influences on sexuality in Hispanic Latin women: Implications for psychotherapy. In C. Vance (Ed.), *Pleasure and danger: Exploring female sexuality* (pp. 149–171). London: Rutledge.

Gavey, N. (1989). Feminist poststructuralism and discourse analysis: Contributions to feminist psychology. *Psychology of Women Quarterly, 13,* 459–475.

Gergen, M. M. (Ed.). (1988). *Feminist thought and the structure of knowledge.* New York: New York University Press.

Gergen, K. J. (1985). The social constructionist movement in modern psychology. *American Psychologist, 40,* 266–275.

Hare-Mustin, R. T., & Marecek, J. (1987). The meaning of difference: Gender theory, postmodernism and psychology. *American Psychologist, 43,* 455–464.

Harre, R. (Ed.). (1986). *The social construction of emotion.* Oxford, England: Basil Blackwell.

Hooks, B. (1981). *Ain't I a woman? Black women and feminism.* Boston: South End Press.

Hooks, B. (1984). *Feminist theory: From margin to center.* Boston: South End Press.

Horney, K. (1967). *Feminine psychology.* New York: Norton. (Original work published in 1924).

Hubbard, R. (1988). Some thoughts about the masculinity of the natural sciences. In M. M. Gergen (Ed.), *Feminist thought and the structure of knowledge.* New York: New York University Press.

Hurtado, A. (1989). Relating to privilege: Seduction and rejection in the subordination of white women and women of color. *Signs: Journal of Women in Culture and Society, 14*(4), 833–855.

Jaggar, A. (1983). *Feminist politics and human nature.* Totowa, NJ: Rowman & Allanheld.

Jordan, J. (1984). *Empathy and self boundaries* (Work in Progress, No. 16). Wellesley, MA: The Stone Center.

Joseph, G. I., & Lewis, J. (Eds.). (1981). *Common differences: Conflict in black and white feminist perspectives.* New York: Anchor.

Katoppo, M. (1979). *Compassionate and free.* New York: Orbis.

Komarovsky, M. (1987). *Blue-collar marriage.* New York: Random House.

Lerman, H. (1986). *A mote in Freud's eye: From psychoanalysis to the psychology of women.* New York: Springer.

Levine, R. (1981). Personal communication.

Lombardi, A. (1988). *Entre madres e hijas: Acerca de la opresion psicologica.* Buenos Aires, Argentina: Paidos.

Lykes, M. B. (1985). Gender and individualistic vs. collectivist bases for notions about the self. *Journal of Personality, 53,* 357–383.

Lykes, M. B. (1989a). Dialogue with Guatemalan Indian women: Critical perspectives on constructing collaborative research. In R. Unger (Ed.), *Representations: Social constructions of gender* (pp. 167–185). Amityville, NY: Baywood.

Lykes, M. B. (1989b). The caring self: Social experiences of power and powerlessness. In M. Brabeck (Ed.), *Who cares? Theory, research and educational implications of the ethic of care* (pp. 164–179). New York: Praeger.

Marcos, L. (1976). Bilinguals in psychotherapy: Language as an emotional barrier. *American Journal of Psychotherapy, 30,* 522–560.

Marcos, L. (1977). Bilingualism and sense of self. *American Journal of Psychoanalysis, 37,* 285–290.

McIntosh, P. (1988). *White privilege and male privilege: A personal account of coming to see correspondence through work in Women's Studies* (Working Paper, No. 189). Wellesley, MA: Center for Research on Women, Wellesley College.

Miller, J. B. (1986). *Toward a new psychology of women* (2nd ed.). Boston: Beacon Press.

Morawski, J. G. (1988). Impasse in feminist thought? In M. M. Gergen (Ed.), *Feminist thought and the structure of knowledge* (pp. 182–194). New York: New York University Press.

Ostrander, S. A. (1984). *Women of the upper class.* Philadelphia: Temple University Press.

Rogoff, B. (1990). *Apprenticeship in thinking: Cognitive development in social context.* New Jersey: Oxford University Press.

Rubin, L. B. (1976). *Worlds of pain: Life in the working class family.* New York: Basic.

Sennett, R., & Cobb, J. (1972). *The hidden injuries of class.* New York: Vintage.

Snyder, M., Decker-Tanke, E., & Berscheid, E. (1977). Social perception and interpersonal behavior: On the self-fulfilling nature of social stereotypes. *Journal of Personality and Social Psychology, 35,* 656–666.

Spelman, E. V. (1988). *The inessential woman: Problems of exclusion in feminist thought.* Boston: Beacon Press.

Stack, C. B. (1974). *All our kin: Strategies for survival in a black community.* New York: Harper & Row.

Surrey, J. L. (1983). *Self-in-relation: A theory of women's development* (Work in Progress, No. 13). Wellesley, MA: The Stone Center.

Unger, R. (Ed.). (1989). *Representations: Social constructions of gender.* Amityville, NY: Baywood.

Watson-Franke, M. B. (1988, July). *Siblings vs. spouses: Men and women in matrilineal societies (South America and North America).* Paper presented at The International Congress of Americanists, Amsterdam, Holland.

Weedon, C. (1987). *Feminist practice and poststructuralist theory.* Oxford, England: Basil Blackwell.

Wertsch, J. V. (1985). *Vygotsky and the social formation of mind.* Cambridge, MA: Harvard University Press.

PART II

Feminist Perspectives on Psychopathology

Introduction

LAURA S. BROWN

Although these topics are often not presented in tandem, it is my view that theories of personality, that is, normal development, and models of psychopathology, that is, abnormal development, are inextricably linked. Behaviors can only be defined as deviant relative to an already established criterion of what is normal or healthy. Because feminist psychological theories have been fundamentally concerned with a critique and deconstruction of dominant visions of both health and illness, my coeditor and I believed that a juxtaposition of these two issues in one volume would serve to more completely delineate feminist disagreements with mainstream norms.

Part II of this volume examines traditional views of psychopathology and provides feminist critiques of its models and conceptualizations. The feminist analysis of what constitutes psychopathology has a long history within feminist theory, predating to some degree the development of feminist therapy. For example, early second-wave American feminist activists questioned traditional views of female sexual dysfunction (Koedt, 1970; Lydon, 1970), and critiqued psychoanalytic notions of the "normal" female pathologies of masochism and dependency (Chesler, 1971; Weisstein, 1970). Clearly, an early concern of the American women's movement was the reevaluation of what was meant by mental health and normalcy. Some of the responsibility for women's oppression was ascribed to the work of mainstream psychopathologists, who had described certain aspects of women's normative distresses under oppressive conditions as evidence of mental illness or neuroticism.

Inevitably, such a challenge to mainstream norms raises questions of how, or even whether, feminist therapy does conceive of mental health and psychopathology. This is a complex problem, given the tendency of feminist therapy theory to rely heavily on a combination of phenomenological reports and political analyses as sources of data regarding what would constitute distress and wellness. It is this author's sense that what emerges from the chapters in this section is the notion that psychopathology does not simply constitute inner distress; in fact, Maria Root argues, in her chapter on trauma, that certain forms of distress may be highly adaptive means of coping with intolerable situations. A feminist vision of psychopathology also includes the pathology of oppressiveness, a state in which the individual may feel little discomfort but inflicts distress on others. A prime example of this feminist vision can be found in Caplan's (1991) proposed diagnostic category of Delusional Dominating Personality Disorder, in which the primary criteria for the diagnosis constitute the social and interpersonal expressions of extreme sexism and misogyny, even or especially when these behaviors do not distress or disturb the person manifesting them. Health, in this model, is thus defined not simply as an absence of distress, but also as the presence of nonoppressive attitudes and relationships towards other humans, animals, and the planet. In this model, as several of the authors in Part II will suggest, certain types of distress may be more appropriate responses to external reality; in a feminist therapy conceptualization, mentally "healthy" and "unhappy" may at times be synonymous.

Part II of this volume emerges from the tradition of feminist deconstruction and critique of traditional images of health and pathology. These chapters address current mainstream models of several large categories of psychopathology, and present feminist revisions for differently understanding these sets of observed behaviors. While our authors do not disagree with the existence of the syndromes observed and described by standard nosologies, their interpretations of the phenomena and their beliefs regarding possible etiologies vary considerably from mainstream views. Several dominant themes emerge from this work which, taken together, constitute one possible feminist model for understanding distressed behavior.

A common thread in these chapters is that mainstream models are overly narrow in their focus. Hamilton's and Jensvold's chapter on depression, Fodor's chapter on agoraphobia, and Greenwald's on schizophrenia, for example, each describe how attempts have been made to reduce such disorders to purely biogenic phenomena; Brown's chapter on personality disorders and Root's on posttraumatic phenomena describe how mainstream perspectives have tended to strip context and complexity away from the study of these entities. Each of these authors have identified tendencies within mainstream models toward describing distress as a highly individualized phenomenon, rather than as a manifestation of larger social and cultural forces. Standard models of psychopathology have tended to look for a prime cause of the observed entity, rather than allowing for the possibility that similar phenomena may have multiple causations that interact with person and context in somewhat unique ways. Whatever the particular nature of the narrow focus in a given mainstream model, feminist critiques push for a broader, more complete and therefore more diagnostically and clinically adequate conceptualization of the etiology of psychopathology. Parallel with feminist models of normal personality development, feminist visions of what constitutes pathology require a biopsychosocial perspective that allows for a thorough examination of the interaction of person and context in the creation and expression of psychological distress. Feminist models, unlike mainstream ones, also rely on a political analysis of the meaning and appearance of certain symptom patterns within certain groups in a culture, and inquire as to the significance for the body politic of the co-occurrence of group membership and certain forms of distress.

The emphasis on the social and interpersonal context and the meaning given by context to an individual's or group's behavior is another theme that resonates throughout these chapters. As Fodor points out in Chapter 8, behavior that was valued for women in one social context and time period (not leaving the house) has become pathologized in another time and place. While certain symptoms may be distressing to people regardless of their context (e.g., suicidal ideation), others may only be a source of distress if there exists no cultural explanation to make them seem abnormal. For example, Ross (1990) has commented that the hearing of voices or the seeing of ghosts is not a distressing symptom in those cultures that describe such experiences as signs of divine favor rather than of psychosis. Additionally, as Root (Chapter 10) and Brown (Chapter 9) point out, behaviors and experiences that currently reside in the diagnostic manual may, from a feminist perspective, represent healthy strategies for staying alive and sane in dangerous and insane places. Feminist critiques demand cultural relativity in diagnosis and require that we ask what is normal for this individual, in this time and place. Feminist analysis, with its emphasis on sensitivity to cultural differences, finds inadequate a single, supposedly "objective" standard of mental health being imposed on all persons when such a standard fails to adequately comprehend the nuances and meanings of the interaction between a particular person–situation and a specific sociocultural setting.

This questioning of the pathological nature of so-called psychopathology in turn raises questions of who possesses the authority to make determinations of health and illness. As Ballou points out in her introduction to our section on theories of personality, the assignment of such expertise to those who represent dominant cultural norms has led to a tendency to overvalue experiences common to the white/male/heterosexual/Christian/middle-class dominant group. The authorities to whom appeal is made to support mainstream models are themselves inherently tied to the status quo and tend to exclude alternative explanations or marginalized knowledge. This has led, in American psychopathology, to a hierarchy of values in which reductionistic biological models develop greater believability because the proponents of these models receive more funding for their research and are more likely to have their findings taken seriously and published, even when the effects of biology are somewhat weak (Rothblum, Solomon, & Albee, 1986). Feminist critiques, by their nature, require the extension of expertise regarding the meanings of behavior to those who experience it, rather than only to societally-sanctioned "experts" whose roles in labeling certain behaviors as pathological often serve primarily to uphold dominant hierarchies of power and control.

Thus, a feminist model of psychopathology requires reliance on a wide variety of sources, including life stories as told by people from diverse and marginalized groups within a culture and data collected outside the framework of logical positivist empiricism. A challenge to taken-for-granted notions regarding health and illness is a central aspect of this undertaking, which asks: Who is benefited and who harmed, in the greater social context, by a behavior being labeled as pathological or normal? Feminist models of pathology analyze the political significance of certain explanatory fictions and attempt to discover whether a particular frame for understanding behavior risks the further oppression of groups in the culture who are already at risk because of devalued status. Similarly, feminist models seek to have potentially subversive impact on the culture at large by leading to a reassessment of the contributions of external reality to internal distress, thus leading to calls for social change as a strategy for treating the distress being described.

A final theme that emerges within these critiques is that of the importance of understanding the contribution of gendered experiences and gender norms to the development of subjective perceptions of distress. The American Psychiatric Association's *Diagnostic and Statistical Manual* (DSM), in its various revisions, stops short at listing gender prevalence of specific diagnoses, but fails to comment on what this means. Nor does the DSM give us information about how gender, interacting with such phenomena as race, class, or experience, can account for large percentages of what is observed and defined as "pathology." A feminist vision of distressed behavior is, ultimately, one that asks such questions about gender, and about how the privileging of male experience leads inexorably to the pathologizing of female experiences in any sexist society. A feminist model also asks how and if gender membership can be protective or a source of greater resilience for either women or men, and factors this question into its resulting conceptualizations of distress and wellness.

What these chapters present are what Ballou, in her introduction, describes as a new, feminist set of "building codes" for constructing our model of pathology in human behavior. These codes tell us that distress must be understood in a complex, contextual manner. They question the foundations of current standard models of psychopathology. To borrow a phrase from Audre Lorde, feminist models attempt to avoid using the "master's tools" and inhabit uneasily, if at all, the "master's house." This section introduces the reader to a different structure and invites a remodeling of mainstream images of pathology.

REFERENCES

Caplan, P. (1991). Delusional dominating personality disorder. *Feminism and Psychology, 1,* 171–174.

Chesler, P. (1971). Patient and patriarch: Women in the psychotherapeutic relationship. In V. Gornick & B. Moran (Eds.), *Woman in sexist society* (pp. 362–392). New York: Signet.

Koedt, A. (1970). *The myth of the vaginal orgasm.* In S. Firestone & A. Koedt (Eds.), *Notes from the second year: Women's liberation* (p. 39). New York: Editors.

Lorde, A. (1979, September). The master's tools will never dismantle the master's house. Presentation as part of the panel *The personal and political* at the Second Sex Conference, New York.

Lydon, S. (1970). The politics of orgasm. In R. Morgan (Eds.), *Sisterhood is powerful* (pp. 197–205). New York: Vintage.

Rothblum, E. D., Solomon, L. J., & Albee, G. W. (1986). A sociopolitical perspective of DSM-III. In T. Millon & G. L. Klerman (Eds.), *Contemporary directions in psychopathology: Toward the DSM-IV* (pp. 167–189). New York: Guilford.

Ross, C. A. (1990). *Multiple personality disorder: Diagnosis, clinical features, and treatment.* New York: Wiley.

Weisstein, N. (1970). "Kinder, kuche, kirche" as scientific law: Psychology constructs the female. In R. Morgan (Ed.), *Sisterhood is powerful* (pp. 205–220). New York: Vintage.

CHAPTER SIX

Personality, Psychopathology, and Depressions in Women

JEAN A. HAMILTON
MARGARET JENSVOLD

There is general agreement that rates of depression are about twice as high in women than men. The gender difference in depression appears to be a "real" finding, and not simply an artifact of any one type of assessment or of differences in help-seeking or willingness to report symptoms (Nolen-Hoeksema, 1987; Weissman & Klerman, 1977). From an epidemiological perspective, the observed sex difference in depression must be accounted for if we are to claim an understanding of depression.

There has been considerable interest in the relationship between personality and depression. Sex differences in rates of depression have fostered interest in theories of female development. One hypothesis has been that certain aspects of female personality development, at least in our society, are "depressigenic."

Before reviewing the link between personality and depression, several terms deserve definition. While there are numerous definitions of *personality*, in the current diagnostic nomenclature of the American Psychiatric Association (1987, p. 335), personality traits are "enduring patterns of perceiving, relating to, and thinking about the environment and oneself." Personality disorders occur when these traits are inflexible and maladaptive, resulting in impaired functioning or subjective distress. In general, personality traits are considered to be lifelong in duration once one reaches maturity, and are believed to be relatively consolidated by adolescence.

In depression research and clinical practice, a critical distinction exists between an isolated symptom of depression and a persistent set of symptoms, or syndrome. Moreover, numerous types, or subtypes, of depressive syndromes have been recognized. That is, depression is a heterogeneous disorder. Sex-related differences in rates of depression are substantiated for certain subtypes (e.g., unipolar), but not for others (e.g., bipolar or manic-depressive illness).

CONCEPTUALIZATIONS OF THE LINK BETWEEN PERSONALITY AND DEPRESSION: EMPIRICAL FINDINGS

The possible link between personality and depression has been conceptualized in at least four ways (Klerman & Hirschfeld, 1988). The first "direction" of the relationship is that personality promotes (or protects one from) certain subtypes of depression. The reciprocal direction is that certain depressive syndromes affect personality or, at least, assessments of personality. Alternatively, personality and depressive syndromes may co-occur in relationship to a third variable, such as life-event stress, which contributes to both. And finally, what appears to be characterological—that is, a depressigenic personality— may actually be a variant of a depressive syndrome, albeit an attenuated version. Empirical evidence for and against each of these conceptualizations is presented below. We will argue that the strongest evidence is for the third conceptualization, which becomes especially salient when one considers gender-based victimization as the third variable that contributes both to depression and to personality assessments. Biological risk factors are reviewed and are discussed in terms of the third variable conceptualization.

Personality as a Promotive or Protective Risk Factor

Despite the fact that most research has focused on this direction of the relationship, the empirical evidence regarding personality as a risk factor for depressive syndromes is inconclusive. Selecting from among the leading theoretical perspectives, the following hypotheses are especially prominent: (1) sex-role socialization largely accounts for gender-related personality features, and these contribute to the female excess of depression, (2) gender-related attributional styles give rise to depressive symptoms associated with "learned helplessness," and (3) a gender-related set-response bias promotes depression in women and protects against it in men. Following an examination of these three hypotheses, primarily in nonpatient populations, data from psychiatric studies will be examined.

Studies in Nonpatient Populations

Social Roles

Socialization for male and female gender roles begins in infancy. Gender roles can be defined as the sum of socially designated behavior that differentiates between men and women. There is marked consistency in the way that adults describe gender roles. As examples, the male gender role has been described by words such as "active," "independent," and "objective" or "logical" (not at all emotional); whereas, the female role has been described as "passive," "not at all independent" (dependent), and "subjective" or "emotional" (Bem, 1974; Broverman, Vogel, Broverman, Clarkson, & Rosenkrantz, 1972). The male gender role forms a positive cluster entailing "competence," while the female role reflects the positive traits of "warmth–expressiveness." Another description of this polarity is in terms of "instrumentality" (a trait that reflects a sense of agency or mastery) and "expressiveness" (a trait reflecting a sense of communion or concern). Personality traits such as these are highly gendered.

Status inequality refers to the fact that the male gender role is more valued in our society than the female role (Carmen, Russo, & Miller, 1981). For example, in a classic study (Broverman et al., 1972), practicing mental health clinicians were given the authors' Sex-Role Questionnaire with one of three sets of instructions. One group was asked to indicate on each item the characteristics of a healthy, mature, and socially competent adult person. Others were asked to do the same for an adult man or an adult woman. Not surprisingly, healthy adults were described as having characteristics congruent with those of the healthy male; whereas, mental health clinicians described the mentally healthy female as differing from the healthy male by being more submissive, less independent, less adventurous, less objective, less aggressive, less competitive, more excitable in minor crises, more emotional, more easily influenced, more conceited about their appearance, and more likely to have their feelings hurt. The investigators discuss these findings in terms of the "hypothesis that a double-standard of health exists for men and women . . . the general standard of health (adult, sex-unspecified) is actually applied to men only, while healthy women are perceived as significantly *less* healthy by adult standards" (p. 71).

One implication is that women's sense of identity develops within a framework that devalues women. Boys are encouraged to construct and to firmly anchor their self-worth around a pattern of actions with real-world tasks, where clear and immediate feedback from the task itself can enhance their sense of self-reliance (see Block,

1983). In contrast, girls are encouraged to build their sense of worth more upon acceptance by and approval from others. Because adult males ultimately hold greater power and authority, females in theory are rewarded for developing characteristics that accommodate and please men, for example, submissiveness and passivity (Miller, 1976). At issue are the mental health consequences of gender differences in social roles, especially in terms of personality traits and depressive syndromes.

In theory, at least, it is not difficult to extrapolate from the female gender role to special risks for depressive syndromes that are embedded in that role. As suggested by the Broverman et al. study (1972), simply conforming to the female role tends to be pathologized because a person cannot simultaneously be a healthy adult and female. Especially when taken literally, the female role would seem to be a caricature of and a prescription for depression. As examples, several theories of depression specifically suggest that nonassertiveness, dependency, and the tendency to be self-effacing (incompetence) predisposes individuals to depression. Since the female role is consistent with these traits, an obvious hypothesis is that sex differences in these personality characteristics lead to the sex difference in rates of depression (Nolen-Hoeksema, 1990). Unfortunately, personality-based hypotheses have received more attention in theory (e.g., Chodoff, 1972; Kaplan, 1986; Rehm, 1977) than in empirical research. As one example, some psychoanalysts have proposed that there is a "depressive personality," characterized by dependency, obsessionality, low self-esteem, and narcissism, that predisposes to clinical depression (Arieti & Bemporad, 1978). In comprehensive reviews, however, Nolen-Hoeksema (1987, 1990) critically evaluated data pertinent to these theories and found that there was no conclusive evidence to support them. Here we will briefly review key data on assertiveness, aggression, dependency, and the need for approval. The reader is referred to the original reviews for further details.

Assertiveness and Aggression

With regard to sex differences in assertiveness, Eagly and Carli (1981) performed a meta-analysis on studies of "influenceability" and found that women are more likely to be persuaded and to conform than men, but that the effect size is minimal: only 1% of the variability was accounted for by sex. This suggests a negligible contribution, if any, by sex difference in rates of depression. Moreover, influenceability and conformity cannot be considered as inviolate personality traits, because strong contextual effects have been demonstrated; an important variable, for example, is the presence or absence of group pressure (Eagly, 1978). There may also be a historical cohort effect, in that greater influenceability was reported in studies published prior to 1970 than in those published in the '70s (Eagly, 1978).

A related construct is aggression, where the sex difference also has strong contextual determinants. Despite gender role stereotypes to the contrary, women are not always less aggressive than men. Women are more likely to show aggressive behavior if they believe that there will not be physical harm to themselves or the target (Eagly & Steffen, 1986). Based on empirical data, the possible relationship of aggression to depression is difficult to assess at this time. One problem is that laboratory measures of aggression are biased in favor of demonstrating an excess of aggression in males (vs. females), because of an emphasis on studying short-term encounters with strangers.

Dependency and Need for Approval

With regard to sex differences in dependency, women have been thought to be more concerned with relationships than men, which would be expected to contribute to the excess of depression in women. A major theory of depression holds that relationship loss or disruption gives rise to depression. The empirical data, however, suggest that men, not women, are more likely to become depressed with the loss of an intimate relationship (Bernard, 1972; Stroebe & Stroebe, 1983). In a study of college student dating couples, women also tended to leave romantic relationships more readily than men (Rubin, Peplau, & Hill, 1981).

A remaining possibility is that women are more dependent than men on the approval of others, which could lead to lowered or unstable self-esteem. To the extent that someone's identity and sense of worth are highly dependent on the approval of others, we can predict that the person highly vulnerable to disapproval will have difficulty in relying on their own perceptions and tolerating and expressing anger. The latter effect may be of importance since psychoanalytic theory has held that depression is "anger turned inward" (against the self). There is some evidence to support the claim that women's self-evaluations are more reactive to feedback than men's (Roberts & Nolen-Hoeksema, 1990). As noted by Nolen-Hoeksema (1990), others have found that males are more likely than females to engage in self-enhancing estimates of their own competence and control (Golin, Terrell, Weitz, & Drost, 1979). This bias, along with an illusion of control, has been associated with protection against depression (Alloy & Abramson, 1982) in males.

There is also evidence that low self-esteem is related to depressive symptoms in nonpatient adolescent females, but not in males (Gjerde, Block, & Block, 1988); moreover, in girls, but not in boys, early intellectual competence predicts depressive symptoms at 18 years of age (Block & Gjerde, 1990). This may be relevant to the subsequent onset of depression, since depressed women are more likely than depressed men to be characterized by self-dislike (Hammen & Padesky, 1977).

In summary, there is no conclusive evidence to support the hypothesis that personality traits thought to be stereotypically female, such as nonassertiveness or dependency, contribute substantially to the female excess of depressive symptoms in nonpatient populations. Limited data, however, do support the hypothesis of lowered self-esteem in women, along with greater reactivity to feedback compared to men.

In addition, some theorists have observed that there are positive as well as negative aspects of traits like dependency, and that these apply to both males and females (Lerner, 1983). It is of interest that males may be protected from depression by biased self-assessments, although the effect size and relevance to clinical depressive syndromes are unknown and deserve further investigation. More recent feminist contributions to theory will be discussed in a later section (Chernin, 1986; Gilligan, 1982; Jordan & Surrey, 1986; Lerner, 1987).

Attributional Styles and Learned Helplessness

The reformulated *learned-helplessness theory* of depression (Abramson, Seligman, & Teasdale, 1978) predicts that individuals who characteristically explain negative events by causes that are internal to them ("it's my fault"), stable in time ("it's going to last forever"), and global in effect ("it will undermine everything that I do")—and who do the reverse for positive events ("it came out okay this time by chance")—are prone to depression. Optimism seems to have a protective effect and pessimism a permissive effect on depression (Peterson & Seligman, 1983; Nolen-Hoeksema, 1990). Overall, meta-analysis has shown considerable support for the association between these attributional patterns, particularly for negative events, and depression (Sweeney, Anderson, & Bailey, 1986). In an all-female sample, continuity between childhood and adult ratings of helplessness has been observed, with a high correlation between the degree of helplessness remembered just prior to and during current episodes of depression (Harris, Brown, & Bifulco, 1990).

Contrary to cognitive or attributional theory, Miranda and Persons (1988) have reviewed several studies showing that dysfunctional thinking remits as the patient recovers from depression. These studies challenge the hypothesis that dysfunctional attitudes or attributional styles are stable (personality) traits. Miranda and Persons (1988) tested an alternative hypothesis: that an individual's ability to access and report dysfunctional attitudes is mood-state dependent, while the attitudes themselves are indeed stable traits. Using a negative mood-induction procedure, subjects who reported previous episodes of depression demonstrated more dysfunctional attitudes than subjects without a depressive history. The study is consistent with the hypothesis that stable (personality) traits associated with dysfunctional attitudes exist, and that these can be reconciled with studies that superficially appear to be contradictory if mood-state dependent thinking is taken into account. Because the study population was composed entirely of females, however, possible gender-related differences were not assessed.

The empirical evidence for a sex difference in attributional style is, to our surprise, quite limited. Nolen-Hoeksema (1990) reviewed studies on attributions and behavioral persistence under challenge. The literature on sex differences in explanatory style has received some support in studies of children. Overall, however, the literature on sex differences in attributions has been criticized on several grounds. Some studies have found that females are more likely than males to show lowered expectations of success following failures (e.g., Dweck & Bush, 1976; Eccles, 1983). But even when there were sex differences in expectancies, there was not a difference in behavioral performance, as would have been expected by the learned-helplessness hypothesis (Eccles, Adler, & Meece, 1984). In addition, many other studies have found little evidence for consistent sex differences in reaction to failure (e.g., Dweck & Repucci, 1973). A final criticism is that many studies have asked subjects about attributions during laboratory tasks, which may or may not be relevant to behaviors in daily life.

Instrumentality, however, may interact with explanatory style and thereby moderate women's risk for depression (McGrath, Keita, Strickland, & Russo, 1990). For high-instrumentality women, success facilitated performance on subsequent tasks, but failure did not affect it. But for low-instrumentality women, failure impaired subsequent task performance, and success did not (Baucom & Danker-Brown, 1984). High-instrumentality women were also more likely than low-instrumentality women to attribute success to effort and ability, and failure to task difficulty.

Set-response Bias

Nolen-Hoeksema (1987) has hypothesized that responses to one's own depressed moods are gender-related, and that these traits contribute to the excess of depression in women. According to this hypothesis, males as a group are more likely to respond behaviorally, and thereby to "dampen" depressive symptoms. This tendency may be related to Angst's and Dobler-Mikola's finding (1984) that males are less likely to recall depressive symptoms compared to females. In contrast, females as a group show more ruminative responses to depressive experiences and moods, and this may tend to "amplify" the symptoms. While the hypothesis is highly interesting, the data thus far are quite limited, and do not yet demonstrate the relevance for clinical depressive syndromes.

In nonpatient populations, however, Ingrams and colleagues (1988) have shown that women have a greater tendency to report paying attention internally to thoughts and feelings, as opposed to externalizing their feelings into action, that is, to "self-focus," than do men, as assessed by a subscale of the Self-Consciousness Scale (Fenigstein, Scheier, & Buss, 1975). An experimental manipulation of self-focus (using a TV monitor) showed an interaction of gender role, as assessed by Bem's Sex Role Inventory (1974), and self-focus in determining negative mood. "Feminine" individuals who received a self-focusing manipulation responded with greater levels of negative affect than did any other group.

In a study (Gjerde, Block, & Block, 1988) of 18-year-old adolescents, scores on a measure of depressive symptoms, the Center for Epidemiological Studies–Depression (Radloff, 1977), were correlated with trait measures of "rumination" for females but not for males. Rumination was assessed by an aggregation of individual items on the Observer-Based California Adult Q-Sort (Block, 1978).

Psychiatric Studies on Personality and Depression

While data in nonpatient populations are inconclusive, stronger evidence for a link between personality and depression comes from psychiatric studies. For example, there is evidence linking cyclothymic temperament to bipolar illness (Klerman & Hirshfeld, 1988). The essential feature of cyclothymia is a chronic mood disturbance of at least 2 years' duration, involving numerous hypomanic episodes and numerous episodes of depressed mood or dysthymic symptoms, that does not meet the criteria listed in the *Diagnostic and Statistical*

Manual of Mental Disorders, Third Edition–Revised (DSM-III-R) for a major depressive or manic episode (American Psychiatric Association, 1987).

Dysthymic disorder, a chronic, low-grade—and perhaps characterological—form of depressive disorder, appears to be a risk factor for development of major depressive disorder (Akiskal, 1987; Weissman, Myers, Thompson, & Bellanger, 1986). Historically, dysthymic disorder replaced previous categories such as depressive neurosis and "depressive personality" (Phillips, Gunderson, Hirschfeld, & Smith, 1990). These findings will be discussed further in the section on personality as a depressive variant.

In a large study where personality was assessed prospectively, lower emotional strength and resiliency differentiated the first-onset depressives from the never-ill group; but, contrary to expectations, overall differences were not found on interpersonal dependency—a gender-linked trait—nor on extraversion. Among older subgroup members (31–41 years of age), however, decreased emotional strength, increased interpersonal dependency, and increased thoughtfulness were associated with the first onset of depression (Hirschfeld et al., 1989). There is also evidence that more severe personality disorders are associated with more severe depression. These findings, however, are not unique to women.

Depressive Symptoms or Syndromes Affect Personality

It is well-established that the clinically depressed state will strongly influence the assessment of interpersonal dependency, extraversion–introversion, and emotional strength (Hirschfeld, Klerman, Clayton, Keller, McDonald-Scott et al., 1983; Hirschfeld et al., 1989). While not unique to females, this suggests the importance of assessing personality after recovery from depression or prior to the first episode of depression.

In a study of 31 female depressives with primary nonbipolar depressive disorder, recovered depressives were introverted, submissive, and passive, with increased interpersonal dependency as compared to the normal population and to never-ill relatives (Hirschfeld, Klerman, Clayton, & Keller, 1983). Similar studies need to be completed for males, as well as females, in order to allow assessment of possible sex differences.

As mentioned earlier, several studies have shown that "dysfunctional" thinking remits as patients recover from depression (Eaves & Rush, 1984; Hamilton & Abramson, 1983; Persons & Rao, 1985; Silverman, Silverman, & Eardley, 1984; Simons, Garfield, & Murphy, 1984), although state-dependent cognitive functioning may account for this discrepancy (Miranda & Persons, 1988). In a prospective study, however, Lewinsohn, Steinmetz, Larson, and Franklin (1981) demonstrated that individuals who later developed a clinical depression were no more likely to have previously evidenced depressive thinking than were individuals who did not become depressed. While these studies do not speak to the question of gender differences per se, they do weaken the hypothesis that personality traits linked to dysfunctional thinking precede, and possibly give rise to, depression. Instead, they support alternative hypotheses, such as the possibility that depressive thinking is a result of depression, rather than an antecedent.

How might depression lead to personality change? One mechanism would be for the hopelessness and helplessness associated with clinical depression to be remembered and incorporated into one's self-image. Since these experiences are thought to be congruent with the female social role (vs. the male), they may be preferentially recalled by females. The finding that women are more likely to recall having been depressed compared to men (Angst & Dobler-Mikola, 1984) is intriguing with respect to this hypothesis, but not conclusive.

A Third Variable May Be Contributory: Victimization

In the American Psychological Association's *Task Force Report on Women and Depression* (McGrath et al., 1990), a number of possible moderating variables are discussed, including: family and employment roles, victimization, and poverty. Victimization is a critically important issue for two reasons: (1) it is a risk factor for depression and posttraumatic stress disorder in women, and the types of abuse that are most highly related to psychiatric sequelae occur in disproportionate excess in women; and (2) it can both complicate the course and clinical management of depressions and confound attempts to diagnose personality disorders in women, leading to a misunderstanding about the relationship between personality and depression in women. For these reasons, the present discussion will focus on victimization.

What Is Victimization?

Victimization is a life event that is highly salient to women's lives. Women are the primary victims of all forms of gender-based abuse. The spectrum of gender-based abuse encompasses physical and sexual violence or exploitation, as well as the psychological and economic abuse of sexual harassment and other forms of discrimination.

Sexual and physical abuse are so prevalent that they have been characterized as normative aspects of female development (Carmen, 1985; Johnson, 1980). Based on a randomized, community-based survey, there is a 46% life-time probability that a woman will be a victim of completed or attempted rape, and a 26% probability of a completed rape (Russell, 1984). In an epidemiologic study that included both sexes, women were about twice as likely to experience a sexual assault as were men (Sorenson, Stein, Siegal, Golding, & Burnam, 1987).

Because of gender role stereotypes and unequal social roles, even those women who do not directly experience gender-based abuse have reason to fear it. There has been speculation, for example, that unequal social roles are reinforced in part by threats of physical and sexual violence. Some of the harm associated with gender-based crimes may be related to the meaning of these events, given the gender roles in our society. In a randomized, community-based survey on mental health correlates of criminal victimization (Kilpatrick et al., 1985), victims of attempted or completed rape had serious mental health problems more frequently than did victims of attempted or completed robbery, or aggravated assault.

In discussing prevalence studies, Sorenson and colleagues (1987) observed that studies with a higher completion rate had lower prevalence rates, suggesting that nonresponders may have been less likely than responders to have been sexually assaulted, a bias that would tend to inflate prevalence estimates. On the other hand, it is more likely that rates overall are underestimated, because individuals often do not identify themselves as sexual assault victims. By using behaviorally specific questions and a large number of questions, subjects may become desensitized to the topic and memories of sexual assault may be stimulated. In Russell's (1984) study, use of behaviorally specific questions doubled the rate of rape or attempted rape from that reported by the initial self-identification of victims alone. Experts in women's mental health have found that a history of victimization often cannot be elicited in the initial evaluation, and may not be reported for upwards of 3 to 6 months.

Mental Health Correlates or Consequences of Victimization

Brown (1989) reviewed data on the connection between various types of victimization and mental health symptoms or syndromes. Several studies have found that psychiatric inpatients have relatively high rates of victimization, but the available data do not suggest a specific link to depressive disorder per se (Carmen, Reiker, & Mills, 1984; Jacobsen & Richardson, 1987). Data from a community sample of women also fail to identify a link to a specific psychiatric disorder (Winfield, George, Swartz, & Blazer, 1990). Here we will discuss depression, posttraumatic stress disorder (PTSD), and personality disorders as possible sequelae of victimization.

Depression. In the community-based survey of Kilpatrick and colleagues (1985), nearly 20% (19.2%) of rape victims had attempted suicide, compared to only 2.2% of nonvictims, suggesting a link to depression and despair. Importantly, completed rape victims' mental health problems were 14 times more likely to occur after their victimizations than before (with a pre-assault base rate of 1.1%). In another epidemiologic sample, crime victims who were mugged, sexually assaulted, or who experienced repeated victimization were at the greatest risk for depression; whereas those who were mugged were at greatest risk for suicidality (Sorenson & Goulding, 1990). The focus in the remaining discussion will be on sexual assault, specifically rape and incest, as prime examples for understanding the effects of victimization in women.

Most assessments of depressive symptomatology after rape have not been sufficient to determine whether or not a depressive disorder exists. When psychiatric assessments were made, however, 24% of rape victims met standard research diagnostic criteria (RDC) for a depressive disorder (Frank, Turner, & Duffy, 1979). In a replication by the same group, 90 recent victims of sexual assault were assessed within 4 weeks of the assault using RDC criteria (Frank & Stewart, 1984). Forty-three percent of the subjects met criteria for depression. Older subjects and those who previously had been assaulted were at increased risk for depression. More than 25% reported post-rape suicidal ideation. Taken together, these data suggest that rape can be associated with the onset of depressive symptoms, including suicidality, and in a substantial proportion of cases, with a depressive syndrome. The data from Frank and Stewart's group requires replication, however, before these findings could be considered well-established.

Posttraumatic Stress Disorder. PTSD consists of reexperiencing a traumatic event in recurrent and intrusive recollections, dreams, or dissociative episodes (e.g., flashbacks); avoidance of reminders of the event or a generalized constriction of affect; and persistent symptoms of increased arousal, particularly in response to reminders of the event. Rape has been recognized as a stressor sufficient to give rise to PTSD (see Hamilton, 1989). However, several other psychiatric disorders share prominent psychological processes and symptoms with PTSD, as described below. In an urban population of young adults from a large health maintenance organization (Breslau, Davis, Andreski, & Peterson, 1991), the prevalence of PTSD was greater in women than in men (11.3% vs. 6%). Among persons exposed to traumatic events, women developed PTSD at significantly higher rates than did men (30.7% vs. 14%).

Personality Disorders and Trauma. Victimization is thought to play an etiologic role in the development of multiple personality disorder (MPD) (Ross et al., 1990) and borderline personality disorder (BPD) (Bryer, Nelson, Miller, & Krol, 1987; Herman, Perry, & van der Kolk, 1989). Extreme trauma may give rise to dissociative processes, and these processes may play a role in symptom formation in a variety of disorders, ranging from flashbacks in PTSD (Spiegel, 1988; van der Kolk, 1988; van der Kolk & van der Hart, 1989) to frank dissociations in MPD. Moreover, both MPD and BPD occur or are diagnosed excessively in women when compared to men. A prospective, representative sample of children were assessed for physical abuse (Dodge, Bailes, & Pettit, 1990). Abused girls were especially at risk for the development of internalizing problems, such as withdrawal and isolation, which are hypothesized to be precursors of depression. In a comparison of abused and nonabused children, teacher assessments of internalizing problems were 19% higher in abused boys, but 87% higher for abused girls.

Trauma, Comorbidity and the Problem of Misdiagnosis. The current diagnostic nomenclature assumes that several disorders may co-occur, a phenomenon referred to as "comorbidity," and that clinicians are able to adequately assess comorbidity. Depressive symptoms are frequent in patients with PTSD, and these, not uncommonly, are sufficient to meet criteria for a depressive disorder. Personality disorders and depressive disorders are highly correlated, with comorbidity rates in clinical populations of 23% to 53% (Shea, Glass, & Pilkonis, 1987). As summarized elsewhere (Hamilton & Jensvold, 1991), the presence of a personality disorder in a depressed patient typically is associated with a persistent, severe, and treatment-resistant course.

While trauma may indeed give rise to personality disorders, an alternative possibility is that personality disorders are misdiagnosed when trauma has occurred. For example, it may be more parsimonious and helpful to diagnose PTSD, rather than BPD, when there is a history of victimization (Bryer et al., 1987). Another caveat in making personality disorder diagnoses is that criteria may appear to have been met, even though the onset may have occurred in adulthood subsequent to physical or sexual abuse. This clearly goes against the view of personality disorders as being life long, inflexible traits, and suggests a high risk for misdiagnosis.

Failure to understand victimization confounds the evaluation and treatment of depressions in women. Some women with child-hood abuse histories present with premenstrual dysphoria. Except for the cyclic exacerbation and remission of their symptoms, these women would meet criteria for dysthymic disorder. While some of the depressive symptoms may resolve with antidepressant therapy, a confusing clinical picture may remain or emerge. Unless the clinician is familiar with victimization and dissociative processes, the remain-ing symptoms (e.g., sleep disorder) may be misunderstood as indicat-ing a partially treated or treatment-resistant depression. Formulating the particular case will be especially difficult if the clinician is overly reliant on utilizing diagnostic categories, as opposed to also recogniz-ing fundamental psychological processes. For example, even when a woman does not meet the precise criteria for a diagnosis of PTSD, dissociative experiences and both waking and sleeping flashbacks related to incest may be observed to persist premenstrually. In some cases, residual symptoms are better understood as features of PTSD rather than depression.

Jensvold and Putnam (1990) documented a premenstrual in-crease in PTSD symptoms over the course of 3 months in a patient with premenstrual dysphoria (PMS). Of nine patients with current PTSD symptoms, four experienced only premenstrual symptoms and four reported symptoms throughout the cycle that worsened before the menses. Only one reported that symptoms were independent of the menstrual cycle. Dissociative experiences, as measured by the Dissociative Experiences Scale (DES) (Bernstein & Putnam, 1986), were higher in patients than controls across the menstrual cycle, but were significantly increased by over one third (38%) in the luteal (premenstrual) phase when compared to the follicular (postmen-strual) phase in PMS patients.

While in need of replication, observations such as these may have treatment implications. For example, depression and PTSD symptoms may have special characteristics in women. In addition to showing a link between the timing of various symptoms and syn-dromes and the menstrual cycle, women appear to have more cyclic depressions overall than do men. Examples of cyclic disorders showing a female excess include seasonal affective disorder (SAD) and the rapid-cycling variant of bipolar disorder (Hamilton, Parry, & Blumenthal, 1988; Parry, 1989), and recurrent unipolar depression (Perugi et al., 1990). Cyclicity requires more frequent evaluations to monitor treatment and complicates attempts to assess risk for relapse. A treatment trial for antidepressants will typically last for 5 to 6 months past the last evidence of mild to moderate symptoms (Prien & Kupfer, 1986), and recent evidence suggests that maintenance therapy may be advisable. It is not clear, however, whether mild symptoms confined to the premenstrual phase require extended treatment in order to decrease risk for a depressive relapse (Hamilton & Jensvold, 1991).

In summary, it appears that depression and personality disorders can co-occur because of a third variable related to both. A likely candidate for such a variable is victimization, since trauma can be associated not only with PTSD, but also with depression and with at least several personality disorders. The possible role of PTSD as an intervening variable is unclear, but deserves further research attention. Biological risk factors are discussed in a later section, although these could also be conceptualized as a third variable, and may, in fact, be linked to victimization and PTSD.

Personality as a Depressive Variant

Several depressive disorders tend to begin at an early age and to show a periodic, somewhat chronic, lifelong course, much like that described for personality disorders. In such cases, the distinction between personality and depressive disorders is tenuous at best. The examples of cyclothymia and dysthymia have already been discussed. If these are conceptualized as depressive disorders, then it is likely that the resultant instability of moods would affect personality development; and if conceptualized as personality disorders, then the resulting instability of mood may be said to reach the level of a depressive syndrome.

An instructive example of the need for greater clarity around these issues is bipolar II (hypomania) disorder, since it may appear to be characterological and can be confused with BPD. The problem with erring diagnostically on the side of a personality disorder is that treatment options will appear to be limited; whereas many of these individuals actually are responsive to lithium, and have a family history of bipolar disorder. Partly because drug-responsiveness is not typically recognized as a feature of personality disorders, Akiskal

(1987) recommends that we preferentially conceptualize certain "characterological" conditions as depressive variants until proven otherwise.

Biological Risk Factors and Theories of Depression

A remaining possibility is that there are biologically based, sex-related differences in "temperament." If so, the biological substrate for temperament, or other biological risk factors for depression, could be conceptualized as a third variable, that is, as related to both personality and to depressions occurring in women. A variety of substances in the brain have been hypothesized to be neurotransmitters (NTs)—the chemical mediators of neuronal transmission. Many of these agents have been investigated as etiologic for depression, but, despite years of study, data are mixed and inconclusive.

It is of interest, however, that many NTs, or NT metabolites vary directly with levels of sex steroid hormones, such as estrogen, progesterone, and testosterone. Halbreich, Vital-Herne, Goldstein, and Zander (1984) reviewed sex differences in biological factors thought to be related to depression. Prominent examples include brain dopamine and serotonin, which are catecholamines. Sex differences have also been observed in cerebrospinal fluid, blood, and urine metabolites of these and other NTs. While data are inconclusive overall, these findings are interesting because women with a history of depression are at increased risk for having episodes of illness precipitated around times of hormonal change. Examples include premenstrual, postpartum, and surgical-menopause- or oral-contraceptive-induced depressions (Hamilton et al., 1988; Parry, 1989). It is not clear, however, to what extent these changes are due to direct biological effects, versus effects having to do with the stress of reproductive-related life events, for example, becoming a parent (Hamilton, 1984) or undergoing an infertility work-up.

It is beyond the scope of this paper to detail biological findings that may be related to depressions in women. Here we will limit our discussion to the leading theoretical model at present as it relates to sex differences in depression. In the *New England Journal of Medicine,* Gold, Goodwin, & Chrousos (1988) summarized evidence supporting the theory that depression results when natural mechanisms meant to adapt to stress go awry. The normal response to acute stress includes the release of cortisol and a variety of adaptive changes in catecholamines; high cortisol and catecholamine changes are also seen in depression. There are striking similarities between the general adaptational response to chronic stress and the syndrome of depression.

Several characteristics of stress have been linked to animal models of depression. In particular, behavioral and physiological responses to chronic, intermittent, and uncontrollable stress have been described by the learned-helplessness theory of depression. One of the physiological findings is "stress-induced analgesia," or lessened responsivity to pain. The learned-helplessness model may be especially pertinent to females, since estrogen modulates the stress-induced analgesia in rats that is mediated by endogenous opiates (Rayn & Maier, 1988). In the absence of estrogen, the adaptive analgesic effect is impaired or lost; whereas moderate, but not high, levels of estrogen enhance the analgesic effect. These data suggest that the human menstrual cycle may have effects on risk for stress-induced analgesia and learned helplessness, since only diestrus female rats—that is, those with relatively low to moderate estrogen—are expected to show strong learned-helplessness effects.

In addition to the link between opiate pathways and depression, similar models have been proposed for PTSD (van der Kolk, Greenberg, Boyd, & Krystal, 1985). Naloxone, a drug that blocks opiate effects, will reverse stress-induced analgesia in persons with PTSD (Pitman, van der Kolk, Orr, & Greenberg, 1990). Possible hormonal effects have not been studied experimentally in humans.

Elsewhere, we have summarized ways that some of these findings may have implications for understanding dysphoria and depressions occurring in women (Gallant & Hamilton, 1988; Hamilton & Gallant, 1990). Specifically, cognitive processes are sensitive to effects of sex-steroid hormones. State-dependent learning (SDL), for example, is seen with hormones such as progesterone in animal studies (Stewart, Krebs, & Kaczender, 1967). SDL refers to recall that is enhanced in situations—or in neurochemically defined states—that are congruent with those in which encoding occurs. Preliminary studies and clinical observations (Hamilton, Alagna, & Sharpe, 1985) suggest that SDL occurs across the human menstrual cycle. SDL has been explored as a model for understanding dissociative processes and PTSD (Spiegel, 1988), and these symptoms may be exacerbated premenstrually (Jensvold & Putnam, 1990). Taken together with reports that women are more susceptible to PTSD than are men, these data suggest a sex-related effect on the biological substrate for PTSD and depression.

CRITIQUE OF THEORIES OF
PSYCHOPATHOLOGY AND DEPRESSION

Long-held theories about gender, personality, and depression have not been well-supported by empirical data. Lerner (1988), a leading feminist clinician and theorist, has critically examined two of the more recent contributions (Chernin, 1986; Jordan & Surrey, 1986) that attempt to reinterpret traditional psychoanalytic thinking. The following discussion will focus on one of these, the self-in-relation theory as formulated by Jordan and Surrey (1986), who built upon the earlier work of Miller (1976). The present review is informed by Lerner's critique (1988), and the reader is referred to the original for a more extensive discussion.

The central thesis of self-in-relation theory is that "women organize their sense of identity, find existential meaning, achieve a sense of coherence and continuity, and are motivated in the context of a relationship (Jordan & Surrey, 1986, p. 102). While models for male development focus on autonomy and separation, female development is said to be characterized by the development of mutual empathy in the mother–daughter dyad, which is seen to facilitate women's special focus on relatedness (see Lerner, 1988; Gilligan, 1982). An important contribution of the theory is its emphasis on positive aspects of traits that are stereotypically female (e.g., empathy).

Lerner (1988) has two primary concerns with self-in-relation theory: the model's mother–daughter focus and the acceptance of extreme gender dichotomies in identity development. As in previous theories (e.g., Chernin, 1986), the exclusive focus on the mother–daughter dyad does not do justice to the actual complexity of interrelatedness in the family, including the father. And the theory seems to accept a highly polarized view of healthy adults. Even if unintended, the model appears to be based on and to reinforce gender stereotypes (see Mednick, 1989, on Gilligan, 1982). An alternative conceptualization suggested by Lerner (1988) is that mature and successful intimacy requires similar development in males and females, including both separation and relatedness.

Lerner (1988) has made several specific recommendations for improving feminist theory building. First, we need to be more precise in our statements, so as to avoid stereotyping. For example, we might say that "More women than men root their identity in nurturance and caretaking."

Second, we need to recognize the complexity and interactive

dynamics of relationships in the family, for example, the "circular reciprocity" when a woman (or man) "overfunctions" and the partner "underfunctions" in relating and caretaking. One of Lerner's (1987) contributions to understanding depression in women comes from her analysis of our behavior in relationships, specifically loss of the self ("de-selfing") and self-betrayal. While further description of these processes is beyond the scope of the present paper, the reader is referred to Lerner (1987, 1988) for an eloquent discussion and for clinical examples that are rich in detail.

And finally, Lerner (1988) reminds us that we must continually recontextualize our thinking, for example, to recognize that gender differences do not occur in a vacuum, and that in our society they occur in the context of dominant and subordinate social-role status. Instead of seeing relatedness as an "inherent" or "natural" part of our development as women qua women, Lerner sees it as reflecting larger patterns of socialization. Socialization is situationally defined, and a special part of our socialization as women happens to include subordinate role status. According to Lerner (1988), it is "not women's affiliative needs or relationship orientation that predisposes females to depression, for emotional connectedness is a basic human need as well as a strength. Rather, *it is what happens to women in relationships that deserves our attention*" (italics added except for "happens").

TOWARD A FEMINIST CONTRIBUTION

As discussed by Mednick (1989), the evidence for gender differences in stereotypes is strong, whereas the evidence for actual differences is less clear (Greeno & Maccoby, 1986). Strong popular perceptions of gender differences are one reason why recent feminist theories often resonate so well with our own experiences, as Mednick (1989) has illustrated by reference to Gilligan's (1982) work on female development. That is, there is "face validity" to notions about differences, despite weaknesses in the relevant data (Colby & Damon, 1983; Thoma, 1986). The lack of conclusive data about assertiveness and dependency, however, challenges hypotheses about personality and depression that—intuitively—have strong validity.

According to Mednick (1989), part of the problem has to do with the nature of human thought: there is a "well-documented tendency to underestimate the role of situations as determinants of a person's behavior and to overestimate the importance of personal or dispositional factors" (p. 1121). Social psychologists have called this "the fundamental attribution" error (Watson, de Bortali-Tregerthon, & Frank, 1984).

A critical review of the empirical literature and theory on personality and depressions in women has led us to conclude that gender-stereotyped "personality" factors have likewise, been overestimated. Even the statement of the problem itself—personality and depression—suggests a "personal," intrapsychic approach, shifting the focus away from important alternative conceptualizations.

By restating the question, "do personality and depression co-occur in relation to a third variable, such as a life event stressor," we were better able to explore and understand situational determinants of the observed link between personality measures (if not personality itself) and depression. Victimization appears to be a critical determinant of depression in women.

Moreover, there are strong contextual effects on gender-stereotyped personality traits, a finding that challenges traditional conceptualizations of personality. A crucial distinction is that between personality as an enduring, stable trait, and assessments of personality including diagnoses and standardized rating instruments. Many of our so-called "trait" measures are in fact affected by changes in clinical state. That is, these measures are "state-dependent." In addition, we now know that development is not indelibly fixed once and for all upon reaching "maturity." Instead, relatively enduring traits can continue to be formed in adulthood, affecting both measurements of personality, and in some cases, personality itself. For example, battered women may present with what appears to be a personality disorder but is better conceptualized as a form of PTSD. Similarly, rape-trauma syndrome may be misdiagnosed as depression alone or as a personality disorder.

Empirical data have been flawed because of biases in the laboratory measures used to investigate possible sex differences in gender-stereotyped traits. In addition, the preference for laboratory measures has led to a lack of ecological validity in the measures used.

And finally, both empirical data and theory affirm the need for more complex models. One example is investigation of the interaction of instrumentality with explanatory style. Another is the effect of subordinate role status on women's behavior in relationships.

Feminist Models for Research

A promising feminist research strategy would be to combine and integrate a contextual, life-events approach with study of hypothesized mediating variables, using a prospective design, with depression and PTSD as outcome measures (Lloyd, 1989). Mediating variables would be derived, in part, from studies of normal adaptation to threatening events (Taylor, 1983), as suggested by conceptualizations of PTSD as a normal response to trauma. For example, do women who become depressed following physical or sexual assault, compared to those who do not become depressed, show a pre- [minus] post-assault change in the areas of: (a) control and mastery, self-esteem, ability to find meaning in the experience, and ability to use self-enhancing evaluations and illusions (Taylor, 1983); (b) use of rumination (Nolen-Hoeksema, 1987, 1990); and (c) types of attributions or laboratory assessments of learned-helplessness-related behaviors (see Follingstad, Neckerman, & Vormbrock, 1988) or stress-induced analgesia? If so, are there interactions between these variables and gender-related factors such as instrumentality? There is also a need to assess PTSD and dissociative experiences, and state-dependent learning in women on and off estrogen or progesterone and before and after surgical menopause. The study by Jensvold and Putnam (1990) deserves replication.

Clinical Implications of Feminist Research and Theory

In the meantime, the immediate clinical implications of a contextualized approach have been elaborated by Lerner (1987) and by others (Brown, 1987; Rieker & Carmen, 1986), and have been summarized by the American Psychological Association's *Task Force Report on Women and Depression* (McGrath et al., 1990). In particular, feminist therapists believe in the importance of attending to power in relationships, both in society at large, in the family, and in the therapeutic relationship (Feminist Therapy Institute, 1987). Brown (1990) has detailed a feminist approach to evaluation of the client that addresses issues such as gender roles and history of abuse.

Elsewhere (Hamilton, Alagna, King, & Lloyd, 1987; Institute for Research on Women's Health, 1988), we have suggested that the clinical picture will be clouded unless the therapist is sensitive to issues of victimization. Depression, if present, must be recognized and treated in order to further clarify the clinical picture and the underlying issues. A hierarchy for decision making is suggested, such that depression must be ruled out or treated before a definitive personality diagnosis is made and a diagnosis of personality disorder is deferred for at least 6 months if PTSD, or significant features of PTSD, is present. In some cases, PTSD does not clearly emerge until the depression is treated. And finally, it should be recognized that the evaluation of depression and PTSD can be confounded, especially when there is a premenstrual pattern for some of the symptoms.

REFERENCES

Abramson, L., Seligman, M., & Teasdale, J. (1978). Learned helplessness in humans: Critique and reformulation. *Journal of Abnormal Psychology, 87*, 102–109.

Alloy, L. B., & Abramson, L. Y. (1982). Learned helplessness, depression, and the illusion of control. *Journal of Personality and Social Psychology, 42*, 1114–1126.

American Psychiatric Association (1987). *Diagnostic and statistical manual of mental disorders* (3rd ed., revised), Washington DC: Author.

Angst, J., & Dobler-Mikola, A. (1984). Do the diagnostic criteria determine the sex ratio in depression? *Journal of Affective Disorders, 7*, 189–198.

Akiskal, H. S. (1987). The milder spectrum of bipolar disorders: Diagnostic characteristic, and pharmacologic. *Psychiatric Annals, 17*, 32–37.

Arieti, S., & Bemporad, J. R. (1978). The psychological organization of depression. *American Journal of Psychiatry, 137*, 1360–1365.

Baucom, D. H., & Danker-Brown, P. (1984). Sex role identity and sex-stereotyped tasks in the development of learned helplessness in women. *Journal of Personality and Social Psychology, 46*, 422–430.

Bem, S. L. (1974). The measurement of psychological androgyny. *Journal of Consulting and Clinical Psychology, 42*, 155–162.

Bernard, J. (1972). *The future of marraige.* New York: Bantam.

Bernstein, E. M., & Putnam, F. W. (1986). Development, reliability, and validity of a dissociation scale. *Journal of Nervous and Mental Disease, 174*, 727–735.

Block, J. (1978). *The Q-sort method in personality assessment and psychiatric research.* Palo Alto, CA: Consulting Psychologists Press.

Block, J. H. (1983). Differential premises arising from differential socialization of the sexes: Some conjectures. *Child Development, 54*, 1335–1354.

Block, J., & Gjerde, P. F. (1990). Depressive symptomatology in late adolescence: A longitudinal perspective on personality antecedents. In J. E. Rolf, A. Masten, D. Cicchetti, K. Neuchterlein, & S. Weintraub (Eds.), *Risk and protective factors in the development of psychopathology* (pp. 334–360). Cambridge, Eng.: Cambridge University Press.

Breslau, N., Davis, D. C., Andreski, P., & Peterson, E. (1991). Traumatic events and posttraumatic stress disorder in an urban population of young adults. *American Journal of Psychiatry, 48*, 216–222.

Broverman, I. K., Vogel, S. R., Broverman, D. M., Clarkson, F. E., & Rosenkrantz, P. S. (1972). Sex-role stereotypes: A current appraisal. *Journal of Social Issues, 28*, 59–78.

Brown, L. (1987). From alienation to connection: Feminist therapy with post traumatic stress disorder. *Women and Therapy, 5,* 13–26.

Brown, L. (1989, August). *The contribution of victimization as a risk factor for the development of depressive symptomatology in women.* Paper presented at the Annual Convention of the American Psychological Association, New Orleans, LA.

Brown, L. (1990). Taking account of gender in the clinical assessment interview. *Professional Psychology, 21,* 12–17.

Bryer, J. B., Nelson, B. A., Miller, J. B., & Krol, P. A. (1987). Childhood sexual and physical abuse as factors in adult psychiatric illness. *American Journal of Psychiatry, 144,* 1426–1430.

Carmen, E. H. (1985, November 11). *Masochistic personality disorder DSM-III-R: Critique.* Paper presented at the Work Group to Revise DSM-III, American Psychiatric Association, New York.

Carmen, E. H., Rieker, P. P., & Mills, T. (1984). Victims of violence and psychiatric illness. *American Journal of Psychiatry, 141,* 378–383.

Carmen, E. H., Russo, N. F., Miller, J. B. (1981). Inequality and women's mental health: An overview. *American Journal of Psychiatry, 138,* 1319–1330.

Chernin, K. (1986). *The hungry self: Women, eating and identity.* New York: Perennial.

Chodoff, P. (1972). The depressive personality: A critical review. *Archives of General Psychiatry, 27,* 666–673.

Colby, A., & Damon, W. (1983). Listening to a different voice: A review of Gilligan's *In a Different Voice. Merrill-Palmer Quarterly, 29,* 473–481.

Dodge, K. A., Bates, J. E., & Pettit, G. S. (1990). Mechanisms in the cycle of violence. *Science, 250,* 1678–1683.

Dweck, C. S., & Bush, E. S. (1976). Sex differences in learned helplessness: I. Differential debilitation with peer and adult evaluators. *Developmental Psychology, 12,* 147–156.

Dweck, C. S., & Repucci, D. (1973). Learned helplessness and reinforcement responsibility in children. *Journal of Personality and Social Psychology, 25,* 109–116.

Eagly, A. H. (1978). Sex differences in influenceability. *Psychological Bulletin, 85,* 86–116.

Eagly, A. H., & Carli, L. L. (1981) Sex of researchers and sex-typed communications as determinants of sex differences in influenceability: A meta-analysis of social influence studies. *Psychological Bulletin, 90,* 1–20.

Eagly, A. H., & Steffen, V. J. (1986). Gender and aggressive behavior: A meta-analytic review of the social psychological literature. *Psychological Bulletin, 100,* 309–330.

Eaves, G., & Rush, A. J. (1984). Cognitive patterns in symptomatic and remitted unipolar depression. *Journal of Abnormal Psychology, 93,* 31–40.

Eccles, J. (1983). Sex differences in mathematics participation. In M. Steinkamp & M. Maehr (Eds.), *Women in science* (pp. 80–100). Greenwich, CT: JAI Press.

Eccles, J., Parsons, Adler, T., & Meece, J. L. (1984). Sex differences in achievement: A test of alternate theories. *Journal of Personality and Social Psychology, 46,* 26–43.

Fenigstein, A., Scheier, M. F., & Buss, A. (1975). Public and private self-consciousness: Assessment and theory. *Journal of Consulting and Clinical Psychology, 43,* 522–527.

Feminist Therapy Institute (1987). *Feminist therapy ethical code.* Denver, CO: Author.

Frank, E., & Stewart, B. D. (1984). Depressive symptoms in rape victims. A revisit. *Journal of Affective Disorders, 7,* 77–85.

Frank, E., Turner, S. M., & Duffy, B. (1979). Depressive symptoms in rape victims. *Journal of Affective Disorders, 1,* 264–277.

Follingstad, D. R., Neckerman, A. P., & Vormbrock, J. (1988). Reactions to victimization and coping strategies of battered women: The ties that bind. *Clinical Psychology Review, 8,* 373–390.

Gallant, (Alagna), S.J., & Hamilton, J. A. (1988). On a premenstrual psychiatric diagnosis: What's in a name? *Professional Psychology: Research and Practice, 19*(3), 271–278.

Gilligan, C. (1982). *In a different voice: Psychological theory and women's development.* Cambridge, MA: Harvard University Press.

Gjerde, P. F., Block, J., & Block, J. H. (1988). Depressive symptoms and personality during late adolescence: Gender differences in the externalization-internalization of symptom expression. *Journal of Abnormal Psychology, 97,* 475–486.

Gold, P. W., Goodwin, F. K., Chrousos, G. P. (1988). Clinical and biochemical manifestations of depression. Relation to the neurobiology of stress. *New England Journal of Medicine, 319,* 413–420.

Golin, S., Terrell, T., Weitz, J., & Drost, P. L. (1979). The illusion of control among depressed patients. *Journal of Abnormal Psychology, 88,* 454–457.

Greeno, C. G., & Maccoby, E. E. (1986). How different is the "different voice"? *Signs: Journal of Women in Culture and Society, 11,* 310–316.

Halbreich, U., Vital-Herne, J., Goldstein, S., & Zander, K. (1984). Sex differences in biological factors putatively related to depression. *Journal of Affective Disorders, 7,* 223–233.

Hamilton, E. W., Abramson, L. Y. (1983). Cognitive patterns and major depressive disorder: A longitudinal study in a hospital setting. *Journal of Abnormal Psychology, 92,* 173–184.

Hamilton, J. A. (1984). Psychobiology in context: Reproductive-related events in men's and women's lives. *Contemporary Psychiatry, 3,* 12–16.

Hamilton, J. A. (1989). Emotional consequences of victimization and discrimination in "special populations" of women. *Psychiatric Clinics of North America, 12,* 35–51.

Hamilton, J. A., Alagna, S. W., & Sharpe, K. (1985). Cognitive approaches to understanding and treating premenstrual depression. In H. J. Osofsky & S. J. Blumenthal (Eds.), *Premenstrual syndromes* (pp. 69–83). Washington, DC: American Psychiatric Press.

Hamilton, J. A., Alagna, S. W., King, L., & Lloyd, C. (1987). The emotional consequences of gender-based abuse in the workplace. *Women and Therapy, 6,* 155–182.

Hamilton, J. A., & Gallant, S. J. (1990). Problematic aspects of diagnosing premenstrual phase dysphoria: Recommendations for psychological research and practice. *Professional Psychology: Research and Practice, 21*(1), 60–68.

Hamilton, J. A., & Jensvold, M. (1991). Pharmacotherapy for complicated depressions in Women. *The Psychiatric Times, 8*(5), 1, 48–53.

Hamilton, J. A., Parry, B., Blumenthal, S. (1988). The menstrual cycle in context: I. Affective syndromes associated with reproductive hormonal changes. *Journal of Clinical Psychiatry, 49,* 474–480.

Halbreich, U., Vital-Herne, J., Goldstein, S., & Zander, K. (1984). Sex differences in biological factors putatively related to depression. *Journal of Affective Disorders, 7,* 223–333.

Hammen, C. L., & Padesky, C. A. (1977). Sex differences in the expression of depressive responses on the Beck Depression Inventory. *Journal of Abnormal Psychology, 86,* 609–614.

Harris, T. O., Brown, G. W., & Bifulco, A. T. (1990). Depression and situational helplessness/mastery in a sample selected to study childhood parental loss. *Journal of Affective Disorders, 20,* 27–41.

Herman, J., Perry, J., & van der Kolk, B. (1989). Childhood trauma in borderline personality disorder. *American Journal of Psychiatry, 146,* 490–495.

Hirschfeld, R. M. A., Klerman, G. L., Clayton, P. J., & Keller, M. B. (1983). Personality and depression. *Archives of General Psychiatry, 40,* 993–998.

Hirschfeld, R. M. A., Klerman, G. L., Keller, M. B., Andreasen, N. C., & Clayton, P. J. (1986). Personality of recovered patients with bipolar affective disorder. *Journal of Affective Disorders, 11,* 81–89.

Hirschfeld, R. M. A., Klerman, G. L., Clayton, P. J., Keller, M. B., McDonald-Scott, P., & Larkin, B. H. L. (1983). Assessing personality: Effects of the depressive state on trait measurement. *American Journal of Psychiatry, 140,* 695–699.

Hirschfeld, R. M. A., Klerman, G. L., Lavori, P., Keller, M. B., Griffith, P., & Coryell, W. (1989). Premorbid personality assessments of first onset major depression. *Archives of General Psychiatry, 46,* 345–350.

Ingram, R. E., Cruet, D., Johnson, B. R., & Wisnicki, K. S. (1988). Self-focused attention, gender, gender role, and vulnerability to negative affect. *Journal of Personality and Social Psychology, 55,* 967–978.

Institute for Research on Women's Health (1988). *Sexual harassment and employment discrimination against women: A consumer handbook.* Bethesda, MD: The Feminist Institute Clearinghouse.

Jacobsen, A., & Richardson, B. (1987). Assault experiences of 100 psychiatric inpatients: Evidence of the need for routine inquiry. *American Journal of Psychiatry, 144,* 908–913.

Jensvold, M., & Putnam, F. (1990, March). *Postabuse syndromes in premenstrual syndrome patients and controls.* Paper presented at the National Conference of the Association of Women in Psychology, Tempe, AZ.

Johnson, A. G. (1980). On the prevalence of rape in the United States. *Signs,* 6(1), 136–146.

Jordan, J., V., & Surrey, J. L. (1986). The self-in-relation: Empathy and the mother-daughter relationship. In T. Bernay and D. W. Cantor (Eds.), *The Psychology of today's woman: New psychoanalytic visions.* Hillsdale, NJ: Analytic Press, 81–104.

Kaplan, A. G. (1986). The "self-in-relation": Implications for depression in women. *Psychotherapy: Theory, Research, and Practice, 23,* 235–242.

Kilpatrick, D. G., Best, C. L., Veronen, L. J., Amick, A. E., Villeponteaux, L. A., & Ruff, G. A. (1985). Mental health correlates of criminal victimization: A random community survey. *Journal of Consulting and Clinical Psychology, 53,* 866–873.

Klein, D. N., Harding, K., Taylor, E. B., & Dickstein, S. (1988). Dependency and self-criticism in depression: Evaluation in a clinical population. *Journal of Abnormal Psychology, 97,* 399–404.

Klerman, G. L., & Hirschfeld, R. M. A. (1988). Personality as a vulnerability factor: With special attention to clinical depression. In S. Henderson, & G. Burrows (Eds.), *Handbook of Social Psychology* (pp. 41–53). Blackwell, Melbourne, Australia: Elsevier.

Lerner, H. G. (1983). Female dependency in context: Some theoretical and technical considerations. *American Journal of Orthopsychiatry, 53,* 697–705.

Lerner, H. G. (1987). Female depression: Self sacrifice and self betrayal in relationships. In R. Formanek and A. Guiran (Eds.), *Women and Depression: A lifespan perspective.* New York: Springer.

Lerner, H. G. (1988). *Women in therapy.* New York: Harper and Row.

Lewinsohn, P. M., Steinmetz, J. L., Larson, D. W., & Franklin, J. (1981). Depression-related cognitions: Antecedent or consequence? *Journal of Abnormal Psychology, 90,* 213–219.

McGrath, E., Keita, G. P., Strickland, B. R., & Russo, N. F. (1990). *Women and depression: Risk factors and treatment issues.* Washington, DC: American Psychological Association.

Mednick, M. T. (1989). On the politics of psychological constructs: Stop the bandwagon, I want to get off. *American Psychologist, 44,* 1118–1123.

Miller, J. B. (1976). *Toward a new psychology of women.* Boston: Beacon.

Miranda, J., & Persons, J. B. (1988). Dysfunctional attitudes are mood-state dependent. *Journal of Abnormal Psychology, 97,* 76–79.

Nolen-Hoeksema, S. (1987). Sex differences in unipolar depression: Evidence and theory. *Psychological Bulletin, 101,* 259–282.

Nolen-Hoeksema, S. (1990). *Sex differences in depression.* Stanford, CA: Stanford University Press.

Parry, B. (1989). Reproductive factors affecting the course of affective illness in women. *Psychiatric Clinics of North America, 12,* 207–220.

Perugi, G., Musetti, L., Simonini, E., Piagentini, F., Cassano, G. B., & Akiskal, H. S. (1990). Gender-mediated clinical features of depressive illness: The importance of temperamental differences. *British Journal of Psychiatry, 157,* 835–841.

Persons, J. B., & Rao, P. A. (1985). Longitudinal study of cognitions, life events, and depression in psychiatric inpatients. *Journal of Abnormal Psychology, 94*, 51–63.

Peterson, C., & Seligman, M. E. P. (1983). Learned helplessness and victimization. *Journal of Social Issues, 2*, 103–116.

Phillips, K. A., Gunderson, J. G., Hirschfeld, R. M. A., Smith, L. E. (1990). A review of the depressive personality. *American Journal of Psychiatry, 147*, 830–837.

Pitman, R. K., van der Kolk, B. A., Orr, S. P., & Greenberg, M. S. (1990). Naloxone-reversible analgesic response to a combat-related stimuli in postrraumatic stress disorder. *Archives of General Psychiatry, 47*, 541–544.

Prien, R., & Kupfer, D. (1986). Continuation drug therapy for major depressive episodes: How long should it be maintained? *American Journal of Psychiatry, 143*, 18–23.

Radloff, L. S. (1977). The CES-D Scale. A self-report depression scale for research in the general population. *Applied Psychological Measurement, 1*, 385–401.

Rehm, L. P. (1977). A self-control model of depression. *Behavior Therapy, 8*, 787–804.

Rieker, P. P., & Carmen, E. H. (1986). The victim-to-patient process: The disconfirmation and transformation of abuse. *American Journal of Orthopsychiatry, 56*, 360–370.

Roberts, T. A., & Nolen-Hoeksema, S. (1989). Sex differences in reactions to feedback. *Sex Roles, 21*(11/12), 725–747.

Ross, C. A., Miller, S. D., Reagor, P., Bjornson, L., Fraser, G. A., & Anderson, G. (1990). Structured interview data on 102 cases of multiple personality disorder from four centers. *American Journal of Psychiatry, 147*, 596–601.

Rubin, Z., Peplau, L. A., & Hill, C. T. (1981). Loving and Leaving: Sex differences in romantic attachments. *Sex Roles, 7*, 821–835.

Russell, D. E. H. (1984). Sexual exploitation. Beverly Hills, CA: Sage.

Ryan, S., & Maier, S. F. (1988). The estrous cycle and estrogen modulate stress-induced analgesia. *Behavioral Neuroscience, 102*(3), 371–380.

Shea, T., Glass, D., Pilkonis, P., et al. (1987). Frequency and implications of personality disorders in a sample of depressed outpatients. *Journal of Personality Disorders, 1*, 27–42.

Silverman, J. S., Silverman, J. A., & Eardley, D. A. (1984). Do maladaptive attitudes cause depression? *Archives of General Psychiatry, 41*, 28–30.

Simons, A. D., Garfield, S. L., & Murphy, G. E. (1984). The process of change in cognitive therapy and pharmacotherapy for depression. *Archives of General Psychiatry, 41*, 45–51.

Sorenson, S. B., & Golding, J. M. (1990). Depressive sequelae of recent criminal victimization. *Journal of Traumatic Stress, 3*, 337–350.

Sorenson, S. B., Stein, J. A., Siegal, J. M., Golding, J. M., & Burnam, A. (1987). The prevalence of adult sexual assault: The Los Angeles epidemiologic catchment area project. *American Journal of Epidemiology, 126*, 1154–1164.

Spiegel, D. (1988). Dissociation and hypnosis in post-traumatic stress disorders. *Journal of Traumatic Stress, 1*(1), 17–33.

Stewart, J., Krebs, W. H., & Kaczender, E. (1967). State-dependent learning produced with steroid. *Nature, 216*, 1223–1224.

Stoebe, M. S., & Stroebe, W. (1983). Who suffers more? Sex differences in health risks of the widowed. *Psychological Bulletin, 93*(2), 279–301.

Sweeney, P. D., Anderson, K., & Bailey, S. (1986). Attributional style in depression: A meta-analytic review. *Journal of Personality and Social Psychology, 50*, 974–991.

Taylor, S. E. (1983). Adjustment to threatening events: A theory of cognitive adaptation. *American Psychologist, 38*, 1161–1173.

Thoma, S. (1986). Estimating gender differences in the comprehension and preferences of moral issues. *Developmental Review, 6*, 165–180.

van der Kolk, B. A. (1988). The trauma spectrum: The interaction of biological and social events in the genesis of the trauma response. *Journal of Traumatic Stress, 1*, 273–290.

van der Kolk, B. A., Greenberg, M., Boyd, H., & Krystal, J. (1985). Inescapable shocks, neurotransmitters, and addiction to trauma: Toward a psychobiology of posttraumatic stress. *Biological Psychiatry, 20*, 314–325.

van der Kolk, B. A., & van der Hart, O. (1989). Pierre Janet and the breakdown of adaptation in psychological trauma. *American Journal of Psychiatry, 146*, 1530–1530.

Watson, D. L., de Bortali-Tregerthon, G., & Frank, J. (1984). *Social psychology: Science and application*. Glenview, IL: Scott, Foreman.

Weissman, M. M., Klerman, G. L. (1977). Sex differences and the epidemiology of depression. *Archives of General Psychiatry, 34*, 98–111.

Weissman, M., Myers, J., Thompson, W., & Bellanger, A. (1986). Depressive symptoms as a risk factor for mortality and for major depression. In L. Erlenmeyer-Kimling and N. Miller (Eds.), *Life span research on the prediction of psychopathology* (pp. 251–260). Hillsdale, NJ: Lawrence Erlbaum.

Winfield, I., George, L. K., Swartz, M., & Blazer, D. G. (1990). Sexual assault and psychiatric disorders among a community sample of women. *American Journal of Psychiatry, 147*(3), 335–341.

CHAPTER SEVEN

Psychotic Disorders with Emphasis on Schizophrenia

DEBORAH GREENWALD

Many traditional approaches to schizophrenia have focused on parent–child interaction as the main causal factor, emphasizing the hypothesized poor parenting of the child by the mother (Bateson, Jackson, Haley, & Weakland, 1956; Fromm-Reichmann, 1948; Lidz, Fleck, & Cornelison, 1965). These theories variously held that the mother's personal psychopathology, her wish to control her child for her own needs, and/or her inability to respond to her child with love and mutuality caused or laid the basis for the child's disorder. Such thinking attends to one particular aspect of the environmental surroundings in which a schizophrenic develops, and, by this direction of attention, finds primary responsibility with the mother.

It is likely that wherever the intense gaze of scientific research is directed, deviation from the norm will be found. It may be easy to attribute responsibility for the emergence of psychological disorder to such deviation. The types of questions asked and the area chosen for research in themselves represent the implicit values and orientation of the researcher. The traditional approaches to schizophrenia indicate that the theorists held the mother at fault for her children's disorders and, in addition, reflected the prevailing social values of the time regarding a woman's role in raising a family. The assumption, often implicit and almost always unquestioned, seemed to be that the family's emotional well-being was solely, or at least primarily, the responsibility of the woman, and anything that went amiss was by definition her fault. This attitude often led to research that focused solely on mothers and their psychological state and interaction with the children.

In more recent times, predominant trends in research on psychopathology have changed. This was partly in reaction to the scapegoating tendency to blame the mother. Furthermore, when the research began to include both parents, it became clear that the correlations for mothers with child psychopathology were no greater than those for fathers. These trends have diverged into two major directions. The family, or systems, approach has moved from examining the individual parent to examining the entire family context. The locus of culpability was shifted from the mother to the entire family, whose level of functioning was seen to have major effects upon how individual members cope with development and change. Another trend has focused on the biochemical make-up of those with severe mental disorders and their families. This approach, too, removes the focus from the mother's behavior in producing pathological children. If she is to blame for her child's disorder, it is, in this model, due only to her unwitting transmission of predisposing genetic material, and in this the child's father is equally involved. Neither parent, however, is held responsible for the eventual pathological outcome. In fact, the emphasis on genetic causes for mental disorder lets everyone off the hook. Prevention of serious disorder becomes a matter for biogenetic and pharmaceutical research.

A feminist approach to schizophrenia focuses upon the social milieu in which schizophrenia arises. Such a focus can help clarify what specific social conditions and stresses are associated with increased incidence and prevalence of the disorder. Numerous studies (Hollingshead & Redlich, 1958; Kohn, 1973) have found that schizophrenics are more common in the lower social classes. Though research has begun to explore the parameters of this connection, this is an area in which much work remains to be done. The factors related to social class that are associated with an increase in schizophrenia are not likely to be inconsistent with other approaches to the development of the disorder, such as familial or genetic theories, but may well provide a crucial understanding of the predisposing conditions that are potentially under social control.

DSM-III AND DSM-III-R: DIAGNOSES OF SCHIZOPHRENIA

Rosenhan's (1973) devastating critique of the *Diagnostic and Statistical Manual of Mental Disorders, Second Edition* (DSM-II) (American Psychiatric Association [APA], 1968) and challenging reliability studies (e.g., Helzer et al., 1977) helped pave the way for an improvement in psychiatric diagnosis. The APA's long-awaited DSM-III and its recent revision, DSM-III-R, arrived in 1980 and 1987, respectively. In the DSM-III-R, as before, psychosis is defined as a general category of mental disorders involving the loss of reality testing. Specific psychoses are defined by medical-model-inspired descriptions of syndromes: sets of signs and symptoms that seem to appear in regular groupings among the cases presenting for treatment. The DSM-III purports to offer only descriptive characterizations of each disorder, eschewing causal inferences regarding the syndromes described. However, as pointed out by Schacht and Nathan (1977), the assumption underlying most of the syndrome definitions in the DSM-III and DSM-III-R is that of genetic or biochemical causation.

The DSM-III-R (APA, 1987) describes schizophrenia's essential features as: (1) characteristic psychotic symptoms during an active phase of disturbance, (2) functioning below the highest level previously achieved, and (3) a duration of acute, prodromal, and/or residual symptoms for at least 6 months. The stipulation of 6 months' duration makes it more likely that a relatively chronic group of patients with poor prognosis will be identified. This conceptualization was made in deference to the ideas of Kraepelin (1919), who claimed that a deteriorating course over the long run was the primary indication of a valid diagnosis of schizophrenia. In identifying such a chronic group, DSM-III-R also hopes to distinguish "true" schizophrenics (who may well have a very specific etiology) from those patients who appear similar, but are really experiencing other psychiatric syndromes or disorders. Thus, the authors of the DSM-III-R emphasize careful differential diagnosis and provide distinctions between schizophrenia and each of the following: psychotic mood disorders (mood-congruent delusions or hallacinations), schizoaffective disorder (full mood syndrome and schizophrenic characteristics without the predominance of one over the other), schizophreniform disorder (less than 6 months of the schizophrenic syndrome), delusional/paranoid psychosis (absence of prominent hallucinations, incoherence, or bizarre delusions), personality disorders with transient psychotic symptoms (schizotypal, schizoid, paranoid, and borderline), and other disorders less often linked with schizophrenia.

This careful delineation of schizophrenia has predictably decreased the frequency of schizophrenic diagnoses in the United States to about half of what it was prior to DSM-III (Harrow, Westermyer, & Marengo, 1987). Schizophrenia is, nonetheless, related to the disorders from which it must be distinguished. In fact, in the classification of personality disorders, DSM-III-R identifies a Cluster A of schizotypal, schizoid, and paranoid disorders, which some (Kety, Rosenthal, Wender, & Schulsinger, 1968; Meehl, 1962) have theorized share a common genetic etiology with schizophrenic psychoses. Borderline personality disorders have sometimes been interpreted (Stone, 1980) as not sharing the same genetic causes with the schizophrenic spectrum disorders. However, since 54% of patients with borderline personality disorder are also diagnosed as having schizotypal personality disorder (Spitzer, Endicott, & Gibbon, 1979), borderline disorders have also appeared in the manual's paragraphs on differential diagnosis.

Since the DSM-II did not make such careful distinctions, and much of the research used diagnostic systems predating DSM-III, this chapter will speak of schizophrenia as a spectrum of disorders roughly twice as large as the cohort of patients identified as such by DSM-III-R, reflecting the populations being studied in that earlier research. A recent study (Harrow et al., 1987) comparing outcomes for two groups of patients, one diagnosed as schizophrenic according to DSM-III and another as schizophrenic according to DSM-II but not according to DSM-III, suggests that either set of criteria defines a group characterized by relatively poor outcome, such that the distinctions may not be prognostically crucial. In addition, the broader concept of schizophrenia seems appropriate if one does not automatically adopt the narrow medical (genetic/biochemical) causation approach of DSM-III-R. The material that follows invites the consideration of such alternative approaches along with the model adopted by the DSM-III-R.

SCHIZOPHRENIA: ONE DISORDER, ONE ETIOLOGY?

One major approach to understanding schizophrenia involves conceptualizing it as a specific disorder with a specific cause (or possibly causes) leading in a more or less direct route to the symptoms termed "schizophrenia." This way of viewing the disease is commonly referred to as the "medical model." The notion of one disease, one cause, is indeed applicable to diseases attributable to specific organisms, such as scarlet fever or malaria. However, even in those instances, issues of vulnerability to contracting the diseases and of the virulence/effect with which the symptoms manifest themselves vary from individual to individual. There are models, equally medical, which apply to other diseases (e.g., heart disease), that may well be more appropriate as models for schizophrenia, because they do not posit causation by a single external agent but rather by a malfunction in a bodily system in conjunction with environmental factors. In heart disease, diabetes, or ulcers, to name a few such illnesses, there are a variety of causal factors, some genetic, others associated with diet, life patterns, personality style, bacteria and/or stress (Weiner, 1977). In turn, these various factors relate in complex ways to create different manifestations of illness, disease courses, and outcomes in different patients.

The latter medical model, the diathesis–stress model, has more application to mental disorders than does the single-causation paradigm. The approach, often used in the study of schizophrenia, of searching for the exclusive cause or using rigid diagnostic definitions, may not be the most promising one for furthering the understanding of the disorder (Zubin & Spring, 1977).

It may be useful to consider the possibility that, not only may there be multiple pathways to schizophrenia, but that there may be no one-to-one correspondence between the pathway and the form and course of the illness. In certain instances, such as in symptoms that apparently have their origin in drug ingestion or organic illness, such as syphilis, the "schizophrenic" symptoms are thought to be mimetic and not truly schizophrenic (DSM-III-R, 1987). However, the fact that the symptoms can be caused by such factors suggests that a multiplicity of pathways for expression of the disease may produce the genuine article, rather than an ersatz one, and that what we call schizophrenia may be, like fever, a response with different causes.

Critical Individual Characteristics

Much research has focused on the establishment of critical markers or diagnostic criteria for schizophrenia that are specific to this disorder and not to other psychoses. In this context, "critical" refers to an essential or basic trait or symptom that differentiates schizophrenics from other groups. Such a group can then be studied closely to reveal what is centrally causal to the disorder. This approach is taken by the DSM-III-R (1987) in describing the external, clinical phenomena of the disorder to enhance diagnostic agreement.

The first-rank symptoms described by Schneider (1959) were one earlier attempt to establish critical characteristics. These included the delusions of thought broadcasting or insertion, of reference, and of being controlled. To some extent these have now been incorporated into the DSM-III-R criteria. However, the characteristics by which a clinician diagnoses a syndrome are not necessarily the best markers for the disease, but rather are only those clinically presented. For example, a child with Down's syndrome does not present his or her chromosomal abnormality to the pediatrician. The characteristics of schizophrenic that are most striking—the psychotic symptomatology—are shared by other psychotics, especially by persons with bipolar disorders (Carlson & Goodwin, 1973). Hence, the search for specifically schizophrenic characteristics has also been made in numerous other areas.

One of the earliest approaches to understanding schizophrenia was based on the concept of a critical flaw in personality organization. The term "schizophrenia," literally "split mind," itself reflects an early version of this concept. Various authors, from Fromm-Reichman (1950) to Laing (1960), speak of the schizophrenic as someone who does not possess an integrated sense of self, but instead has a psychologically symbiotic relationship with others. Such an individual has trouble recognizing his or her body boundaries in both physical and psychological senses (hence the experience of delusions and hallucinations, in which inner events are mistakenly experienced as external). Schizophrenics often have a very diffuse, limited sense of their own thoughts and needs, which are experienced in a very intense, undifferentiated way. According to this view of schizophrenia, the quality of relationships and thinking is seen to spring from and to reflect a basic inner defect in personality organization.

While the view that schizophrenia reflects a critical defect is seen to be most consistent with an emphasis on environmental etiology, it is also in accord with the hypothesis that the disorder is genetically caused. The defect would be one that prevented the individual from developing a normal sense of self, for whatever reason.

Thus, one general viewpoint of the essential characteristics of schizophrenia focuses on the person's internal psychological organization and sees the various symptoms of the disorder as emerging from this deficit. While other psychological views may emphasize different aspects than those cited here, all tend to see the schizophrenic symptoms as being the outer manifestations of an inner difficulty, which in itself is the central characteristic of the disorder.

Other theories of schizophrenia focus on cognitive dysfunction. Cognitive confusion, distortion, and slippage are seen as diagnostic hallmarks of the disorder. For some theorists, difficulties in reality testing, for example, in processing and integrating information, are thought to be central, not merely diagnostic. Shakow (1977; Rodnick & Shakow, 1940), one of the earliest experimental psychopathologists to concentrate on this area, believed that the schizophrenic's difficulties in paying attention and processing information are crucial, in contrast to the self-defect theorists, who viewed such difficulties as secondary. Shakow emphasized problems with shifting sets in the attentional and cognitive processing of everyday, complex reality.

Recent variants of this general approach—to identify critical attentional–cognitive deficits in schizophrenia—have focused on possible neuropsychological indicators of processing difficulties (Mirsky, 1987), on hypothesized deficits in perceptual organization (Knight, 1987), and on possible deficits occurring under conditions of distraction (Asarnow, 1987; Spring et al., 1987). However, despite the extent of interest in this approach, it still remains, as it did in 1978 (Cromwell, 1978a), an area with as yet unproven importance in attempts to establish the critical characteristics of schizophrenia. Many questions still remain unanswered by attempts to relate schizophrenic symptomatology to attentional–cognitive differences between schizophrenics and normal individuals or other controls (George & Neufeld, 1985).

Another approach to defining what is critical in a schizophrenic disorder has been to hypothesize the centrality of language difficulties (Cohen, 1978; Rochester, 1978), which are presumed to lead to the cognitive, perceptual, and emotional aspects of the disorder. Recent research efforts in this area (Harvey, 1987) have focused on "reference failures," or unclear referents, in the speech of schizophrenics.

The critical characteristics of the disorder have also been sought on the biological level of neurotransmitters and other brain substances. Dopamine has been a favorite of investigators (e.g., Davis, 1978; Sachar, Gruen, Altman, Langer, & Halpern, 1978) because of its blockage in the brain by phenothiazine-based antipsychotic drugs. The persistence of important behavioral problems after such drugs have been ingested (Matthysse, 1978) argues against the sufficiency of the neurochemical hypothesis. Other biochemical hypotheses, positing various metabolic deficits, have been advanced (Wyatt & Bigelow, 1978), but none have received definitive support (Cromwell, 1978b).

Others (Gruzelier & Venables, 1972; Mednick, 1970) have theorized that autonomic responsivity, measured by electrodermal reactivity, could be the critical characteristic of schizophrenia. Such heightened reactivity could account for the high degree of anxiety observed clinically and the apparent attentional aberrations reported by many researchers to be present in schizophrenic persons.

Most critical-characteristic theories assume that a genetic defect, or physiological event such as birth anoxia (Mednick, 1970), leads to neurological consequences and the development of schizophrenic symptoms. Other critical-characteristic theories hypothesize physiological deficits related to the disorder that are presumed to be markers for schizophrenia. Markers are genetic traits, not symptoms, that indicate the presence (on the same gene segment) of other physiological traits directly related to the disorder. Holzman's (Holzman, Levy, & Proctor, 1978) eye-tracking hypothesis is one example. This theory holds that schizophrenics and some of their nonschizophrenic family members will show nonsmooth eye pursuit of a swinging pendulum.

However, it is not an inevitable conclusion that a posited genetic or physiological cause for any of these critical-characteristic theories will survive future research. As stated earlier in this chapter, emotional states might create neurotransmitter dysfunctions; or acute disturbance, rather than genetic inheritance, may cause difficulties in eye-tracking (Salzman, Klein, & Strauss, 1978). Also, attentional or cognitive processing deficits can be produced by high anxiety levels (Rapaport, Gill, & Schafer, 1968; Wechsler, 1958).

Similarly, electrodermal reactivity deviations could be the result, rather than the cause, of schizophrenia. Thus, the core of the disorder, whether defined by its most identifying characteristic(s) or by its causal agent(s)—whatever their nature—is not conclusively identified at this time.

Evidence for Genetic Predisposition

Though the assumption that schizophrenia results from an inherited tendency has waxed and waned in strength over time, exploration of this area is currently experiencing a renaissance. This is partly in accord with the sociocultural atmosphere of the times, but it is also a response to increases in our ability to interpret the new scientific data available. As noted earlier, one of the sociocultural implications of the current emphasis on inherited predisposition is that the family is not held responsible for having produced a schizophrenic (e.g., through faulty parenting). The cause is seen to lie beyond the individual or family but is within the potential control of scientifically trained experts. According to one view, a biologically oriented explanation for schizophrenia treats the disorder as a disability rather than as a character flaw. This is comparable to viewing alcoholism as a disease, which many alcoholics find supportive rather than discouraging. Others point out that to regard schizophrenia as having a substantial genetic component places an even heavier, permanent burden on those so diagnosed and their offspring. The label of "schizophrenic," given the belief in a genetic basis for the disorder, is permanent. The schizophrenic remains a schizophrenic, and the genetic taint persists

"unto the generations." A label of mental illness focuses social attention on the illness and can prevent even highly trained professionals from being aware of contradictory (e.g., "healthy") behavior
(Rosenhan, 1973; Rothblum, Solomon, & Albee, 1986).

With regard to the genetic evidence for schizophrenia, it is tauto-
logically obvious, at one level, that if human beings can develop
schizophrenia, it is a disorder with a genetic predisposition. The
question is whether there is a differential predisposition and to what
extent inborn differences affect an individual's likelihood of becoming
schizophrenic. One extreme possibility would be that schizophrenia
results from a single defective gene that produces the disorder, but
which has incomplete penetrance, so that even when the gene is
present, it does not invariably produce schizophrenia (Cromwell,
1978a). The concept of incomplete penetrance, according to which
even dominant genes have their effect only under specific conditions,
could explain the variability with which the disorder is transmitted.
Factors affecting the degree of penetrance could stem either from the
physical or social environment of the individual. In this view, the
gene inherited could be a gene "for" schizophrenia—in the sense that
the gene results in cognitive and affective disruptions—or, alternate-
ly, the gene could reduce protective factors or increase vulnerability
factors, which in turn make the likelihood of schizophrenic symptoms higher (Wynne, 1970). For example, a gene that heightens
reactivity to stress might make a person more likely to become severely disorganized (Mednick, 1970). What is inherited would not be the
disorganizing factor per se, but the susceptibility to a type of stress
that in most individuals leads to disorganization and, in a particular
individual, leads to it so frequently and/or overwhelmingly that a
reaction of schizophrenic proportions is the result.

Alternatively, schizophrenia could be hypothesized to be the
result of two or more genes acting in concert to produce symptoms
(Gottesman & Shields, 1973; Kidd, 1978). Again, the extent of the
pathologic effect of these genes would be modified by the environment. These views are in contrast to the notion that the incidence of
schizophrenia is unrelated to genetic variation and is entirely a response to environmental stresses, a position at the other extreme.

There are three avenues of research often cited in support of the
genetic-predisposition hypotheses: epidemiological studies, biochemical studies, and studies of familial incidence and characteristics.
Only the first of these directly relates to the issue, while the other two
offer, or may potentially offer, indirect support.

Epidemiological research, for example, finds that the cross-
cultural lifetime prevalence of schizophrenia in widely varying pop-

ulations is similar (APA, 1987; Draguns, 1973; Yolles & Kramer, 1969). Such an unvarying incidence is strongly suggestive of an inherited predisposition to the disorder and, furthermore, tends to suggest that environment is not significant, even interactively, in the development of disease symptoms. However, family consanguinity evidence, which will be discussed separately, does suggest that environmental factors are also involved. The relatively unvarying number of cases is surprising, too, in light of the epidemiological research on social class. There are significant differences in schizophrenia rates across social classes, with the lowest classes having a disproportionately higher incidence of the disorder (Hollingshead & Redlich, 1958; Srole, Langer, Michael, Opeler, & Rennie, 1962). Furthermore, there have been differential rates in the diagnoses of schizophrenia cross-culturally (Professional Staff of the United States–United Kingdom Cross-National Project, 1974).

Given these findings, it is puzzling that across widely disparate cultures (the United States, the western European nations, Iran, India, Korea, Formosa, and Japan), with great variation in degree of economic complexity, socioeconomic status, diagnostician training, quality of hospitals, etc., that the incidence of the disorder is more or less the same. In other words, is this a "real" parallel across cultures, akin to similarities in rates of twinning (though, in fact, twinning differs across racial groups, as schizophrenia apparently does not), or an artifact? Torrey's (1973) review suggests the latter, since much of the cross-cultural data has been collected in urbanized centers undergoing a great deal of disruptive sociocultural change. The rural areas, more representative of these societies and less subject to disruptions, are underrepresented in the studies. This is not to assert that differences in incidence across cultures would necessarily contradict evidence of genetic transmission. In fact, diseases with known genetic components, such as diabetes, will show varying incidence in different countries and under different environmental conditions. This may also be the case with schizophrenia.

When a biochemical difference, such as dopamine level (Davis, 1978), is observed between a normal control sample and schizophrenics, it is often used to support the hypothesis of differential genetic predisposition. This is a very important line of research, but findings of correlations between the presence of schizophrenia and an elevation or decrease in the level of a particular neurotransmitter does not constitute support for causation. The production of various biochemical substances is highly correlated with affective state and varies along with changes in that state. It is only plausible to assume that the powerful emotional experiences of the schizophrenia will be signaled by equally powerful alterations in neurochemicals. Such changes would then be indications of the presence of the disorder, rather than the cause.

The final line of research supporting a genetic-causation hypothesis looks at familial incidence of the disorder. If schizophrenia is transmitted genetically, then distant relatives of schizophrenics will have a higher incidence of the disorder than does the general population, immediate family members (who are blood-related) will have a still higher incidence, and monozygotic twins of schizophrenics will have the highest incidence. This pattern has been found (Gottesman, 1978; Mayer-Gross, Slater, & Roth, 1969).

Comparisons of monozygotic and dizygotic twins for concordance of schizophrenia show that the monozygotic twins are far more likely to show concordance for the illness. Though the figures vary considerably, the rates are generally between 33% and 50% (Gottesman & Shields, 1976), when schizophrenia is broadly defined. For fraternal twins, the concordance rates are generally between 10% and 20%. It is interesting that the more recent studies, with the most careful methodology, have produced the lowest percentages (White & Watt, 1981). The results offer support for a significant genetic contribution, although, in both twin and family studies, it is also possible to attribute the findings to environmental effects.

Adoption studies offer further evidence on this issue. In the study by Kety et al. (1968), adopted schizophrenics and normals were compared with a sample of schizophrenics reared by their biological parents. The biological relatives of both the adopted and the non-adopted schizophrenics had the highest levels of pathology, the adoptive parents of the schizophrenics had intermediate levels of psychopathology, and the adoptive parents of normal offspring had the lowest. This is what one would predict on the basis of a theory of genetic predisposition to schizophrenia, with environment having an interactive effect in the incidence of the disorder. However, Kety et al. (1975) note that schizophrenia was found to be more common in the biological relatives of only the chronic schizophrenics in the sample, not the acute cases. This evidence suggests that the two groups represent different etiological pathways to schizophrenia. Other data offer support for this distinction as well, in that perinatal difficulty and birth trauma are found more commonly in the histories of chronic schizophrenics (McNeil & Kaij, 1978; Mednick, 1970; Mishler & Waxler, 1968) than in those of normals or acute schizophrenics. Such findings have contributed to the DSM-III restriction of confining schizophrenic diagnosis to patients with at least 6 months of relatively chronic symptoms. Perhaps chronic schizophrenia is more likely to occur when there are organic precipitating factors, whether genetic or traumatic in origin.

It is important to note that, even when the data provide clear support for one aspect of the nature–nurture debate, they do not necessarily indicate a loss for the other side. For example, the Wender, Rosenthal, and Kety (1968) sample was reexamined by Singer, Wynne, and Toohey (1978) and Wynne (personal communication, May 1978). The Rorschach tests taken by the three sets of parents involved in the Wender et al. study—two sets of adoptive parents (of normal and schizophrenic offspring) and one set of parents who had raised their schizophrenic biological child—were scored for "communication deviance" (Singer & Wynne, 1966), a measure of the clarity of focus and meaning in verbal communications. Singer (1967) has found communication deviance (CD) to be higher in parents who have a schizophrenic or borderline-personality child. She and her colleagues used a measure of CD to predict which of the three sets of parents would have children with schizophrenia. Blind to the status of the parents in the original Wender et al. sample, Singer et al. were able to distinguish, on the basis of the Rorschach test CD scores, which parents had schizophrenic offspring and which had normal offspring. Singer found no significant differences in the level of CD between biological and adoptive parents of schizophrenics, while these groups differed significantly from the parents of normals in their communication patterns.

In summary, the above findings suggest that there is a genetic predisposition associated with some forms of (chronic) schizophrenia. However, even for these forms, there is likely to be considerable input by environmental factors. For other, less chronic forms of schizophrenia, the status of genetic predisposition is not clear.

ENVIRONMENTAL INFLUENCES: THE FAMILY

Most of the studies of environmental factors associated with the development of schizophrenia have focused on factors within the family. In particular, research has focused on communication, affect, power, and capacity for change.

Communication

Communication was one of the earliest-examined factors, beginning with the Bateson, Jackson, Haley, and Weakland (1956) theory of the double bind. This theory focused on contradictory and confusing levels of communication. However, it also postulated, as an important element, a sense of threat that the child is presumed to experience while attempting to decipher the mixed messages correctly. According to Bateson et al., the child in a schizophrenic family is given messages that contradict each other and are not mutually reconcilable. The child is unable to allow realization of the contradiction to come to full awareness because if he or she does the mother's love will be lost. Thus, this is a communication theory with a vital affective component. Smith (1976), in his research with normal women, found support for this hypothesis, but work with schizophrenic families has not found direct confirmation or disconfirmation of the presence of double binds in their communication processes.

Bateson's (Bateson et al., 1956) theory is generally thought (Dell, 1980) to represent an important shift in thinking from the earlier, linear theories. These attributed responsibility for the development of schizophrenia to pathology on the part of the mother, rather than to the child's abnormality, on the one hand, or to the larger social system within which mother functioned, on the other. Even if the earlier theorists (e.g., Fromm-Reichman, 1948) acknowledged the extent to which the mother was the recipient herself of noxious agents within the environment, for example, her own mother, she was nonetheless portrayed in the early literature as the essential transmitter of the disorder. Bateson, referring to the double bind as a reverberating process in which both mother and child participate, proposed a nonlinear theory. Even so, his emphasis was first and foremost on the way the mother interacts with her child. The child's response was viewed as being secondary to maternal initiations. The father's participation was not directly noted by Bateson, except as a potential protector, and any possible influences from the social surroundings were left unmentioned. Only with additions to the theory by Weakland (1960) and Haley (1963) did the double-bind theory become less mother-blaming and dyadic and more truly systemic. Weakland (1960) suggested that contradictory messages are often given by two emotionally significant people, rather than by one, so that the child is torn between loyalties to each. In these developments of the theory, the mother is no longer solely responsible for the child's confusion. Rather, unresolved conflicts between those responsible for the child's upbringing lead to the communication of mixed messages.

Singer and Wynne (1966) developed the related concept of communication deviance to assess clarity of communication. They found that the communications of parents of schizophrenics (and, to a somewhat lesser degree, those of the schizophrenics themselves) could be characterized by both failure to establish a shared focus of attention and failure to clarify meaning. The listener was left wondering what precisely was being discussed and what precisely was being said about it. An interesting aspect of this theory and research is that CD characterizes the parents' speech when they are talking to anyone, not only to their offspring. Goldstein, Rodnick, Jones, McPherson, and West (1978) and Doane, West, Goldstein, Rodnick, and Jones (1981), studying a high-risk population, offer additional support for the importance of CD in the etiology of schizophrenic spectrum disorders. In their research, data obtained from adolescents being treated at an outpatient mental health facility and from their parents were compared with the 5-year outcome. Initially none of the adolescents was diagnosed as being schizophrenic or within the schizophrenia spectrum. Parental CD, however, predicted the children's status, in terms of severity of disorder, at follow-up. Those couples in which both parents had high levels of distorted communication were significantly more likely to have offspring diagnosed in the schizophrenia spectrum. Other data (Mishler & Waxler, 1968; Goldstein et al., 1978) suggest that members of families with schizophrenic (or schizophrenia-spectrum) offspring tend not to respond to or acknowledge each other's comments in conversation. There is a disjointed, unconnected quality to the communication within the family. Mishler and Waxler report other differences in communication patterns between control families (e.g., those without seriously disturbed offspring) and those with schizophrenic offspring. The control families interrupted each other frequently in discussion, tuning their input closely to what had been said by others. In families of schizophrenics, there was less interruption and more questioning, together with a tendency for each speaker to maintain his or her position without integrating what others were saying. The style suggested sounds closer to that of a public debate than to that of an intimate sharing.

Mishler and Waxler's (1968) study was done after the offspring had been diagnosed as schizophrenic. Thus, it is possible that differences between their familial discussions and those of control families were caused by the presence of the schizophrenic member, rather than being causal factors in the development of the disorder. However, the parents of schizophrenics showed similar, though somewhat less deviant, communication patterns when conversing with their non-schizophrenic offspring. This suggests that the communication style is more a characteristic of the parent than a response to the child. Goldstein et al.'s (1978) work was done before the child had been diagnosed as having a thought disorder. Again, this suggests that the parents' deviant communication was not in response to the child's disordered cognition, but rather the other way around. Liem (1974), however, offers contrary evidence. He found that parents of schizophrenics did not differ from normals in terms of the adequacy of their descriptions of common objects or roles, while their schizophrenic and normal male offspring did differ in terms of description intelligibility. Schizophrenic sons, as expected, gave inadequate descriptions. In contrast to the previously cited family research, which required discussion or somewhat ambiguous material (projective test stimuli, for example), Liem's study focused on specific, unambiguous objects. The findings suggest that parents of schizophrenics are not necessarily less clear than parents of normals when describing well-defined facts, but they are less clear when presenting and discussing their opinions on ambiguous phenomena.

In summary, research on communication in families with schizophrenic offspring indicates that the parents of schizophrenics have difficulty in clearly establishing their focus of attention and their opinions and thoughts, though they can communicate adequately when the focus is set and unambiguous. Further, such parents do not regularly acknowledge, respond to, or integrate the ideas of others. This is consistent with the findings of Reiss (1971), which indicate that the members of schizophrenic families are intent on reaching an appearance of agreement with each other and will do so at the expense of attending to information that a member provides, even when that information is discrepant with what they already think to be true. Thus it is predictable that, when confronting clear, factual situations, families of schizophrenics will express themselves clearly, as there is little chance of disagreement. When dealing with more ambiguous situations, such as interpersonal relationships, families will be more ambiguous and less clear, to ensure that they will be in a position that agrees with others.

Affect

Data on affective difference between schizophrenic families and families without schizophrenic members are somewhat less clear than data on communication, responsiveness, and attention. Still, there is substantial evidence that families with members diagnosed as schizophrenic or having schizophrenic spectrum disorder have an emotional climate that differs from that in families without such members. Vaughn and Leff (1976) found that, in their sample of schizophrenics, the relapse rate was higher for those who returned to a family that was critical, hostile, or emotionally overinvolved with them. Criticism and hostility were indicated by negative tone of voice or by obviously critical statements. Overinvolvement was based on "excessive anxiety, overconcern or overprotectiveness toward the patient" (Vaughn & Leff, 1976, p. 125). In fact, the relapse rate for those in critical and/or overinvolved families (parents or spouse) was 91% for those who spent more than 35 hours per week in contact with their families and were not taking antipsychotic medication. This contrasts with relapse rates of 12% for those in less critical or intrusive families, who also spent more than 35 hours per week in the home and were not taking medication. In critical, intrusive families, spending time away from the family or avoiding them while at home, and/or taking medication, offered significant protection against relapse.

Doane et al. (1981) used a modified version of the same measure of criticism and overinvolvement, which they termed "negative affective style." They found that families with such a style and high levels of communication deviance all had offspring that were diagnosed as being within the schizophrenia spectrum at 5-year follow-up, while those with a positive affective style and low or intermediate CD had offspring with no, or less severe, disturbance. This study suggested that affective climate and CD are most powerful in predicting schizophrenia or schizophrenic-like disorders when combined, a result highly consistent with the Bateson double-bind hypothesis. Mishler and Waxler (1968) reported that their control families were more emotionally expressive than the families of schizophrenics. The more detached families with schizophrenic offspring seemed to be guarding against hostility within the family, while the control families could more freely express anger, toward both family members and targets outside the family, but did so in a context of warmth and humor.

Power

Lidz et al. (1957) saw schizophrenic families as falling into two types. In one, the schismatic families, there is constant struggle and unresolved conflict between the parents. Frequently, the children are strongly pushed into taking sides in the marital battles. In these families, power is not shared by the parents jointly, as a tool for managing the family tasks, but rather is wielded as a weapon in a struggle between two mistrustful people. Lidz found this pattern more characteristic of families with schizophrenic daughters, while those with schizophrenic sons tended to have one parent with highly disproportionate power, while the other parent tended to be passive. Other research (Mishler & Waxler, 1968) into the families of schizophrenics finds that the parent in power overtly denies his or her control. Thus, these families differ from the control families with regard to power in two ways: the power, rather than being shared by two parents functioning as an executive team, is either hotly contested and used as a weapon against the other; or the power is lodged in one parent, who denies that he or she is, in fact, wielding this power.

The issue of consensus is another important one that has been found to distinguish power management in families with and without schizophrenic members. Schizophrenic families can be characterized by a false consensus (Wynne, 1970; Reiss, 1971). The dominant person enforces his or her own wishes but continually iterates that these wishes are held by all the members of the family. Disagreement is perceived as betrayal, and family members feel pressure to agree with each other, rather than to recognize their own feelings. Members are not permitted to be aware of their own directions, so though they all claim that each decision reflects the true desires of all, this actually is not the case. In the schismatic families described by Lidz et al., where parents use power as a weapon, the power of the children is also reduced since they are constantly pulled to take sides. Thus, what they truly want and need is not of interest to their parents. This greatly reduces the freedom for growth among the children.

Mishler and Waxler (1968) found that the power balance in schizophrenic families differed from that of controls. For example, in families with a male schizophrenic offspring, this son had a family position of relatively greater power, shared with the mother, while his father had a less powerful or important position. Such a family power structure deviates from the traditional, patriarchal one. The "dominating mother" is implicitly blamed for the mental health problems of her offspring, as though her control over the family—and her husband's lack of it—are in themselves harmful. However, it is very likely that a family that differs from the socially acceptable norm will experience both internal and external pressure to conform. It is not clear what effect such pressure has on the family's functioning and on the mental health of its members. However, it seems very possible that pressure to conform to societal norms with regard to power assertion could induce those families that do not fit the norm to give confusing and contradictory messages with regard to power, and, in less overt ways, how it is exercised, in order to disguise the "inappropriate" power structure. This could well contribute to the communication difficulties described earlier.

It seems possible, even likely, that styles of power and communication may be linked in the families of schizophrenics. The evidence reviewed earlier suggests that, in part, communication in schizophrenic families has the goal of maintaining alliances and power rather than transmitting meaning. That is, when a member of a family with a schizophrenic takes a position on an issue, he or she is concerned with the relationship, not with the issue (Wynne, 1970).

On the other hand, the affective and communicative styles of the family appear, from the data of Doane et al. (1981), to be orthogonal. A family may be critical but communicate directly and clearly, or may have a benevolent affective style along with communication deviance. It is the two in conjunction, consistent with the double-bind hypothesis (Bateson et al., 1956), that seem to result in a schizophrenic disorder.

Change

Although freedom to change is not generally measured directly in families, a number of authors (Bateson et al., 1956; Hoffman, 1981; Wertheim, 1973) have considered whether the ability to make appropriate shifts in family rules, expectations, interpersonal styles, etc., is a parameter that distinguishes the healthy family from a dysfunctional one. In families in which consensus is extremely important, as in the families of schizophrenics (Reiss, 1971), children would be discouraged from becoming aware of what they really want because of the potential for conflict. These families have a very low tolerance for conflict and will avoid it at all costs, including neglect of the very real needs and wishes of family members. Children are not free to alter their behavior and family roles, so that there is insufficient adaptive development or change.

Hoffman (1981) has speculated that symptoms occur when a change is needed within the family, but for one reason or another the system is rigid and unable to make the appropriate shift. Transition points in a family are therefore especially difficult, not simply because of the stress, but because some type of adjustment is needed. While well-functioning families are likely to have temporary difficulties at such times, they have an interactional style that makes such adaptations possible. As individual family members react to the new status quo, they are free to voice their thoughts, even when these thoughts conflict with previously developed patterns for the family or with the expressed opinion of the more dominant family members. Though they will still experience stress, the struggle is likely to end in productive coping and a satisfactory resolution of the friction between their previous adjustment and the one demanded by the change in circumstances.

According to this scheme of thought, members of dysfunctional families are constricted by an outmoded way of experiencing and responding to what is going on around them. The gap between how they need to be and how they actually are widens, until there is very little overlap and they are quite unprepared to function on their own. Only within the unchanging family does their rigid adjustment style make sense. Outside of the family, their mode of adjustment does not cope adequately with reality. It is consistent with this explanation that most schizophrenics first develop the florid symptoms of their illness around when they are expected to leave their parents' home and become more autonomous.

The issue of change in families is particularly important at this time. The norms regarding gender roles and what constitutes a family, for example, have not kept pace with societal changes. Recent shifts in the concept and function of the family clearly indicate a need for a corresponding shift in the goals and expectations for both males and females. Murphy and Lemieux (1967), writing of traditional French Canadian women 3 decades ago, linked their greater rates of schizophrenia to a conflict between their traditional values and newer values that stress autonomy and educational success. While there is no evidence of increasing incidence of schizophrenia among women overall, it is nonetheless possible that those women who are most subject to irreconcilable conflict are most vulnerable to schizophrenia. In this light, some of the findings regarding power distributions in families that produce schizophrenics may be relevant. In these families the management of power is reportedly different from that in families that do not have schizophrenic offspring. It is worth investigating whether the risk in such families is heightened because of culturally induced conflicts.

Katz, Sanborn, Lowery, & Ching (1978) found that schizophrenics were described within their culture as most deviant in terms of behaviors least tolerated in that particular culture. These characteristics were not thought to be salient by professionals who were not members of the culture, who saw the schizophrenics exhibiting the universal symptoms of the disease. Katz et al. hypothesize that the schizophrenic is both vulnerable to breakdown and, at the same time, acting out against the culture. Such a model of schizophrenia is both individual and societal in its origin.

In summary, aspects of family interactional style have been discussed for their relevance to schizophrenia. Theoretical and empirical approaches have examined communication, affective style, and power management, and found evidence that the families of schizophrenics differ from families without schizophrenic members across these three dimensions.

The possibility that communication and power issues are integrally related was raised, with affective style as an orthogonal dimension that interacts with the others in fostering schizophrenia. The issue of flexibility, or freedom to develop, was presented as a possible mediator between the effects of poor communication and negative affect, on the one hand, and the development of schizophrenia, on the other.

To a very large extent, the research cited above on familial factors and schizophrenia investigated intact families. There is no reason to assume that schizophrenics are more likely to come from such families. Holding to a norm of two-parent family seems particularly inappropriate in this context. It would appear far more useful in further research to broaden the concept of family to include non-normative families, such as those headed by a single parent, a parent and grandparent, remarried parents, etc. A less narrow approach not only makes better sense from a scientific point of view, but also would support a more inclusive view of what constitutes a family.

SOCIAL CLASS

The incidence and prevalence of schizophrenia are strongly and inversely related to social class (Hollingshead & Redlich, 1958; Kohn, 1973) and are markedly greatest in the lowest social class (Gift, Strauss, Ritzler, Kokes, & Harder, 1988), defined by education and occupation. The fundamental nature of this relationship has long been the subject of controversy. Does it represent the effects of stress, known to be higher among lower-status groups (Dohrenwend, 1974), or does it result from "downward drift" of genetically impaired preschizophrenic individuals? Dohrenwend and Dohrenwend (1969) and Kohn (1973) have addressed the complexities of this issue and found it difficult to choose unequivocally between the two competing hypotheses. In fact, there may be subgroups of schizophrenics who match each of the causal models (Turner & Wagenfeld, 1967). Srole et al. (1962) found that social class significantly correlated with both stress and mental illness. Whatever the level of stress, mental disorders were more common in the lower social classes. Hence, numerous possible influences of social class (Kohn, 1973) separate from stress level deserve extensive further research.

Increasingly, single-parent families headed by women are finding themselves economically within the lower social classes. It is not known what effect, if any, this will have on the very large number of children raised in such families. It is an area that merits particular attention with regard to prevention strategies that attempt to ameliorate the very stressful conditions associated with poverty in our culture.

Even for individuals who presumably carry a genetic predisposition for the disorder and who might show downward drift, social class factors and environmental stressors may still play an important role (Zubin & Spring, 1977). Though the stresses that precipitate the disorder in schizophrenics may not be experienced as highly stressful for less-vulnerable people (Beck & Worthen, 1972; Lahniers & White, 1976), the role of environmental pressures continues to be important in the emergence and course of the disorder.

Both social class and stress present possible avenues for intervention/prevention with regard to schizophrenia. Interventions aimed at these influences would be quite different from those aimed at a presumed biochemical or genetic imbalance. In the former case, the schizophrenic, while perhaps seen as especially vulnerable, is nonetheless viewed as importantly affected by factors outside him/ herself. These factors could be explored by research and addressed through prevention and treatment programs. For example, Hogarty et al. (1974) found that treatment focusing on successful performance of major social and occupational roles was successful in reducing relapses among a sizeable subgroup of schizophrenics. Programs aimed at the lower social classes could provide, for example, increased aid to beleaguered community mental health facilities, walk-in centers and hotlines, serving inner city populations, where the incidence and prevalence of schizophrenia are higher than elsewhere. Other prevention programs could be aimed at those who are in high-stress situations, especially those most closely associated with the disorder.

While a great deal of research has been done on links between schizophrenia and genetic predisposition, relatively little research has been conducted on stresses that might trigger schizophrenic episodes. What is emphasized frequently is that such stressors, while they may be disastrous for the schizophrenic, are well within the coping capacities of less vulnerable individuals. This may be true, but the emphasis is on the frailty of the schizophrenic rather than on potential areas of intervention. Medical experts search diligently for the environmental source of an allergy attack even though the allergen is expected to be a substance most people are not allergic to. With mental disorder, it is common to look within the individual psyche or genetic makeup rather than to explore the wider environmental surroundings. The values reflected by research on stress or social class and schizophrenia are quite different from those reflected by research on the genetic basis for schizophrenia. The former suggests an orientation to extraindividual causes and influences in schizophrenia, while the latter locates the predisposition within the individual.

Locating the source of schizophrenia within the individual has important implications for the treatment of schizophrenics. Some of these relate to the emphases of treatment, whether on medication and institutional care, on the one hand, or on prevention and focused support on the other. In addition, however, there are other implications. Murphy (1978), on the basis of cross-cultural comparisons in the occurrence and course of schizophrenia, suggests that cultures that view the disorder as a permanent handicap are more likely to have patients who are more chronically ill and who deteriorate. In cultures that perceive schizophrenia as being externally caused, schizophrenics are likely to remain stable or to improve. Thus, our conceptualizations in approaching the disorder may well affect its manifestation and outcome.

GENDER DIFFERENCES

Physiological data on males and females suggest there may be gender-related differences in vulnerability. For example, for males, but not for females, difficulties experienced by the mother during pregnancy or birth and unusual patterns of autonomic nervous system responsivity are associated with the development of schizophrenia (Mednick, Schulsinger, Teasdale, Schulsinger, Venables, & Rock, 1978).

Gender differences have been also noted in the premorbid behavior of schizophrenics. Females show a higher level of social competence premorbidly than do males (Kokes, Strauss, & Klorman, 1977). Watt (1978) reported that preschizophrenic boys typically displayed more aggressive, acting-out behaviors during their school years, while preschizophrenic girls were more quiet and withdrawn. These patterns, of course, are parallel to the culturally sanctioned differences in gender roles. It seems likely that, when males act out aggressively or females act in by withdrawing, they are simply availing themselves of the avenues for deviation that are, relatively speaking, more socially acceptable. Watt contrasts this premorbid finding with the findings for diagnosed schizophrenics. After being di-

agnosed, males are found to show flat affect and to be more withdrawn, while females are more active and have more florid and more
affective symptoms (Lewine, 1981; Burbach, Lewine, & Meltzer,
1984). Greater affective involvement for schizophrenic women is consistent with the higher incidence of affective disorders among women
(Boyd & Weissman, 1981). In fact, this symptomatic difference between men and women, with women showing more emotional
symptomatology and men being more withdrawn, is much like the
differences attributed to men and women generally.

Precipitating events or stress appear to be more clearly important
in the histories of female schizophrenics. Early familial disturbance,
including separation from or loss of parents, is more prominent
among female schizophrenics than among male schizophrenics or the
general female population. Similarly, the course of schizophrenia for
adult women is also more vulnerable to loss of love objects than for
men (Al-Issa, 1982).

Consistent differences have been found in age of onset for males
and females, with males becoming symptomatic and being hospitalized for schizophrenia at a significantly earlier age than females
(Lewine, 1981). The later onset does not appear to be an artifact of
greater familial or social tolerance for schizophrenia among females,
and leads to later hospitalization. The data (Anderson & Holder,
1989; Lewine, 1981) indicate that the interval between the onset of
symptomatology and hospitalization is the same for both males and
females. These same investigators have hypothesized that the early-
male/late-female onset is associated with hormonal differences.

Research (APA, 1987) prior to 1987 found schizophrenia to be
equally common among men and women. A recent study (Harrow et
al., 1987) using the more narrow, chronicity-oriented DSM-III (APA,
1980) diagnostic criteria for schizophrenia found a difference in the
sex ratio of the disorder. While there were twice as many men as
women carrying the diagnosis when the DSM-III criteria were applied, the ratio was approximately equal in the same sample when
using the DSM-II criteria for inclusion. However, this sample excluded schizophrenics over 30 years of age. This most likely underrepresented the number of female schizophrenics because of their
later onset.

Several investigators (Lewine, 1981; Sartorius, Jablensky, Stromgren, & Shapiro, 1978; Westermeyer, Harrow, & Marengo, 1988) have
reported less severe episodes and better outcome for women, even
with strict diagnostic criteria. Female schizophrenics are also more
likely to be married and have higher levels of premorbid occupational
status than do males (Al-Issa, 1982; Farina, Garmezy, & Barry, 1963).

This may be partly due to later onset, which permits them to develop more competent functioning. Females also show better social and occupational recovery (Huber, Gross, Schuttler, & Linz, 1980) and have a lower relapse rate (Hogarty et al., 1974; Sartorius et al., 1978; Vaughn & Leff, 1976).

The fact that women more typically receive diagnoses of atypical or schizoaffective schizophrenia (Tsuang, Dempsey, & Rauscher, 1976) and affective disorders suggests the possibility that schizophrenia in women may show itself in a more affective form and therefore be misdiagnosed. The model for what constitutes schizophrenia may be based on male schizophrenics' typical clinical picture.

In summary, the data suggest that there are numerous gender-related differences in schizophrenia. Female schizophrenics tend to develop the disorder later in life, experience higher premorbid and recovery level of functioning, need fewer rehospitalizations, show more clear evidence of important environmental influences, and display more florid and affective symptomatology. This different clinical picture may suggest that males show a more physiologically based predisposition to schizophrenia, whereas, for females, schizophrenia may be more environmentally based. Alternatively, the hormonal hypothesis mentioned earlier might also explain some of the differences noted.

An additional possibility is that differential environmental influences affecting males and females—such as family roles, interaction patterns, and cultural expectations—strongly shape psychological/behavioral vulnerability along differential lines. These environmental influences may also interact with differing physiological vulnerabilities.

However, what emerges distinctly from the data on gender differences is that there are distinct male and female patterns in schizophrenia. Although these differences have been neglected until recently, they have potentially important implications for treatment and follow-up planning (Anderson & Holder, 1989). For example, the significance of important relationships in worsening or improving the clinical picture for women needs to be addressed specifically in treatment programs. The relationship factor appears to be less crucial for males. In fact, Hogarty's own data and his review of the expressed emotion literature (Hogarty, 1985) suggest that, for males, a high level of family criticism is significantly associated with relapse. Reduced contact with such families appears beneficial (Vaughn & Leff, 1976). It may be important for males to effect a reduction in contact with their families, while for females it may be important to reunite with those they love. Other differences in treatment planning may be appropriate for male and female schizophrenics, as the latter generally have a better prognosis.

In attempting to develop a model for schizophrenia in which symptoms are distinct from other psychotic diseases, diagnosticians may have formulated a description of the disorder that is more true for males than for females. That is, men may tend to exhibit more of the "pure" form of the disease, with a relative absence of affective components. It is worth considering whether this pure form represents a disease that is essentially different from schizoaffective disorder, or whether distinctions are not essential to the nature of the disorder and reflect, rather, the tendency of men to exhibit less emotionality than women.

It is vital that data on schizophrenics be examined separately by gender, so that any differences can emerge clearly. This appears to be the current trend, which parallels the trend in psychological research more generally in recent years. Such a development is clearly indicated by the abundance of data in many areas indicating distinct gender-linked patterns of behavior and experience.

CONCLUSIONS

The evidence surveyed in this chapter suggests several general conclusions:

1. Traditional approaches to understanding schizophrenia focused on poor parenting, especially poor mothering, as a central causal factor in the disorder. From a feminist perspective, the assumption underlying this focus is that the mother is solely responsible for psychological disabilities in her offspring. Consequently, the traditional approach seriously neglected social and interactive factors that are important causal influences in the development of the disorder and/or parental behavior. Negative reaction to the mother-blaming approach may be a large factor in the recent swing toward a more exclusively biological model for schizophrenia.

2. Much recent research in schizophrenia has been based on the assumption that the disorder is a specific disease entity with a specific cause (or possibly a few causes), leading more or less directly to the symptoms observed clinically. This approach also neglects the importance of social and interaction influences.

3. There are other, broader conceptualizations of the "medical model" that consider the possibility that multiple pathways converge within the range of symptoms labeled schizophrenic. Such models

permit the inclusion of various causal factors in complex and interdependent ways.

4. Research evidence suggests that there are meaningful subgroups within the schizophrenia spectrum that have important clinical, prognostic, and possibly etiological implications. For example, those patients exhibiting chronic disturbance provide the most convincing evidence for genetic causation, while more acute cases show very different patterns of family pathology and outcome.

5. The research on communication deviance, critical emotional family climate, and differential family patterns for preschizophrenics of the two sexes combine to suggest that environmental influences are important for onset and course, even in the chronic instances of disorder where the genetic contribution is presumed to be the greatest.

6. Males and females show distinctly different patterns with regard to age of onset, premorbid functioning and personality, precipitating stress, symptoms, and prognosis. This indicates that gender needs to be taken into account in diagnosing and treating this disorder. Women are more likely than are men to receive diagnoses of schizoaffective disorder or atypical schizophrenia. Indeed, it may be that the paradigmatic model for schizophrenia is based on males.

7. Chronicity may prove to be a less useful way of grouping patients than other dimensions. For example, clinical and etiological characterizations of the disorder, such as positive (hallucinations and delusions) versus negative (withdrawal and affective flattening) symptoms (Dworkin et al., 1987), high versus low critical emotional family background, or high versus low similarity to neurological–psychological testing profiles (Mirsky, 1987) might prove to be extremely important. A concatenation of such "risk" factors, for example, history of birth trauma, male sex, neurological testing deficits, communicatively deviant parents, and a critical family climate, may predict better and reveal more about causality than a rigid adherence to a simple model of one disease, one cause. Zubin and Spring (1977) illustrate the general framework of such a multifarious diathesis–stress paradigm and point out that schizophrenia may result from various combinations of vulnerability factors. Some patients may carry high loadings of genetic risk, others may be schizophrenic more by virtue of environmental factors, and still others may be the victims of moderate levels of both working in concert.

8. The current dominant research trend of looking for the biological underpinnings of schizophrenia may well reinforce the neglect of social-class, stress, and gender factors. These are extremely important areas for investigation that can produce significant contributions

to the field. An emphasis on social-class issues, for example, might have considerable impact on social policy, not only in the treatment of diagnosed schizophrenics but also on policy aimed at reducing the incidence and prevalence of the disorder.

REFERENCES

Al-Issa, I. (1982). Gender and schizophrenia. In I. Al-Issa (Ed.), *Gender and schizophrenia* (pp. 154–177). New York: Academic Press.

American Psychiatric Association. (1968). *Diagnostic and statistical manual of mental disorders.* (2nd ed.). Washington, DC: Author.

American Psychiatric Association. (1980). *Diagnostic and statistical manual of mental disorders* (3rd ed.). Washington, DC: Author.

American Psychiatric Association. (1987). *Diagnostic and statistical manual of mental disorders* (3rd ed., Revised.) Washington, DC: Author.

Anderson, C. M., & Holder, D. P. (1989). Women and serious mental disorders. In M. McGoldrick, C. M. Anderson, & F. Walsh (Eds.), *Women in Families* (pp. 381–406). New York: Norton.

Asarnow, R. F. (1987, November). *Visual information processing in children with schizophrenic and attention deficit disorders.* Paper presented at the second annual meeting of the Society for Research in Psychopathology.

Bateson, G., Jackson, D. D., Haley, J., & Weakland, J. (1956). Toward a theory of schizophrenia. *Behavioral Science, 1,* 251–264.

Beck, J. C., & Worthen, K. (1972). Precipitating stress, crisis theory, and hospitalization in schizophrenia and depression. *Archives of General Psychiatry, 26,* 123–129.

Boyd, J., & Weissman, M. M. (1981). Epidemiology of affective disorders: A re-examination and future directions. *Archives of General Psychiatry, 38,* 1039–1046.

Burbach, D. J., Lewine, R., & Meltzer, H. Y. (1984). Diagnostic concordance for schizophrenia as a function of sex. *Journal of Consulting and Clinical Psychology, 52,* 478–479.

Carlson, G. A., & Goodwin, F. K. (1973). The stages of mania. *Archives of General Psychiatry, 28,* 221–228.

Cohen, B. D. (1978). Self-editing deficits in schizophrenia. In L. C. Wynne, R. L. Cromwell, & S. Matthysse (Eds.), *The nature of schizophrenia* (pp. 313–319). New York: Wiley.

Cromwell, R. L. (1978a). Concluding comments (on genetic transmission). In L. C. Wynne, R. L. Cromwell, & S. Matthysse (Eds.), *The nature of schizophrenia* (pp. 76–83). New York: Wiley.

Cromwell, R. L. (1978b). Attention and information processing: A foundation for understanding schizophrenia? In L. C. Wynne, R. L. Cromwell, & S. Matthysse (Eds.), *The nature of schizophrenia* (pp. 219–224). New York: Wiley.

Cromwell, R. L. (1978c). Concluding comments (on biochemical approaches to schizophrenia). In L. C. Wynne, R. L. Cromwell, & S. Matthysse (Eds.), *The nature of schizophrenia,* (pp. 151–156). New York: Wiley.

Davis, J. M. (1978). Dopamine theory of schizophrenia: A two-factor theory. In L. C. Wynne, R. L. Cromwell, & S. Matthysse (Eds.), *The nature of schizophrenia* (pp. 105–115). New York: Wiley.

Dell, P. F. (1980). Researching the family theories of schizophrenia: An exercise in epistemological confusion. *Family Process, 19,* 321–335.

Doane, J., West, K. L., Goldstein, M. J., Rodnick, E. H., & Jones, J. E. (1981). Parental communication deviance and affective style. *Archives of General Psychiatry, 38,* 679–685.

Dohrenwend, B. (1974). Social and cultural differences in psychopathology. *Annual Review of Psychology, 25,* 417–452.

Dohrenwend, B., & Dohrenwend, B. (1969). *Social status and psychological disorder.* New York: Wiley Interscience.

Draguns, J. (1973). Comparisons of psychopathology across cultures: Issues, findings, directions. *Journal of Cross-Cultural Psychology, 4,* 9–47.

Dworkin, R. H., Green, S., Small, N., Warner, M., Cornblatt, B. A., & Erlenmeyer-Kimling, L. (1987, November). *Negative symptoms and social competence in adolescents at risk for schizophrenia and affective disorder.* Paper presented at the second annual meeting of the Society for Research in Psychopathology, Atlanta, GA.

Fromm-Reichmann, F. (1948). Notes on the development of treatment of schizophrenics by psychoanalytic psychotherapy. *Psychiatry, 2,* 263–274.

Farina, A., Garmezy, N., & Barry, H. (1963). Relationship of marital status to the incidence and prognosis of schizophrenia. *Journal of Abnormal and Social Psychology, 67,* 624–630.

Fromm-Reichmann, F. (1950). *Principles of intensive psychotherapy.* Chicago: University of Chicago Press.

Gift, T. E., Strauss, J. S., Ritzler, B. A., Kokes, R. F., & Harder, D. W. (1988). Social class and psychiatric disorder: The examination of an extreme. *Journal of Nervous and Mental Disease, 176,* 593–597.

George, L., & Neufeld, R. W. (1985). Cognition and symptomatology in schizophrenia. *Schizophrenia Bulletin, 11,* 264–285.

Goldstein, M. J., Rodnick, E. H., Jones, J. E., McPherson, S. R., & West, K. L. (1978). Familial precursors of schizophrenia spectrum disorders. In L. C. Wynne, R. L. Cromwell, & S. Matthysse (Eds.), *The nature of schizophrenia* (pp. 487–498). New York: Wiley.

Gottesman, I. I. (1978). Schizophrenia and genetics: Where are we? Are you sure? In L. C. Wynne, R. L. Cromwell, & S. Matthysse (Eds.), *The nature of schizophrenia* (pp. 59–69). New York: Wiley.

Gottesman, I. I., & Shields, J. (1973). Genetic theorizing and schizophrenia. *British Journal of Psychiatry, 22,* 15–30.

Gottesman, I. I., & Shields, J. (1976). A critical review of recent adoption, twin and family studies of schizophrenia: Behavioral genetics perspectives. *Schizophrenia Bulletin, 2,* 360–376.

Gruzelier, J. H., & Venables, P. H. (1972). Skin conductance orienting activity in a heterogeneous sample of schizophrenics: Possible evidence of limbic dysfunction. *Journal of Nervous and Mental Disease, 155,* 277–286.

Haley, J. (1963). *Strategies of psychotherapy.* New York: Grune & Stratton.

Harrow, M., Westermeyer, J. F., & Marengo, J. T. (1987, November). *Broad versus narrow concepts of schizophrenia: Evidence from psychopathology research.* Paper presented at the second annual meeting of the Society for Research in Psychopathology, Atlanta, GA.

Harvey, P. D. (1987, November). *A longitudinal examination of reference performance and thought disorder in schizophrenia and mania.* Paper presented at the second annual meeting of the Society for Research in Psychopathology, Atlanta, GA.

Heilbrun, A. B. (1973). *Aversive maternal control: A theory of schizophrenic development.* New York: Wiley.

Helzer, J. E., Clayton, P. J., Pambakian, R., Reich, T., Woodruff, R. A., & Reveley, M. A. (1977). Reliability of psychiatric diagnosis: II. The test/retest reliability of diagnostic classification. *Archives of General Psychiatry, 34,* 136–141.

Hoffman, L. (1981). *Foundations of family therapy.* New York: Basic.

Hogarty, G. E., Goldberg, S. C., Schooler, N. R., Ulrich, R. F., & the Collaborative Group. (1974). Drug and sociotherapy in the aftercare of schizophrenic patients. II—Two-year relapse rates. *Archives of General Psychiatry, 31,* 603–618.

Hogarty, G. E. (1985). Expressed emotion and schizophrenic relapse: Implications from the Pittsburgh Study. In M. Alpert (Ed.), *Controversies in schizophrenia* (pp. 354–365). New York: Guilford.

Hollingshead, A. B., & Redlich, F. C. (1958). *Social class and mental illness.* New York: Wiley.

Holzman, P. S., Levy, D. L., & Proctor, L. R. (1978). The several qualities of attention in schizophrenia. In L. C. Wynne, R. L. Cromwell, & S. Matthysse (Eds.), *The nature of schizophrenia* (pp. 295–306). New York: Wiley.

Huber, G., Gross, G., Schuttler, R., & Linz, M. (1980). Longitudinal studies of schizophrenic patients. *Schizophrenia Bulletin, 6,* 592–605.

Katz, M. M., Sanborn, K. O., with Lowery, H. A., & Ching, J. (1978). Ethnic studies in Hawaii: On psychopathology and social deviance. In L. C. Wynne, R. L. Cromwell, & S. Matthysse (Eds.), *The nature of schizophrenia.* New York: Wiley.

Kety, S. S., Rosenthal, D., Wender, P. H., & Schulsinger, F. (1968). The types and prevalence of mental illness in the biological and adoptive families of adopted schizophrenics. In D. Rosenthal & S. S. Kety (Eds.), *The transmission of schizophrenia* (pp. 345–362). New York: Pergamon Press.

Kety, S. S., Rosenthal, D., Wender, P. H., Schulsinger, F., & Jacobsen, B. (1975). Mental illness in the biological and adoptive families of adopted individuals who have become schizophrenic: A preliminary report based upon psychiatric interviews. In R. Fieve, D. Rosenthal, & H. Brill (Eds.), *Genetic research in psychiatry* (pp. 147–165). Baltimore: Johns Hopkins University Press.

Kidd, K. K. (1978). A genetic perspective on schizophrenia. In L. C. Wynne, R. L. Cromwell, & S. Matthysse (Eds.), *The nature of schizophrenia*, (pp. 70–75). New York: Wiley.

Knight, R. (1987, November). *The information processing dysfunction of poor premorbid schizophrenics: Specifying deficiencies.* Paper presented at the second annual meeting of the Society for Research in Psychopathology, Atlanta, GA.

Kohn, M. L. (1973). Social class and schizophrenia: A critical review and a reformulation. *Schizophrenia Bulletin, 3,* 617–631.

Kokes, R. F., Strauss, J. S., & Klorman, R. (1977). Premorbid adjustment in schizophrenia (Part II). *Schizophrenia Bulletin, 3,* 186–213.

Kraepelin, E. (1971). *Demential praecox and paraphrenia.* (R. M. Barclay, Trans.). New York: Robert E. Krieger. Reprinted with an historical introduction. (Original work published 1919)

Lahniers, C. E., & White, K. (1976). Changes in environmental life events and their relationship to psychiatric hospital admission. *Journal of Nervous and Mental Disease, 163,* 154–158.

Laing, R. D. (1960). *The divided self.* London: Tavistock.

Lewine, R. R. (1981). Sex differences in schizophrenia: Timing or subtypes? *Psychological Bulletin, 90,* 432–444.

Lidz, T., Cornelison, A., Fleck, S., & Terry, D. (1957). The intra-familial environment of schizophrenic patients: II. Marital schism and marital skew. *American Journal of Psychiatry, 114,* 241–248.

Lidz, T., Fleck, S., & Cornelison, A. (1965). *Schizophrenia and the family.* New York: International Universities Press.

Liem, J. H. (1974). Effects of verbal communications of parents and children: A comparison of normal and schizophrenic families. *Journal of Consulting and Clinical Psychology, 42,* 438–450.

Loveland, N. T., Singer, M. T., Wynne, L. C. (1963). The family Rorschach: A new method of studying family interaction. *Family Process, 2,* 187–215.

Matthysse, S. (1978). Missing links. In L. C. Wynne, R. L. Cromwell, & S. Matthysse (Eds.), *The nature of schizophrenia* (pp. 148–150). New York: Wiley.

Mayer-Gross, W., Slater, E., & Roth, M. (1969). *Clinical psychiatry* (3rd ed.). Baltimore: Williams & Wilkins.

Mednick, S. A. (1970). Breakdown in individuals at high risk for schizophrenia: Possible predispositional perinatal factors. *Mental Hygiene, 54,* 50–61.

McNeil, T. F., & Kaij, L. (1978). Obstetric factors in the development of schizophrenic: Complications in the births of preschizophrenics and in reproduction by schizophrenic parents. In L. C. Wynne, R. L. Cromwell, & S. Matthysse (Eds.), *The nature of schizophrenia* (pp. 401–429). New York: Wiley.

Mednick, S. A., & Schulsinger, F. (1970). Factors related to breakdown in children at high risk for schizophrenia. In M. Roff & D. F. Ricks (Eds.), *Life history research in psychopathology* (Vol. 1). Minneapolis: University of Minnesota Press.

Mednick, S. A., Schulsinger, F., Teasdale, T. W., Schulsinger, H. Venables, P. H., & Rock, D. R. (1978). Schizophrenia in high risk children: Sex differences in predisposing factors. In G. Serban (Ed.), *Cognitive defects in the development of mental illness.* New York: Brunner/Mazel.

Meehl, P. E. (1962). Schizotaxia, schizotypy, schizophrenia. *American Psychologist, 17,* 827–838.

Mirsky, A. F. (1987, November). *A model of attention—elements of a complex behavior.* Paper presented at the second annual meeting of the Society for Research in Psychopathology, Atlanta, GA.

Mishler, E. G., & Waxler, N. (1968). *Interaction in families.* New York: Wiley.

Murphy, H. B. M. (1978). Cultural influences on incidence, course, and treatment response. In L. C. Wynne, R. L. Cromwell, S. Matthysse (Eds.), *The nature of schizophrenia* (pp. 586–594). New York: Wiley.

Murphy, H. B. M., & Lemieux, M. (1967). Quelques considerations sur le taux élève de schizophrenie dans un type de communauté canadienne-française. *Canadian Psychiatric Association Journal, 12,* Numero Special S71.

Nameche, G. F., Waring, M., & Ricks, D. F. (1964). Early indicators of outcome in schizophrenia. *Journal of Nervous and Mental Disease, 139,* 232–240.

Neuchterlein, K. H. (1977). Reaction time and attention. *Schizophrenia Bulletin, 3,* 373–428.

Professional Staff of the United States–United Kingdom Cross-National Project. (1974). *Schizophrenia Bulletin, 1* (Experimental Issue No. 11), 80–102.

Rapaport, D., Gill, M. M., & Schafer, R. (1968). *Diagnostic psychological testing* (Rev. ed.). New York: International Universities Press.

Reiss, D. (1971). Varieties of consensual experience. *Family Process, 10,* 1–35.

Rochester, S. R. (1978). Are language disorders in acute schizophrenia actually information processing problems? In L. C. Wynne, R. L. Cromwell, & S. Matthysse (Eds.), *The nature of schizophrenia* (pp. 320–328). New York: Wiley.

Rodnick, E. H., & Shakow, D. (1940). Set in the schizophrenic as measured by a composite reaction time index. *American Journal of Psychiatry, 97,* 214–218.

Rosenhan, D. L. (1973). On being sane in insane places. *Science, 179,* 250–258.

Rothblum, E. D., Solomon, L. J., & Albee, G. W. (1986). A sociopolitical perspective of DSM-III. In T. Millon & G. L. Klerman (Eds.), *Contemporary directions in psychopathology: Toward the DSM-IV* (pp. 167–189). New York: Guilford.

Sachar, E. J., Gruen, P. H., Altman, N., Langer, G., & Halpern, F. S. (1978). Neuroendocrine studies of brain dopamine blockade in humans. In L. C. Wynne, R. L. Cromwell, & S. Matthysse (Eds.), *The nature of schizophrenia* (pp. 95–104). New York: Wiley.

Salzman, L. F., Klein, R. H., & Strauss, J. S. (1978). Pendulum eyetracking in remitted psychiatric patients. In L. C. Wynne, R. L. Cromwell, & S. Matthysse (Eds.), *The nature of schizophrenia* (pp. 289–294). New York: Wiley.

Sartorius, N., Jablensky, A., Stromgren, E., & Shapiro, R. (1978). Validity of diagnostic concepts across cultures: A preliminary report from the International Pilot Study of Schizophrenia. In L. C. Wynne, R. L. Cromwell, & S. Matthysse (Eds.). *The nature of schizophrenia* (pp. 657–669). New York: Wiley.

Schacht, T., & Nathan, P. E. (1977). But is it good for psychologists? *American Psychologist, 32,* 1017–1025.

Schneider, K. (1959). *Clinical psychopathology* (M. Hamilton, trans.). New York: Grune & Stratton.

Shakow, D. (1977). Segmental set: The adaptive process in schizophrenia. *American Psychologist, 32,* 129–139.

Singer, M. T. (1967). Family transactions and schizophrenia: I. Recent research findings. In J. Romano (Ed.), *The origins of schizophrenia* (pp. 147–153). Amsterdam: Excerpta Medica.

Singer, M. T., & Wynne, L. C. (1966). Principles for scoring communication defects and deviances in parents of schizophrenics: Rorschach and TAT scoring manuals. *Psychiatry, 29,* 260–288.

Singer, M. T., Wynne, L. C., & Toohey, M. L. (1978). Communication disorders and the families of schizophrenics. In L. C. Wynne, R. L. Cromwell, & S. Matthysse (Eds.), *The nature of schizophrenia* (pp. 499–511). New York: Wiley.

Smith, E. K. (1976). Effects of the double-bind communication. *Journal of Abnormal Psychology, 85,* 356–363.

Spitzer, R. L., Endicott, J., & Gibbon, M. (1979). Crossing the border into borderline personality and borderline schizophrenia. *Archives of General Psychiatry, 36,* 17–24.

Spring, B., Wagman, A., Kurtz, R., Kirkpatrick, B., Levitt, M., & Lemon, M. (1987, November). *Symptom correlates of distractibility in inpatient and outpatient schizophrenics.* Paper presented at the second annual meeting of the Society for Research in Psychopathology, Atlanta, GA.

Srole, L., Langer, T. S., Michael, S. T., Opeler, M. K., & Rennie, T. A. C. (1962). *Mental health in the metropolis: The midtown Manhattan study.* New York: McGraw-Hill.

Stone, M. H. (1980). *The borderline syndromes.* New York: McGraw-Hill.

Torrey, E. F. (1973). Is schizophrenia universal: An open question. *Schizophrenia Bulletin, 7,* 53–60.

Tsuang, M. T., Dempsey, G. M., & Rauscher, F. (1976). A study of "atypical schizophrenia": Comparison with schizophrenia and affective disorder by sex, age of admission, precipitant, outcome, and family history. *Archives of General Psychiatry, 33,* 1157–1160.

Turner, R. J., & Wagenfeld, M. O. (1967). Occupational mobility and schizophrenia: An assessment of social causation and social selection hypotheses. *American Sociological Review, 32,* 104–113.

Vaughn, C. E., & Leff, J. P. (1976). The influence of family and social factors on the course of psychiatric illness. *British Journal of Psychiatry, 129,* 125–137.

Watt, N. F. (1978). Patterns of childhood social development in adult schizophrenics. *Archives of General Psychiatry, 35,* 160–165.

Weakland, J., (1960). The "double-bind" hypothesis of schizophrenia and three-party interaction. In C. Sluzki & D. Ransom (Eds.), *Double bind: The foundation of communicational approach to the family.* New York: Grune & Stratton.

Wechsler, D. (1958). *Measurement and appraisal of adult intelligence.* Baltimore: Williams & Wilkins.

Weiner, H. (1977). *Psychobiology and human disease.* New York: Elsevier.

Wender, P. H., Rosenthal, D., & Kety, S. S. (1968). A psychiatric assessment of the adoptive parents of schizophrenics. In D. Rosenthal & S. S. Kety (Eds.), *The transmission of schizophrenia* (pp. 235–250). Oxford: Pergamon Press.

Wertheim, E. (1973). Family unit therapy and the science and typology of family systems. *Family Process, 12,* 361–376.

Westermeyer, M., Harrow, M., & Marengo, J. (1988, November). *Gender differences in schizophrenic course and outcome.* Presented at the third annual meeting of the Society for Research in Psychopathology, Boston, MA.

White, R. W., & Watt, N. F. (1981). *The abnormal personality* (5th ed.). New York: Wiley.

World Health Organization. (1973). *The international pilot study of schizophrenia* (Vol. 1). Geneva: Author.

Wyatt, R. J., & Bigelow, L. B. (1978). A survey of other biologic research in schizophrenia. In L. C. Wynne, R. L. Cromwell, & S. Matthysse (Eds.), *The nature of schizophrenia* (pp. 143–147). New York: Wiley.

Wynne, L. C. (1970). Communication disorders and the quest for relatedness in families of schizophrenics. *American Journal of Psychoanalysis, 30,* 100–114.

Yolles, S. F., & Kramer, M. (1969). In L. Bellak & L. Loeb (Eds.), *The schizophrenic syndrome.* New York: Grune & Stratton.

Zubin, J., & Spring, B. J. (1977). Vulnerability–A new view of schizophrenia. *Journal of Abnormal Psychology, 86,* 103–126.

CHAPTER EIGHT

The Agoraphobic Syndrome: From Anxiety Neurosis to Panic Disorder

IRIS G. FODOR

> The Gods created the woman for the indoors functions,
> the man for all the others.
> —Xenophon, Ancient Greek philosopher

Until the 19th century, most women were confined to the home. They were encouraged to focus on the home and family and were discouraged from participating in life outside. No one worried too much about women who could not go out in the world or function independently. However, by Victorian times, woman's roles were beginning to change. A new disorder, agoraphobia—the fear of being out in the world—was named by Westphal in 1871, and further elaborated upon by Freud (1909) and his followers. From that time on, women who followed the cultural directive to stay out of the *agora* and remain confined to the home were considered abnormal. As the 20th century progressed, these agoraphobic women attracted increasing attention from the mental health establishment.

This chapter will focus on agoraphobia as well as its latest variant, panic disorder. Agoraphobia is a representative anxiety disorder that has high prevalence rates among women, and has been the locus of a biological versus psychological etiology debate among contemporary researchers and clinicians.

Overlooked in most writings about this syndrome is that it is mostly females who report having agoraphobic symptoms and panic attacks (65%–85% females). The problem often begins in the late teens or 20s, often after marriage or motherhood. If untreated, it can last a lifetime. Agoraphobics represent half of the phobic population, with recent surveys in the United States and Europe suggesting that agoraphobia may affect many more women than are currently identified, representing all classes and ethnic groups (Fleming & Faulk, 1989; Marks, 1987; Thorpe & Burns, 1983).

During the last decade, there has been a rapid increase in the research and theoretical and clinical literature on anxiety disorders, agoraphobia, and panic disorder (1,000 articles and 47 books per year, according to Marks, 1987). In 1974, this author wrote a comprehensive paper on agoraphobia and hoped to cover the literature. Today, I would not make such an attempt. Instead, I begin with a historical overview in which I summarize the major theoretical positions, discuss the etiology of the syndrome, and explore why women have such a high prevalence rate. Next, I present a feminist model for understanding and dealing with agoraphobia and panic disorder.

Over the past 60 years, there has been a shift from viewing agoraphobia as a variant of anxiety neurosis to a more behaviorally based anxiety-avoidant disorder, and more recently, to a view of agoraphobia as a subcategory of panic disorder. Psychoanalysts from Freud on viewed agoraphobic symptoms as representing neurotic conflicts. In the 1960s and '70s, major researchers and writers in behavior therapy established themselves as the experts on the etiology and treatment of agoraphobia, presenting a view of agoraphobic symptoms as variants of learned-avoidance behaviors (Marks, 1978, 1987; Wolpe, 1958). With the advent of cognitive–behavior therapy, the cognitive aspects of agoraphobia were highlighted. In particular, catastrophic thinking and "fear of fear" were featured as driving panic and avoidance behaviors (Beck & Emery, 1985; Goldstein & Chambless, 1978). At the same time, another shift occurred, when leading biologically oriented psychiatrists presented strong evidence to support a biological basis for agoraphobia. Today, agcraphobia is seen, for the most part, as a variant of panic disorder. In fact, most recent texts on anxiety feature panic as part of the title or subtitle (Barlow, 1988; Hallam, 1985; Marks, 1987; Rachman & Maser, 1988). However, the major controversy today focuses on the opposition of cognitive and biological bases for panic.

When we consider the agoraphobic syndrome, there are five basic questions that need to be addressed: (1) Why does it develop (etiology)? That is, what exists in the constitutional makeup of the agoraphobic, the family, or the environment to create such a syndrome? (2) Why are females more prone to agoraphobic symptoms and panic? (3) What are the immediate triggers/stressors that lead to the development of full-blown symptoms—series of panic attacks and widening avoidance behaviors? (4) What force maintains the symptoms, which can last over a lifetime and are often resistant to conventional therapy? (5) What is the most effective treatment?

As we examine the literature, we see that different schools address one or another of these questions in their theory and have different expectations about what constitutes positive treatment outcome. For the psychoanalysts, the etiology lies in family dynamics and history. What maintains the symptoms is neurotic conflict. The treatment is the standard long-term analytic therapy for resolving conflict, achieving insight, and realigning defense structures. For behavior therapists, the immediate triggers—what set off the symptoms—and the ways to alleviate the symptoms become the prime focus. Successful outcome depends on symptom removal, that is, feared situations are no longer avoided (Barlow, 1988; Marks, 1987; Wolpe, 1958). Recent developments in cognitive–behavior therapy, influenced by cognitive psychology, introduce another emphasis. The focus is on negative cognitions or maladaptive beliefs, for example, a fear of fear and catastrophic thinking that drives panic and maintains avoidance behavior (Beck, 1988; Beck & Emery, 1985; Clark, 1988; Ellis & Harper; 1975, Goldstein & Chambless, 1978). Other cognitive therapists emphasize systems theory: They view the family as being a system that is pivotal in maintaining and reinforcing the agoraphobic person's behaviors (Fodor, 1987; Goldstein, 1982; Guidano & Liotti, 1983; Hafner, 1982; Lazarus, 1966).

Ironically, as behavior therapy broadened and became more cognitive, biologically based theories and treatment also increased in popularity. For these biologically based theorists, the etiology (what causes the symptoms) and the treatment (how to get rid of the symptoms) become primary. An implicit assumption is that something is wrong with the basic organism, the brain or brain functions, or the physiological system. This presumed deficit is also assumed to be hereditary. Hence, families are seen as transmitters of disorders. Most of this research focuses on differentiating between agoraphobia and panic, while drug treatment aims at control of panic and preventing the spread of phobias (Liebowitz & Klein, 1982).

What is most interesting is that the writings on agoraphobia for the past half-century have been a testing ground for all the controversies that rage among mental health professionals. Yet, almost none of the major theorists writing about agoraphobia addresses the question, why are females more prone than males to develop this disorder? What is it about familial and societal structure that makes it more likely that the female will develop and maintain panic and agoraphobic avoidant symptoms?

In this chapter, I will examine all of the differing ways of conceptualizing agoraphobia, arguing for an explanatory system that integrates features of cognitive, behavioral, and psychodynamic systems approaches within a feminist framework. This integrative feminist approach addresses socialization variables, societal reinforcement, and how these factors might account for the high prevalence rate of agoraphobia among women. It will attempt to uncover specific elements in women's lives that might account for the development of agoraphobic symptomology and those aspects of women's lives that serve to maintain and reinforce such symptoms. Based on this knowledge, I will sketch out a feminist model for treatment. Many of the ideas in this chapter are elaborations or revisions of my previous writings, ongoing clinical work with agoraphobics, and my appraisal of the clinical and research literature of the past 20 years (Fodor, 1974, 1983, 1987, 1989).

RECENT HISTORY

The debate over the etiology of agoraphobia, and the consequent ways in which it has been conceptualized over time, can best be seen in the changes in the way it has been described over the past 3 decades in the American Psychiatric Association's (APA) second, third, and revised third editions of the *Diagnostic and Statistical Manual of Mental Disorders* (DSM-II, DSM-III, and DSM-III-R, respectively). Changing diagnostic frameworks reflect the shift in membership on the panels, from a mostly psychoanalytic perspective in the 1960s to increased representation of the behavioral, cognitive, and biological points of view today.

Psychoanalytic Views of Agoraphobia

DSM-II, published in 1968 (APA), places phobias in the category of anxiety neurosis and proposes a psychodynamic etiology. Psychoanalysts view phobias as "symptom neurosis characterized by a pathological fear of a particular object or situation, and the consequent attempts to avoid them. The feared situation or object leads to the feeling of fright by providing stimuli to the activation of repressed wishes, usually oedipal, and the defenses against these wishes" (Eidelberg, 1968, pp. 309–310).

This definition derives from Freud's (1909) psychoanalytic approach to phobias, emerging from his discussion of 5-year-old Little Hans's phobia of horses. Central to the classical psychoanalytic approach is the view elaborated by Fenichel (1945) that "What a person fears, he unconsciously wishes. . . . [There is] an attempt to escape from an internal dangerous impulse by avoiding a specific external condition which represents the impulse" (pp. 196–197). In particular, he suggests that agoraphobia, the fear of being in the outside world, represents latent exhibitionism and describes his analysis of a patient as follows: "Analysis showed the unconscious motive of her exhibitionism was a deep-seated hostility, originally directed toward her mother, then deflected onto herself. 'Everybody look!' her anxiety seemed to proclaim, 'My mother let me come into this world in this helpless condition without a penis'" (p. 200).

Other psychoanalytic theorists highlight interpersonal conflict as the primary translator of anxiety into concrete symbolic symptoms. This view was presented as early as 1929, by Helene Deutsch, who provided the first analytic case description of agoraphobia, which highlighted an ambivalent and conflict-ridden identification with the mother, that is, "the patient reported unconscious death wishes against the mother . . . so she needed to keep her close by" (p. 52). Weiss (1958) sees as central to agoraphobics "a conflict between symbiotic union with the mother and the need for separation from her in order to establish one's own autonomous ego" (p. 386). Sperling (1974) further reported the transfer of mother/daughter conflicts to the marital relationship of an agoraphobic. "The patient . . . expressed feeling like a 'caged animal' . . . she felt trapped in her marriage as she had felt trapped with her mother."

Symonds (1971) broadened this viewpoint by adding a feminist perspective. In a paper entitled *Phobias after Marriage: Woman's Declaration of Dependence,* she says: "For many years I have been interested in a specific clinical problem which occurs when a young woman who was apparently independent, self-sufficient and capable, changes after marriage and develops phobias or other signs of constriction of self. She clings to her husband for constant support, apparently changing from a capable 'strong' person into a classically helpless female" (p. 144). Symonds finds that the ways women are socialized are relevant for the development of agoraphobia.

The Behavioral Approach to Agoraphobia

In the 1960s and '70s, agoraphobia and anxiety disorders became a prime focus of the newly emerging field of behavior therapy, which in turn influenced theorizing about agoraphobia as well as contributed to a more behavioral diagnosis in the DSM-III, published in 1980 (APA).

Behavior-therapy theory developed from the pioneering work of Wolpe (1958), who suggested that phobias arise from classically conditioned autonomic disturbances that are reinforced by developing avoidance behaviors.

Wolpe (1958) viewed phobias as developing by autonomic conditioning from "situations which evoke high intensities of anxiety" (p. 302). He cites the case of an unhappy married woman, exhausted and resentful of her children, who states, "one day when food shopping . . . I felt I wanted to erupt . . . I wanted to scream but didn't. A few days later, I went to the Center City to meet my mother and sister and all of a sudden I began to feel very funny. I told them I had to leave and that was the day I tried to walk home from the bus and I couldn't walk . . ." (p. 303). The phobia is presumed to constitute the avoidance behavior, for example, the woman in Wolpe's study fears leaving the house: "the prospect of taking the action that would lead out of the situation simply adds new anxiety to that which already exists and this is what inhibits action" (p. 303).

The avoidance alleviates the anxiety, but what maintains the avoidance behaviors is usually some form of reinforcement. There is reinforcement in the diminution of the anxiety, and there is usually social reinforcement for the avoided behavior. Lazarus (1966) suggests that it is "impossible to become an agoraphobic without the aid of someone who will submit to the inevitable demands imposed upon them by the sufferer" (p. 97).

Cognitive Theories of Agoraphobia

Spawned by the cognitive revolution in psychology, behavior therapy became more cognitive-oriented in the 1970s and '80s, which in turn affected theorizing about agoraphobia. Most influential were the ideas of Beck (Beck & Emory, 1985; Beck, 1988) and Ellis (Ellis & Harper, 1975). They both presented somewhat overlapping theories. Beck and Emory presented their fully developed cognitive approach to understanding the anxiety disorders. In particular, Beck and Emory emphasized the importance of two types of cognitions central to agoraphobia and panic: *attribution of causality* and *cognitive set*. In panic attacks, there is a misattribution of causality. That is, the person makes an interpretation of symptoms as a threat to life or ability to function, for example, "I am going crazy," which in turn leads to their intensification. Ellis and Harper labeled this misattribution *catastrophic thinking*. Furthermore, as the agoraphobic person approaches the phobic situation, her cognitive set leads to an anticipation that something terrible is about to happen. Central to both Ellis's and Beck's theories is the idea that anxiety-evoking cognitions by themselves simultaneously elicit anxiety, serve to justify fear, and maintain and drive the avoidance behaviors.

Appraisal of Cognitive–Behavioral Therapy Theory of Agoraphobia

Proponents of cognitive–behavioral approaches toward etiology and treatment form the largest block of psychologically oriented therapists and researchers writing about agoraphobia and panic at present. In the 1970s, anxiety disorder clinics and phobia centers were set up widely. Self-help clinics were also spawned by the movement. These clinicians have amassed an impressive array of studies to support claims for a cognitive–behavioral understanding of the symptoms and their treatment, and for the efficacy of exposure therapy as well (Barlow, 1988; Beck, 1988; Clark, 1988; Goldstein, 1982; Marks, 1987; Thorpe & Burns, 1983). However, there have been critics as well, who point to high drop-out and relapse rates (Emmelkamp & van der Hout, 1983).

The current state of theorizing is becoming more influenced by cognitive psychology, which presents an integrative scientific approach for studying brain, behavior, and cognitive functioning. Today's cutting edge of theory addresses emotional processing (i.e., the interface of cognitive appraisal of emotional states and the hierarchical development of fear structures) as central for the development and maintenance of agoraphobia. Also addressed are patterns and underlying cognitive structures that operate outside of awareness and are resistant to the piecemeal approach of behavior therapy (Foa & Kozak, 1986; Lang, 1988). What is neglected, for the most part, in the cognitive–behavioral approaches to agoraphobia is an emphasis on socialization variables. While reinforcement is featured in behavioral theory, what is missing is the link between familial and societal training and the development and maintance of agoraphobic cognitions and avoidance behaviors.

Biological Theories

As behavioral and cognitive–behavioral attention focused on agoraphobia and anxiety disorders over the past 2 decades, there was also an increasing and often competing theoretical and diagnostic focus by biological theorists, who stressed constitutional and physiological factors as a central focus, which in turn was reflected in the diagnostic manuals.

Interestingly, the first use of the term agoraphobia was by Westphal, a neurologist, in 1871. He spoke of agoraphobia as a "physiological sensory disturbance" to diagnose a patient who was afraid to cross a wide, open space (Errera, 1962). Ironically, this first use of the term is now very much in vogue.

Encouraged by new views about panic, biologically based theorizing and research flourished in the mid-1980s. On one end of the spectrum we have biological theories that stress constitutional factors that predispose individuals to panic disorders and anxiety attacks. One such constitutional factor is mitral valve prolapse (MVP). This perspective views women as having an inborn constitutional defect of the cardiovascular system that lowers the threshold for panic attacks. At the other end of the spectrum are pharmacologically based theories, which explore the relationship between drugs and central nervous system functions. Donald Klein (1964) and his associates at the Psychiatric Institute at Columbia University have been in the forefront of the move to focus on panic as central and have provided the major biologically based research paradigms for this orientation. This research falls into three major categories. The first studies constitutional or physiological factors that predispose individuals to panic. The second explores methods to experimentally induce and study panic. The third utilizes a psychopharmacologic approach to study factors leading to the elimination of panic symptoms.

Constitutional Predispositions

Leibowitz and Klein (1982), among others, view MVP as a possible predisposing factor in panic attack. "The principal anatomic defect is a defect in connective tissues of the mitral valve to the heart which cause the valve to prolapse" (p. 158). This defect was observed in female patients with panic attacks. Liebowitz and Klein speculate that MVP may either play a "provocative role in predisposed individuals or [be] linked to panic disorder through a generalized disturbance of the autonomic nervous system" (p. 158).

However, other researchers dispute their claims, finding MVP to be common in asymptomatic, normal women. Furthermore, there does not appear to be a family history of MVP for women with panic disorders. Marks (1987), in his comprehensive review of the research on MVP, concludes that "recent studies argue against the notion that MVP might be a major factor in the etiology or prognosis of agoraphobia" (p. 353).

Endocrine Factors

Liebowitz and Klein (1988) are among those who also implicate estrogen imbalance as influencing panic. They cite 32 cases in which panic attacks occurred following childbirth, hysterectomy, and menstrual irregularity. Furthermore, agoraphobia may be associated with other affective disorders that are possibly affected by estrogen. (See Chapter 6 for further discussion of this issue.) However, other investigators concur in their comprehensive reviews that there appears to be no strong evidence for an endocrine link to agoraphobia and panic disorder (Barlow, 1988; Marks, 1987).

Inducing Panic: Sodium Lactate Infusion

In 1982, Liebowitz and Klein began another line of research to strengthen their case for the physiological underpinnings for panic. They found that intravenous lactate infusions set off panic attacks in patients with a history of spontaneous attacks, and not in controls. Women with and without panic were given an intravenous infusion of sodium lactate, and the women with a history of panic panicked, whereas the others did not. Furthermore, patients assigned to treatment with imipramine—a drug highly effective in blocking panic attacks—did not panic. These findings were cited as evidence to establish the biological primacy of panic.

Research by others did not achieve the same differential effects (Marks, 1987). Margraf, Ehlers, and Roth (1986) report that cognitive and emotional variables appear to have triggered the panic in their panic disorder subjects, since the experimental situation itself was viewed as threatening and dangerous. In other words, patients panicked and began to catastrophize when they began to feel the induced physiological sensations, which in turn triggered further panic.

In a similar line of research, others used carbon dioxide to induce panic. Shear (1988) concludes, from her comprehensive review of both drug induction methods, that "studies to date have failed to provide consistent support for the physiological basis of panic" (p. 63).

Research on Eliminating Panic:
Psychopharmocological Treatment

In the past decade, major investigators, based in medical schools and psychiatric hospitals and funded by the National Institute of Mental Health (NIMH) and various drug company grants, have made major breakthroughs in understanding the biochemistry of panic and its locus in the brain, and have developed psychotropic drugs that can alleviate panic. It is through the differential response to drug treatment that leading researchers such as Klein (1964) proposed the distinction of panic from agoraphobia. Klein's pioneering research demonstrated a blocking of panic attacks by imipramine, a tricyclic antidepressant, which did not effect anticipatory anxiety. However, he reported that benzodiazepines and other tranquilizers eliminated anticipatory anxiety, but had no effect on the panic attacks. He concluded from these findings that "panic attacks appear to represent a form of anxiety biologically distinct from anticipatory anxiety" (Liebowitz & Klein, 1982).

There has been a progression of drug studies that inconsistently show amelioration of anxiety and panic symptoms. Two types of antidepressants have been most often used, the tricyclics and the monoamine oxidase (MAO) inhibitors. A newer antidepressant, Prozac, has also shown promise in alleviating anxiety and panic symptoms.

Appraisal of the Biological Position

While some of the deficits (e.g., MVP) hypothesized as causes seem to have been discounted, one cannot dismiss the mounting evidence that agoraphobic and panic-disorder clients do have differential drug responses, and that their underlying pharmacological patterns appear to be markedly similar to those found in depressed persons. While there is controversy about improvement following drugs, there is growing evidence that drug treatment does enhance behavior therapy. However, just because some panic symptoms are lessened by drugs does not fully support a full biological explanation for panic disorder and agoraphobic symptoms.

Recent research on the brain suggests that the locus ceruleus (LC) may be the center for the physiological, emotional, and behavioral origin of fear and anxiety. "The locus coeruleus [sic] is the brain nucleus containing most of the noradrenergic neuron cell bodies. . . . [P]anic vulnerability may be influenced by pharmacological agents which act on the locus coeruleus [sic]" (Shear, 1988, p. 61).

Recent work also suggests that the emotional centers and pathways for anxiety and depression may be similar. Further work in experimental psychopathology has also highlighted cognitive variables that foster physiological arousal (Clark, 1988).

THE POLITICS OF DIAGNOSIS IN THE 1980s: AGORAPHOBIA VERSUS PANIC DISORDER

In the 1970s and '80s, behavioral and (later) cognitive–behavioral research and writing about agoraphobia attracted increased attention and funding from the NIMH for demonstration programs. These programs, conducted mainly by American, British, or European psychologists, have produced an impressive array of research studies to support claims for a mainly psychological, cognitive–behavioral understanding of the etiology and maintenance of symptoms. They have also conducted a large number of outcome studies, which, for the most part, support psychotherapeutic cognitive–behavioral interventions (Barlow, 1988; Barlow & Wolfe, 1981; Emmelkamp, 1982; Goldstein, 1982; Hallam, 1985; Marks, 1978; Mathews, Gelder, & Johnson, 1986; Thorpe & Burns, 1983). A few of these well-known researchers and theorists were asked to serve on a panel by the American Psychiatric Association to reformulate the diagnostic categories of anxiety and phobic disorders from a more cognitive–behaviorally directed perspective for DSM-III. At the same time, biologically based psychiatrists, who received funding to establish anxiety disorder clinics and research centers within major medical centers—often in competition or in collaboration with the behavior therapists—were appointed to the same panel. Of interest is the jockeying for influence among the various theoretical research groups to reformulate the diagnostic categories, since the psychoanalysts' influence on the anxiety disorders panel was declining. Furthermore, the battles are still continuing, and many of these same researchers will be present on the DSM-IV panel, expected in the mid-1990s. At the heart of the controversy is the question of whether agoraphobic symptoms are triggered by psychological causes or represent a defective biological system. Do the panic symptoms occur spontaneously or are they triggered by cognitions? Another feature of the debate involves the efficacy of drug treatment as opposed to psychotherapy. For the most part, none of the principal researchers, in either of the camps, addresses women's issues or views sociocultural variables as crucial, even though agoraphobia and panic disorders occur primarily in females (Barlow, 1988; Marks, 1987; Liebowitz & Klein, 1982).

Agoraphobia: DSM-III

When we look at DSM-III (APA, 1980), we see that anxiety disorders received a more behaviorally based definition, discarding the language and etiology derived from psychoanalysis and its focus on anxiety neuroses previously emphasized by DSM-II (APA, 1968). The general category of anxiety disorders was established in DSM-III, with two main subcategories: panic disorders and phobias. Agoraphobia was placed under the phobia category and further delineated from panic disorder. For example, it was defined as "A marked fear of being in public places where escape might be difficult. Normal activities are increasingly restricted as the fears or avoidance behaviors dominate the individual's life. . . . The individual develops anticipatory fear of having such an attack and becomes reluctant or refuses to enter a variety of situations that are associated with these attacks" (p. 226). Panic disorder featured untriggered, recurrent, short panic attacks that "typically begin with the sudden onset of intense apprehension, fear or terror. . . . [Associated symptoms include] palpitations . . . chest pain . . . choking or smothering . . . dizziness, vertigo . . . feelings of unreality, hot or cold flashes, sweating, faintness, trembling or shaking and fear of dying or going crazy or doing something uncontrolled during the attacks" (p. 226).

From DSM-III to DSM-III-R: The Ascendance of Panic Disorder

In DSM-III (APA, 1980), there are two disorders with almost identical symptoms, however, one is linked to phobic stimuli and the other triggered by unexplained panic attacks. (Clearly, the work of a committee.) In the 1980s, there was a proliferation of research on panic with the attempt to differentiate it from avoidant-anxiety disorders. The more biologically based researchers presented evidence for panic as central, and the more psychologically oriented behavior and cognitive researchers emphasized learned avoidance and agoraphobic cognitions as central.

In 1987, the American Psychiatric Association published DSM-III-R "because of inconsistencies," with new findings relevant to the diagnostic categories. The manual's approach to agoraphobia was among the changes made. In DSM-III-R, the general category of anxiety disorder (which includes anxiety and phobic neuroses) is maintained. "The characteristic features of this group of disorders are symptoms of anxiety and avoidance behavior" (p. 235). However, panic is now viewed as the central disorder, with agoraphobia secondary. Furthermore, DSM-III-R stresses the hereditary, that is, biological, aspects, stating that panic disorder occurred frequently among "first-degree biological relatives" of diagnosed patients.

The diagnostic manual then presents two categories of panic disorder: panic disorder with agoraphobia and panic disorder without agoraphobia (as central). Furthermore, the "unexpected" aspect of the panic attacks now becomes an essential feature of the disorder. In addition, the manual devotes three pages to differential diagnosis. Central to the discussion are the diagnostic criteria for panic disorder with and without agoraphobia, essentially arguing for the case that all agoraphobic symptoms derive from a previous panic condition. This, in effect, rules out psychological causation.

APPRAISAL FROM A FEMINIST PERSPECTIVE

What is missing from all the previous theories and diagnostic manuals, in their various forms, is a focus on gender and its meaning. Why are women more prone to panic and agoraphobia? The biological position rests on the assumption that women have a constitutional deficit. But nowhere does this literature raise the question: What is it in woman's experiences, beyond their more (supposedly) anxiety-prone brains or nervous systems, that might affect the production of the brain chemicals that produce anxiety attacks? Instead, the literature promotes the long-standing sexist view of women as being more emotional and influenced by their hormones and having a weakened constitution that lowers their threshold for anxiety and panic. We need to ask: What are the triggers that set off the panic and avoidant behaviors in women, and why more often in women? What maintains the symptoms? What is the most effective treatment?

Feminist/Sociocultural Views

Given the long history of women not being allowed to participate in spheres outside the home and, in this time of change, the increasing numbers of women who are expected to perform in the outside world, the disorder of agoraphobia is a quintessential woman's issue. What is surprising, however, is how little attention this disorder has been given by feminist therapists. Anxiety disorders and agoraphobia have not received the attention of feminist therapists, as have, for example, posttraumatic stress disorder, child and spouse abuse, and eating disorders.

In 1974, I wrote an early feminist analysis of agoraphobia that appeared in the first edited book on therapy for women (Fodor, 1974). It was followed up with several other papers over the past decade (Fodor, 1983, 1987). While this work is quoted and referenced under sociocultural variables in some review articles and books on agoraphobia (e.g., Chambless & Goldstein, 1980a; Wolfe, 1984) it is most often ignored by others; the feminist position on agoraphobia has not been taken seriously by mainstream researchers and writers in this field.

Furthermore, agoraphobia has also been overlooked in the feminist literature. I belong to an organization of advanced feminist therapists (the Feminist Therapy Institute) that meets yearly. In a period of 10 years, I presented the only paper on agoraphobia, among the hundreds presented on feminist issues. Furthermore, *Women and Therapy*—the major journal in its field—has rarely dealt with this subject. When one examines feminist therapy and women's mental health books, it becomes clear that feminist writers are not addressing the issues of agoraphobia. However, there are chapters on agoraphobia in books on cases of women in therapy, which for the most part have been written by mainstream cognitive–behavior therapists. (Al-Issa, 1980; Padawer & Goldfried, 1984; Wolfe, 1984). There exists a small, but somewhat persistent, group of cognitive–behavior writers who have addressed women's issues in agoraphobia, but their numbers are not growing and they have not influenced the major thinking in the field (Brehony, 1983; Chambless & Mason, 1986).

Agoraphobia: A High Prevalence Disorder for Women

Etiology: Why Women?

While the symptoms of agoraphobia typically begin in young adulthood, most researchers agree that agoraphobics carry a dependent–avoidant pattern learned in childhood into adult life and that family interactions are central to encouraging and maintaining the symptoms. It is likely that agoraphobia also runs in families. Often, agoraphobics are reported to have an agoraphobic mother, and there are reports of phobias and anxiety disorders in other family members. Furthermore, such families appear to create a family milieu that promotes dependency, inhibition of desire to move too far away from the nest, and mistrust of the outside world. These families foster the development of cognitive styles that perpetuate the dependent–avoidant worldview (Barlow, 1988; Chambless & Goldstein, 1980; Fodor, 1974, 1987; Guidano & Liotti, 1983).

Childhood Antecedents

All theorists, irrespective of their school of therapy, are in agreement that some variant of separation anxiety and a familial pattern of training in avoidance are prominent features of the development of agoraphobia and panic disorders. While almost no literature exists on cultural and class differences, my clinical experiences and analysis of the literature shows that agoraphobics are likely to have families that promote traditional values, for example, they believe that women's place is in the home, or they strongly train female members to put family first. Among my clients in New York and Boston, for example, I have seen many agoraphobics coming from first-generation, working-class and middle-class Italian, Greek-American, Puerto Rican, and Jewish families.

Agoraphobia also runs in families. Agoraphobics are typically found to have mothers who are classified as agoraphobic or who have anxiety disorders. Solyom, Beck, Solyom, and Hugel (1974) reported that 34% of individuals in their sample had a phobic mother, whereas only 6% had a phobic father. Goldstein (1982) reported a number of cases with multigenerational agoraphobia in daughters, mothers, and even grandmothers. Barlow (1988) reviewed twin studies and reported a 31% concordance rate for panic disorder in monozygotic twins, in contrast to a 0% rate for dizygotic twins.

From his clinical studies of agoraphobic families, Bowlby (1973) reported that "it passes from one generation to another . . . it is vital that the neurotic difficulties of the parents of the patients should be looked at sympathetically in the context of their own experiences as children" (p. 304). From the earliest clinical cases, it would appear that mothers of agoraphobics place special demands on their children, which may reflect their own agoraphobic tendencies.

Andrews (1966) provided an extensive review of the literature on phobia, mainly child phobia and adult agoraphobia case descriptions from the psychoanalytic and behavioral literature. He presented strong evidence for phobic symptoms coexisting with personality patterns of dependency and avoidance. In childhood cases, where the parents' behavior was observed, parental overprotection was the rule. Andrews believed that phobics experience early interpersonal familial learning situations in which the avoidant–dependent pattern

is an adaptive role for the child. More recent research supports
Andrews's conclusions (Barlow, 1988). The fathers' role, in this literature, has been for the most part ignored.

School phobia, which shares many features in common with agoraphobia, could be considered a childhood version of agoraphobia
(Bowlby, 1973). Boys and girls develop school phobia with equal
frequency, yet in follow up studies, it is reported that 20% to 30% of
school phobics develop agoraphobia. Since agoraphobics are primarily female, it may be that female school phobics are at risk for developing agoraphobia, with male school phobics developing other symptoms later in life (Fodor, 1983).

Cognitive Variables

Guidano & Liotti (1983) highlight patterns of interactions characteristic of agoraphobic parent–child interactions from an Italian clinical
sample. They report that "agoraphobic patients report having experienced direct obstacles to autonomous exploration of the environment. . . . These include . . . being discouraged by the parents
(usually their mother) from leaving home alone even for a short
outing . . . being kept at home for longer periods of convalescence
than necessary after minor illnesses . . . and not being allowed to go
out and play with friends" (p. 219). They emphasize that such parents
indirectly set up "agoraphobic belief systems." "The core of the
agoraphobic cognitive organization is the tacit knowledge of an experienced limitation of their personal freedom to explore the world
added to an emotional schemata in which the self-image has a
hypothetical state of weakness" (p. 221).

Guidano and Liotti's work is consistent with the recent thinking
of the *self-in-relation* feminist theorists in this country. Chodorow
(1978) sees the growth of the self and the lessening of dependency
occurring by progressive differentiations from the mother. However,
such separation is particularly difficult for daughters and mothers,
because mothers of daughters tend not to experience these daughters
as separate from themselves. Eichenbaum and Orbach (1983) view
agoraphobia as a problem in self-definition, an attempt to disown
unacceptable feelings. Following this line of thinking, we can theorize
that agoraphobic females may be suffering from an exaggerated case
of the prototypical female separation experience. Furthermore, since
some of the mothers of agoraphobics may themselves be agoraphobics, daughters of such women may have even more difficulty separating, in that they identify with their mothers, upon whom they then

model their agoraphobic behavior patterns. Furthermore, both parents may create a climate for the inoculation and continued fostering of the agoraphobic ideology of extreme helplessness and dependency.

Moving beyond Mother-Blaming

Both psychoanalytic and cognitive–behavioral writers put much of the blame on the family, particularly the mother for passing on agoraphobic behavior. However, the syndrome must be viewed within its cultural context. One might think of agoraphobia as analogous to Chinese foot-binding. When women bound the feet of their daughters, they were carrying out cultural prescriptions that maimed as they themselves had been maimed.

In 1974, I argued that agoraphobia was associated with extreme helplessness and dependency and may reflect overtraining in stereotypic aspects of the female role in that women were trained to be fearful, avoidant and non-assertive as part of their socialization into the female role (Fodor, 1974). In this early paper, texts from the media, children's readers, and research on the differential socialization of males and females with respect to fears and mastery were presented. It was argued that agoraphobic women were overly socialized into the female role, and their helplessness, dependency, emotionality, excitability, and tendency to give up under too much stress was part of their "feminization training," that is, the stereotypic way women, at that time, were socialized. Furthermore, such feminine attributes of sex-role stereotyping as "emotionality, submissiveness, excitability, passive, house oriented, not at all adventurous and showing a strong need for security and dependency" could just as well have described agoraphobic behavior (pp. 140–141).

A similar position had been proposed by Symonds (1971), a psychoanalyst, drawing on her clinical work with agoraphobics. "Many women, and men too, equate morbid dependency and helplessness with femininity. My patients all had some confusion and uncertainty about their femininity . . . they feared the ordinary aggression and assertiveness which accompanies growth and involvement . . . such people express fears of self-realization in terms of fear that by their growth they will hurt others" (pp. 151–152).

Several cognitive–behavioral writers have adapted the same basic arguments. Essentially they argue that the sex-role training of women as helpless and dependent leads to their socialization into a prescribed role that promotes fearfulness and nondevelopment of master skills, and leads them to be more vulnerable to phobic conditions (Al-Issa, 1980; Brehoney, 1983; Wolfe, 1984).

Recent research supports these claims. Chambless (1982) in reviewing this literature, reports that when "men report being highly fearful, they are more likely to approach a feared object than women who describe themselves as equally fearful, presumably due to the incongruence of fearful behavior with the male sex-role stereotype" (pp. 3–4). She further concludes that "passively avoiding rather than conquering a feared situation may be more typical of women. Chambless and Mason (1986) conducted a study of gender-role stereotypes in agoraphobics, and found that female agoraphobics and anxiety neurotics were no more stereotypically feminine than normals, but had lower masculinity scores, that is, they were "less instrumental, active, and assertive" (p. 234). Hence, there is partial support for this differential socialization point of view.

A different, feminist perspective is offered by Seidenberg and De Crow (1983) in a book entitled *Women who Marry Houses: Panic and Protest in Agoraphobia*. They propose that the agoraphobic is a "living and acting metaphor, making a statement, registering a protest, effecting a sit-in-strike" (p. 209). They go on to argue that, for centuries, normal women accepted their status, stayed at home, or left the home as the male world allowed it. Today's agoraphobic, they suggest, is engaged in a sit-down strike, calling attention by charicature to woman's limited role. In their book, they discuss several famous recluses who may have been agoraphobic, among them Emily Dickenson, the poet, and Carolyn Wyeth, the painter.

For most of history, women were rewarded for their stereotypic behavior, although some exceptional women obtained their freedom by remaining at home and refusing to participate in a traditional world where rules were made by men. Today, however, we are confronted with a complex and often contradictory situation for women. In the late 20th century, women are still socialized, to some extent, into a role that puts family first, yet they are expected to participate more fully in the world—if only to drive to the market, pick up the kids from school, or earn extra income for the family. Yet, in the 1990s, we are still seeing agoraphobia, and many of these young women are still displaying many stereotypically feminine sex-role behaviors and/or showing signs of conflict. Now, however, such stereotypic behavior is considered somewhat dysfunctional, and even marriage is no longer considered an easy escape route from the "marketplace." Today's women are expected to function more autonomously, by society and often by their mates and significant others, too. We are seeing more single women with agoraphobic symptoms, as well.

Given the changing expectations for women, today's agoraphobics may be under even more stress, have lower self-esteem, and feel even more hopeless and helpless than before. Perhaps they may be "going on strike" against the contradictory messages they are getting, "Be feminine; put family first," as opposed to, "Go out in the world and achieve mastery." As the other chapters in this book suggest, women are still a long way from achieving full equality.

Triggers: Psychological versus Biological Etiology

We are still left with the specific psychological triggers that set off the beginning phase of anxiety and panic attacks that lead to agoraphobia. Does panic occur without warning and then lead to agoraphobic behaviors, or do panic and agoraphobic behaviors similarily originate under stress? Why are women more susceptible than men?

There is considerable agreement among the psychoanalytic, cognitive–behavioral, and biological communities for viewing stress, particularly interpersonal stress, as a trigger for the emergence of panic attacks and agoraphobic symptomology.

Liebowitz and Klein (1982) argue that people with panic disorders "have a lowered threshold to activation of this separation anxiety mechanism," and hence a greater vulnerability to episodic autonomic discharge. They also argue for an "out of the blue" onset of panic. Shear (1988), after reviewing the biological literature, disagreed. She cites a "high prevalence of stresses prior to panic onset" (p. 68). Beck (1988), Clark (1988), and others who have studied this phenomenon carefully do not find evidence to support "out of the blue" onset. Instead, they posit that panic attacks are triggered by psychosocial or physical stress.

> In all of the patients, fixation on somatic or mental experiences triggered panic attacks . . . these internal experiences were typically instigated by social situations, phobic situations . . . but sometimes occurred as the result of physiological factors such as exercise or hypoglycemia. The next step in the genesis of the panic attack was the catastrophic interpretation of the sensations. (Beck, 1988, p. 96)

In a rather comprehensive study of panickers, Beck (1988) found that "they believed that their panic attacks were brought on spontaneously . . . However, once they began to focus on the preliminary symptoms, they recognized some sensation that alarmed them just prior to panic attacks" (p. 97).

Goldstein (1982) suggests that the acute-onset phase of a panic attack is similar to a state of agitated depression: "While there may be a genetic predisposition, it may be that females and males respond differently to these physical signs of stress according to sex-role stereotyping, with women developing avoidance behavior and men 'acting out' behavior, for example alcoholism."

From the earliest case reports on, psychoanalysts described the stress of interpersonal "trappedness" as a factor in the development of agoraphobic symptoms (Deutch, 1929; Terhune, 1949; Wolpe, 1958). Lerner (1984) provides a contemporary update of this position. She sees agoraphobic daughters as "learning to cling to passive-dependent behavior as an 'unconscious oath of fidelity' to remain mother's child, as if the daughter's own moves toward separateness and autonomy constitute disloyalty and betrayal."

On the cognitive–behavioral side, a similar interpersonal trigger is proposed. For example, Chambless and Goldstein (1980b) claim that phobic symptoms are the result of psychological avoidance behavior in conflict situations. "Usually because of his/her unassertiveness the agoraphobic has found him/herself in an unhappy, seemingly irresolvable relationship under the domination of a spouse or parent. The urge to leave and the fears of being on his/her own balance out and the agoraphobic trapped in the conflict is unable to move and lacks the skills to change the situation" (p. 324).

Most writers additionally point to stress in the marital or couple relationship as a prime trigger. Reports from clinical studies suggest that the majority of agoraphobics in treatment report marital difficulties. Padawer and Goldfried (1984), Hafner (1982), and Chambless and Goldstein (1980b) suggest that the conflict centers on unhappiness with marriage and resentment of the spouse's domination. Heterosexual relationships are not the sole source of stress. In my clinical work I have seen a similar pattern in lesbian couples, where one partner assumes the more stereotypic feminine role and becomes helpless, resents her dependency—which is reinforced by the other partner—and feels trapped. It seems reasonable to assume that agoraphobics are not prepared to deal with the realistic stress of adult relationships, and often seek out dominating partners whom they resent. Since they are not good social-problem solvers, the phobias provide another solution to their conflicts.

Recent research by Barlow, O'Brien, and Last (1986) and Hafner (1982), among others, that included spouses in treatment, points to an alleviation of agoraphobic symptoms in such joint therapy.

While the stressor most mentioned in the literature on agoraphobia is interpersonal stress, more recent work has suggested other triggers. Panic disorder and an increase in anxiety and fearfulness have been reported in women following rape. Furthermore, the development of panic symptoms is also a feature of posttraumatic stress disorder (Steketee & Foa, 1987). What is clear is that stress plays a major role in creating a climate that triggers anxiety and panic attacks, and real-life experiences of trauma may contribute to the development of agoraphobia. However, most agoraphobics do not have a history of trauma; for the majority, the major stressor lies in the dynamics of their current relationships.

Maintenance of Symptoms

Maintenance of agoraphobic symptoms seems related to personality and cognitive variables, as well as familial reinforcement. There are suggestions that agoraphobics meet the DSM-III criteria for dependent, avoidant, and histrionic personality disorders. In a recent study, however, only 27% of agoraphobics met these criteria (Mavis-sakalian & Hamann, 1986). If one looks more closely at what constitutes these personality disorders, we do see a distinctive cognitive style common to most agoraphobics that serves to maintain the system. Chambless and Goldstein (1980b) have provided the most elaborate description of this cognitive style and its correspondence to the stereotypically feminine woman. They stress fear of fear, avoidance behavior, lack of self-sufficiency, and a "hysterical cognitive style."

Familial Reinforcement

Many familial childhood patterns are still present in the agoraphobic's ongoing family life. Parents, particularly mothers who are also agoraphobic, may be continuing to support the avoidance behaviors. Goldstein (1982) reports on a number of adult agoraphobic cases with a symbiotic mother–daughter relationship in his clinic sample:

> by far the most consistently difficult cases encountered are those in which the daughter, who is still living with the mother is the identified client. Repeatedly we have seen the mother, who is usually also agoraphobic deteriorate as the daughter improves. The daughter, being overwhelmed with guilt, relapses, and then the mother improves." (p. 200)

Furthermore, spouses often became additionally involved in keeping the agoraphobic at home. Hafner (1982) talks about jealous husbands who become symptomatic themselves as their spouse's phobias improve. In my clinical work, I have often had to deal with anxious mates, who worried about their formerly housebound significant other going into the city and being out in the world.

CONCLUSION

Jack Maser, of the NIMH, asserted in a recent interview that anxiety disorders are the most prevalent of all psychological disorders, affecting as many as 24 million Americans (Launders, 1990). Given the high anxiety-disorder prevalence rate for women, and the fact that only about one quarter of all phobics seek treatment, there are large numbers of unidentified and untreated women in the community.

Given the potentially large number of women who may be affected by agoraphobia or panic disorder, one of the basic issues to be addressed is whether agoraphobia actually exists as a separate disorder or way of being. Does agoraphobic-like behavior exist on a continuum, sharing features common to most women? If we accept the biological model, we tend to think of a disorder—with defective genes or constitutional predisposition to separation anxiety and panic attacks—as passed down in some families. Hence, a large percentage of the female population is seen to be defective and potentially dysfunctional. However, another view holds that anxiety proneness and avoidant behaviors are common for most women. In this view, agoraphobic-like behaviors exist on a continuum, with panic disorder and extreme agoraphobia as the most extreme variants. There is some evidence to support this perspective. Meyer looked at agoraphobics who "gave in" to their anxiety and panic and avoided facing feared situations and those who did not. She discovered a group in the community who met the criteria for agoraphobia, but who pushed themselves to function when anxious. Their expectations and self-efficacy propelled them to override their anxiety. They were less phobic and had fewer panic attacks than the matched agoraphobic controls (Meyer, 1987). In another study, the authors studied avoidance behaviors in a normal population and discovered that they are common in many women, particularly in regard to traveling alone. Brown and Cash (1990) studied panic behavior among a group of normal college students and found that 26% had a past history of panic and 13% had panicked in the previous month. Substantial similar clinical aspects of panic in this nonclinical sample were present, leading the authors to conclude that the parameter of panic might also operate on a continuum.

Thus, the disordered people we have been seeing clinically, who have been the focus of so much research and theorizing, may represent an extreme end of a continuum and share features with much of the female population. From the growing evidence for a physiological basis for panic, it may be that some women may be "wired up" to be more emotional and susceptible to panic attacks and more prone to have attachment problems. However, there is also a long line of other evidence pointing to familial and environment factors interacting with this presumed susceptibility. Many normal women show similar avoidance patterns. If a woman who is at high risk for the development of panic and separation anxiety is raised in an environment that facilitates healthy attachments, provides positive emotional support for independence and mastery, and fosters coping and self-enhancing cognitive styles, then we are less likely to see the development of agoraphobic symptoms, even if there are constitutional tendencies to panic. However, what we are more likely to see in the clinical population are women whose socialization has facilitated dependency. They have lacked training and fostering of positive coping and self-efficacy cognitions. Furthermore, neither their families nor society has provided positive role models. The families may have adopted a narrow, stereotypic role for their daughter or may have required that the daughter or wife stay home to meet other family members' needs. These types of families would also appear to promote agoraphobia in males, who are assumed not to have the same genetic predisposition to anxiety and panic, but who, when reared in these types of families, develop similar symptomology. Furthermore, many of the women we see may also be suffering from posttraumatic stress responses, following rape or other trauma. It sometimes *is* dangerous for women to be out alone on the streets; some fearfulness and avoidance behavior may be appropriate in context.

The "bad news" is that some biological predisposition to agoraphobia and panic may exist, with the family and society reinforcing the avoidant behavior by promoting a traditional female role. It may be easier for a woman in this kind of situation to stay home rather than try to become independent. The "good news" is that this avoidant way of behaving is becoming more and more unacceptable for a modern woman's role. Furthermore, avoidant symptoms appear to be maintained by the client's own cognitions, which are adapted from the culture. We now know better how to change these negative cognitions and to teach positive coping skills to override anxiety and dependent patterning.

More mainstream feminists need to take up the cause of this large number of anxious, helpless, mainly heterosexual, married women, for there is a high risk of passing this syndrome on to the next generation of women. We need to ask why feminists have not been active advocates for these phobics, who have no overt history of trauma or stress. Unlike those women who panic or are anxious following posttraumatic stress incidents, there is usually no outside perpetuator to blame. Another aspect of the problem is that, when one looks closely at the dynamics, one comes into contact with mother-blaming or stereotypic behaviors that we, as feminists, have tried to move away from. Also, agoraphobic women are often hidden in the home as wives and mothers who may not seek help unless their anxiety becomes overwhelming or they become too dysfunctional even within their traditional roles. Feminists need to be more "proactive" in influencing the powerful research establishment to consider sociocultural variables as primary and to counter recent biological claims. This is one of the cases where drugs—which do not alleviate the avoidance behaviors—may be overprescribed.

Sociocultural Variables and the Role of Individual Therapy

In earlier centuries, one did not worry about agoraphobics. When women's prescribed role was to stay at home and not go out in the world alone, agoraphobia was not defined as a problem. In fact, it has been suggested by Seidenberg and De Crow (1983) that agoraphobic behavior, in fact, may have been a healthy form of protest against women's limited lot in life. Certainly, some creative, wealthy women, who had fathers to support and encourage their creativity, chose to live solely within the confines of home. Even Queen Victoria was able to rule an empire while remaining within the confines of her home, seeming to suffer from agoraphobic-like symptoms after her husband's death. Certainly in other countries today, where women's activities outside the home may be unduly restricted, agoraphobia may not be considered a serious problem. A few years ago, I was on a panel at an international conference with a psychiatrist from Saudi Arabia. He was fascinated with my description of agoraphobic women. He said that he had not seen such cases in his country, where women are discouraged from being out of the house alone and are prohibited from engaging in independent activities such as driving. He said that he was more often dealing with depression and suicide.

Today, however, there is a clear message from the mental health establishments in North America and Europe that being in the stereotypic feminine role—staying at home, being anxious and non-functional, depending on a significant other—is becoming more and more an unacceptable and undesirable way of being for the modern woman. However, women are also being told that family comes first. Our society still puts up many barriers to women's achievement of full autonomy over their lives. Women are expected to be "out there" in the world and still put their families first. While the psychiatric establishment posits biological explanations for agoraphobia and panic, we need to consider the stress of a modern woman's life as a possible trigger for panic. "Put family first; be out in the world," is the message, while family and culture have not prepared women or provided support for these multiple roles. Under pressure, experiencing too much conflict or trauma out in the world, it may be easier to retreat to the home. After all, it is in the home that many women can still feel in control and retain a sense of power.

In working with agoraphobics, it is important for the therapist to take into account the many stressors in a modern woman's life and to recognize that succumbing to anxiety and retreating to the home, for a while, is often the agoraphobic's best way of coping with a still very mixed set of expectations and cultural supports. The ultimate goal of such therapy is to foster coping skills and encourage cognitions that counter feelings of helplessness, dependency, and lack of control over one's life. Furthermore, the therapist should strive to support the client's development of self and self-derived goals—aims that are consonant with good feminist therapy.

REFERENCES

Al-lssa, I. (1980). *The psychopathology of women.* Englewood Cliffs, NJ: Prentice Hall.

American Psychiatric Association. (1980). *Diagnostic and statistical manual of mental disorders.* (3rd ed.). Washington, DC: Author.

American Psychiatric Association. (1987). *Diagnostic and statistical manual of mental disorders* (3rd ed., rev.). Washington, DC: Author.

American Psychiatric Association, Committee on Nonenclature and Statistics (1968). *Diagnostic and statistical manual: Mental disorders.* Washington, DC: American Psychiatric Association.

Andrews, J. D. (1966). Psychotherapy of phobias. *Psychological Bulletin, 66,* 455–480.

Barlow, D. H. (1988). *Anxiety and its disorders: The nature and treatment of anxiety and panic.* New York: Guilford.

Barlow, D. H., O'Brien, G. T., Last, C. G. (1986). Couples treatment of agoraphobia. *Behavior Therapy, 15,* 41–58.

Barlow, D. H., & Wolfe, B. E. (1981). Behavioral approaches to anxiety disorders: A report on the NIMH-SUNY, Albany, Research Conference. *Journal of Consulting and Clinical Psychology, 49,* 448–454.

Beck, A. T. (1988). Cognitive approaches to panic disorder: Theory and therapy. In S. Rachman & J. D. Maser (Eds.), *Panic: Psychological perspectives.* Hillsdale, NJ: Erlbaum.

Beck, A. T., & Emery, G. (1985). *Anxiety disorders and phobias: A cognitive perspective.* New York: Basic.

Bowlby, J. (1973). *Separation anxiety and anger.* New York: Basic Books.

Brehony, K. A. (1983). Women and agoraphobia: A case for the etiological significance of the feminine sex role stereotype. In V. Franks & E. Rothblum (Eds.), *The stereotyping of women: It's effects on mental health.* New York: Springer.

Brown, T. A., & Cash, T. F. (1990). The phenomenon of nonclinical panic: Parameters of panic, fear, and avoidance. *Journal of Anxiety Disorders,* 4(1), 15–29.

Chambless, D. (1982). Characteristics of agoraphobics. In D. L. Chambless & A. J. Goldstein (Eds.), *Agoraphobia: Multiple perspectives on theory and treatment.* New York: Wiley.

Chambless, D. L., & Goldstein, A. J. (1980a). Anxieties: Agoraphobia and hysteria. In A. M. Brodsky & R. Hare-Mustin (Eds.), *Women and psychotherapy: An assessment of research and practice* (pp. 113–134). New York: Guilford.

Chambless, D., & Goldstein, A. (1980b). The treatment of agoraphobia. In A. Goldstein & E. Foa (Eds.), *Handbook of behavioral interventions.* New York: Wiley.

Chambless, D. L., & Mason, J. (1986). Sex, sex role stereotyping, and agoraphobia. *Behavior Research and Therapy, 24,* 231–235.

Chodorow, N. (1978). *The reproduction of mothering.* Berkeley, CA: University of California Press.

Clark, D. M. (1988). A cognitive model of panic attacks. In S. Rachman & J. D. Maser (Eds.), *Panic: Psychological perspectives.* Hillsdale, NJ: Erlbaum.

Deutsch, H. (1929). The genesis of agoraphobia. *International Journal of Psychoanalysis,* 51–59.

Ehlers, A., Margraf, J., & Roth, W. T. (1986). Lacate infusions and panics in patients and controls. *Psychiatric Research, 17,* 295–308.

Eichenbaum, L., & Orbach, S. (1983). *Understanding women: A feminist psychoanalytic approach.* New York: Basic Books.

Eidelberg, L. (1968). *Encyclopedia of psychoanalysis. 10,* New York: Free Press.

Ellis, A., & Harper, R. A. (1975). *A new guide to rational living.* Englewood Cliffs, NJ: Prentice Hall.

Emmelkamp, P. M. G. (1982). In vivo treatment of agoraphobia. In D. L. Chambless & A. J. Goldstein (Eds.), *Agoraphobia: Multiples perspectives on theory and treatment.* New York: Wiley.

Emmelkamp, P. M. G., & van der Hout, A. (1983). Failure in treating agoraphobia. In E. B. Foa & Paul M. G. Emmelkamp (Eds.), *Failures in behavior therapy*. New York: Wiley.

Errera, P. (1962). Some historical aspects of the concept of phobia. *The Psychiatric Quarterly*, 36, 325–333.

Fenichel, O. (1945). *The psychoanalytic theory of neurosis*. New York: Norton.

Fleming, B., & Faulk, A. (1989). Discriminating factors in panic disorder with and without agoraphobia. *Journal of Anxiety Disorders*, 3(4), 209–219.

Foa, E. B., & Kozak, M. J. (1986). Emotional processing of fear: Exposure to corrective information. *Psychology Bulletin*, 99,(1).

Fodor, I. G. (1974). The phobic syndrome in women. In V. Franks & V. Burtle (Eds.), *Women in therapy*. New York: Brunner/Mazel.

Fodor, I. G. (1983). Sex differences in phobic anxiety disorders. In I. Al-Issa (Ed.), *Gender and psychopathology*. New York: Academic Press.

Fodor, I. G. (1987). Cognitive behavior therapy for agoraphobic women: Toward utilizing psychodynamic understanding to address family belief systems and enhance behavior change. In M. Braude, (Eds.), *Women, power and therapy:* Issues for women (pp. 103–123). Glencoe, IL: Haworth Press.

Fodor, I. G. (1989). Agoraphobia. In H. Tierney (Ed.). *Women's studies encyclopedia*. Westport, CT: Greenwood Press.

Freud, S. (1909). A phobia in a 5-year old boy. In *Collected works. (vol. 3*, pp. 149–289). London: Hogarth Press.

Goldstein, A. J. (1982). Agoraphobia: Treatment successes, treatment failures, and theoretical implications. In D. L. Chambless & A. J. Goldstein (Eds.), *Agoraphobia: Multiples perspectives on theory and treatment*. New York: Wiley.

Goldstein, A. J., & Chambless, D. L. (1978). A reanalysis of agoraphobia. *Behavior Therapy*, 9, 47–59.

Guidano, V. F., & Liotti, G. (1983). *Cognitive processes and emotional disorders*. New York: Guilford.

Hafner, R. J. (1982). The marital context of the agoraphobic syndrome. In D. L. Chambless & A. J. Goldstein (Eds.), *Agoraphobia: Multiples perspectives on theory and treatment*. New York: Wiley.

Hallam, R. S. (1985). *Anxiety: Psychological perspectives on panic and agoraphobia*. London: Academic Press.

Klein, D. F. (1964). Delineation of two drug-responsive anxiety syndromes. *Psychopharmacologia*, 5, 397–408.

Launders, S. (1990, March 3). Phobias: A stepchild garners new respect. *The APA Monitor*, 21, 18.

Lang, P. J. (1988). Fear, anxiety, and panic: Context, cognition, and visceral arousal. In S. Rachman & J. D. Maser (Eds.), *Panic: Psychological perspectives*. Hillsdale, NJ: Erlbaum.

Lazarus, A. (1966). Broad-spectrum behavior therapy and the treatment of agoraphobia. *Behavior Research Therapy*, 4, 95–97.

Lerner, H. (1984). Female dependency in context: Some theoretical and technical considerations. In P. P. Rierker & E. H. Carmen (Eds.). *The Gender gap in psychotherapy: Social realities and psychological processes.* New York: Plenum.

Liebowitz, M. R., & Klein, D. F. (1982). Agoraphobia: Clinical features, pathophysiology and treatment. In D. L. Chambless & A. J. Goldstein (Eds.), *Agoraphobia: Multiples perspectives on theory and treatment.* New York: Wiley.

Margraf, J., Ehlers, A., & Roth, W. (1986). Biological models of panic disorder and agoraphobia—A review. *Behavioral Research Therapy* 24(5), 553–567.

Marks, I. (1978). Exposure treatments: Clinical studies in phobic, obsessive compulsive and allied disorders. In W. S. Agras (Ed.), *Behavior therapy in clinical psychiatry,* (2nd ed.). Boston: Little Brown.

Marks, I. M. (1987). *Fears, Phobias and rituals: Panic, anxiety and their disorders.* Oxford, England: Oxford University Press.

Mathews, A. N., Gelder, M. G., & Johnson, D. W. (1986). *Agoraphobia: Nature and treatment.* New York: New York University Press.

Mavissakalian, M., & Hamanm, M. S. (1986). DSM-III personality disorders in agoraphobia. *Comprehensive Psychiatry, 27,* 5, 471–447.

Meyer, R. (1987). *The relation of cognition and affect in agoraphobics with differing avoidance patterns.* Unpublished doctoral dissertation, New York University, NY.

Padawer, W. J., Goldfried, M. R. (1984). Anxiety-related disorders, fears and phobias. In E. A. Blechman (Ed.), *Behavior modification with women* (pp. 341–372). New York: Guilford.

Rachman, S., & Maser, J. D. (1988). *Panic: Physiological perspectives.* Hillsdale, NJ: Erlbaum.

Seidenberg, R., & De Crow, K. (1983). *Women who marry houses: Panic and protest in agoraphobia.* New York: McGraw-Hill.

Shear, M. K. (1988). Cognitive and biological models of panic: Toward an integration. In S. Rachman & J. D. Maser (Eds.), *Panic: Physiological perspectives.* Hillsdale, NJ: Erlbaum.

Solyom, L., Beck, P., Solyom, C., & Hugel, R. (1974). Some etiological factors in public neurosis. *Canadian Psychiatric Association Journal, 19*(1), 69–79.

Sperling, M. (1974). Somatic symptomology in phobia: Clinical and theoretical aspects. *Psychoanalytic Forum.*

Steketee, G., & Foa, E. B. (1987). Rape victims: Post-traumatic stress responses and their treatment. *Journal of Anxiety Disorders, 1,* 69–86.

Symonds, A. (1971). Phobias after marriage: Women's declaration of dependence. *The American Journal of Psychoanalysis, 31,* 144–152. Reprinted in E. Howell & M. Bayes (Eds.). (1981), *Women and mental health.* New York: Basic Books.

Terhune, W. (1949). The phobic syndrome: A study of 86 patients with phobic reactions. *Archives Neurological Psychiatry, 62,* 162–172.

Thorpe, G., & Burns, L. (1983). *The agoraphobic syndrome.* New York: Wiley.

Weiss, E. (1958). Psychodynamic formulation of agoraphobia. *The Psychoanalytic Forum, 1*(4), 378–386.

Wolfe, B. E. (1984). Gender ideology and phobias in women. In C. S. Wisdom (Ed.), *Sex roles and psychopathology.* New York: Plenum.

Wolpe, J. (1958). *Psychotherapy by reciprocal inhibition.* Stanford, CA: Stanford University Press.

Wolpe, J. (1970). Identifying the antecents of an agoraphobic reaction: A transcript. *Journal of Behavior Therapy and Experiental Psychiatry, 1,* 299–304.

CHAPTER NINE

A Feminist Critique of the Personality Disorders

LAURA S. BROWN

Since the publication of the third edition of the *Diagnostic and Statistical Manual of Mental Disorders* (DSM-III) by the American Psychiatric Association (APA) in 1980, a new conceptual framework for describing and diagnosing psychopathology has been available to mental health professionals. This new "multiaxial" construction of psychopathology has given a special place in the diagnostic scheme to the diagnostic entities called *personality disorders*. While characterological forms of psychopathology have been described and diagnosed since prior to the inception of the diagnostic manual system, it was only with the DSM-III that such diagnostic entities were considered sufficiently unique and different from other forms of psychopathology as to rate their own category or axis within the DSM-III conceptual framework.

The *Axis II* diagnoses, which are entirely composed of personality disorders, appear to offer great utility to practicing clinicians, and a large body of clinical literature and psychological assessment techniques has sprung up in the intervening 11 years that purports to aid in their diagnosis and treatment. The concept of a disordered personality underlying and influencing other forms of psychopathology appeared, to many mental health professionals, to offer a more potent explanation for many of the clinical syndromes being encountered by practicing psychotherapists than had prior systems of diagnostic thinking. In addition, the implied severity of such a diagnosis presented a rationale for the long periods of treatment many such individuals seemed to require to manifest any changes in functioning, while simultaneously making sense of the fact that many such severely disturbed people functioned adequately, if not well, in certain spheres of their lives. The authors of the DSM-III categories emphasized the empirical research basis for their formulation, as well as the applicability of these diagnoses in a wide variety of other conceptual frameworks regarding psychopathology (Millon, 1981).

The multiaxial system, with its emphasis on characterological pathology, has not been without its critics (despite its popularity). One very common theme of these critiques in the behavioral sciences has consisted of attention to problems in the methodologies by which the categories were constructed, and of their consequent low statistical reliability or validity. Frances and Widiger (1986) point out that "there is in fact very little available data to support the validity of most of the Axis II diagnoses, and virtually no data to support the theoretical speculations regarding specific etiology and treatment" (p. 382). Kutchins and Kirk (1986) note that the reliability studies cited by the authors of the DSM-III contain extremely sloppy research techniques and include misleading interpretations of the data, which imply greater reliability and validity of the Axis II diagnoses than actually exist. Furthermore, the statistics relied upon to demonstrate reliability are suspect, since they were invented specifically for use in evaluating the DSM-III categories, and therefore cannot be meaningfully compared to other, more standard statistical techniques.

Other threats to methodological soundness in studies of reliability in diagnosis include problems with contamination of diagnostic data between clinicians who were being judged on interrater reliability. Often, the diagnostic criteria being evaluated for their reliability had been arrived at in a collaborative rather than autonomous manner; on other occasions, no effort was made to compare reliability of diagnoses between clinicians who were differently trained or worked in different facilities (Kutchins & Kirk, 1986). Since the presumed scientific basis of the Axis II (and other) diagnoses, as formulated in the DSM-III, has been one of the major selling points of its authors, these criticisms of methodology raise serious questions about the usefulness of the concept of personality disorders.

The validity of these diagnoses has also come into question. Blashfield and Breen (1989) found that the 13 personality disorder categories listed in the revised edition of the diagnostic manual (DSM-III-R; APA, 1987) had poor face validity, with high levels of overlap among the criteria for several purportedly distinct disorders. A study by Spitzer, Williams, Kass, and Davies (1989) also found poor validity and inability to make meaningful distinctions between several personality disorder diagnoses in a national field trial. These findings render suspect the notion that the Axis II diagnoses do in fact represent independent entities that can be diagnosed in a predictable manner.

Another major direction in criticism of the Axis II diagnoses has been of their sociopolitical implications. A major strain of this line of thought has come from feminist psychologists and psychotherapists. Kaplan (1983) advanced the first published feminist critique of the categories, suggesting that they were too badly contaminated by sexist concepts and values to be of use for either research or practice. Her central thesis was that Axis II was particularly representative of the androcentric bias regarding mental health that had first been reported by Broverman, Broverman, Clarkson, Rosencrantz, and Vogel (1970), and that the DSM-III tended to label stereotypically feminine behaviors as pathology significantly more frequently than was the case with stereotypically masculine behaviors. More recently, as attempts were being made in the process of revising DSM-III to enlarge Axis II to include diagnoses like self-defeating personality disorder (also known as masochistic personality disorder) and sadistic personality disorder, further criticisms were raised (Brown, 1986; Walker, 1985, 1986; Rosewater, 1986, 1987; Committee on Women in Psychology, 1985). Although these more recent critiques were directed specifically toward the proposed new diagnoses (published in a special appendix to DSM-III-R), they also called the usefulness of the entire personality disorder concept into question. These criticisms also centered on concerns regarding sexism in the diagnostic formulations; additionally, they pointed to evidence of inattention to the impact of certain traumatic life events—that approach normative status in their frequency in the lives of one gender or the other—as factors in the type and intensity of dysfunctional behaviors manifested by an individual.

This chapter will offer a critical review of the conceptualization of personality disorders as a diagnostic entity and will review and expand upon extant feminist critiques of the Axis II diagnoses. Since there are many traditional perspectives on characterological pathology, I will focus upon the models proposed by those authors whose work is most directly reflected in the DSM-III itself, rather than on perspectives on psychopathology and nosology that are less precisely congruent with the DSM-III and the DSM-III-R. For instance, while both Otto Kernberg and James Masterson are considered major contributors to the literature on the treatment of what they each call "borderline" or "narcissistic" disorders of personality, each tends to use these terms more broadly than do writers such as Theodore Millon or Robert Spitzer, both of whom were involved in the actual formulation of the diagnostic manual's personality disorder categories. However, many of the concerns raised regarding the work of the DSM-III nosologists can be found to apply to the concepts put forward by other mainstream writers on the personality disorders. Finally, an attempt will be made to suggest an alternative framework for diagnostic thinking regarding severe or long-term nonpsychotic distress that would have, at its core, a feminist perspective and analysis.

It is my contention that accurate diagnostic thinking is essential to the ethical practice of psychotherapy and research, and that systems for communicating such diagnostic schemata are necessary for the advancement of knowledge and communication between professionals. However, it is also my belief that such diagnostic formulation need not be of a sort that reifies normative aspects of gender, race, or class membership as forms of psychopathology. While the writers of the DSM-III claim that they do not wish to pathologize behaviors that are primarily evidence of conflicts between individuals and society, their analysis lacks—in this writer's opinion—sufficient attention to the very wide and diverse range of conflicts that can result from being powerless, oppressed, and discriminated against in a repetitive and ongoing manner. Additionally, traditional models for understanding characterological pathologies rarely identify as problematic those behaviors of the dominant group that are troubling or even dangerous to nondominant-group persons (Brown, 1991; Caplan, 1991). A feminist analysis does make such observations. This proposed feminist therapy framework will build upon some tentative formulations regarding the presence of a separate diagnostic entity called "abuse disorders," proposed by Lenore Walker and this author in our critiques of the masochistic and sadistic personality disorder diagnoses (Brown, 1988; Walker, 1986). Parallels will be drawn between these formulations and the proposed "disorder of extreme stress not otherwise specified" currently being examined for inclusion in the upcoming fourth edition of the diagnostic manual (DSM-IV). This analysis will also draw upon Hannah Lerman's proposed criteria for a feminist therapy theory of personality (Lerman, 1986), inasmuch as a concept of normative personality is essential to the development of concepts of psychopathology.

TRADITIONAL PERSPECTIVES ON SEVERE DISTRESS

While folk wisdom has long identified people's problems as outcomes of their "personalities" (e.g., "she has a sour disposition" or "he has a sunny personality"), the concept of a disordered personality as a diagnostic entity existing concurrently with other forms of psychopathology is a fairly new one in American psychopathology and nosological systems. Millon (1981) states, "Until recently they (personality disorders) have been categorized in the official nomenclature with a melange of other miscellaneous and essentially secondary syndromes" (p. 3). Indeed, classical approaches to psychopathology have focused on formally naming and describing two classes of disorders, neuroses and psychoses. These classical approaches represent a disease model of psychopathology that perceives emotional distress to be evidence of an illness, an entity alien to the individual. Characterological problems, while acknowledged and treated, are less precisely described in the formal nomenclature.

The concept of a personality disorder, in contrast, assumes that there exists a characteristic and pathological personality substrate that will shape the form and content of the psychopathology manifested, and will serve as a source of psychological dysfunction even in the absence of external stressors. Such a personality disorder can exist concurrently with or separate from the presence of the clinical syndromes of Axis I. DSM-III and DSM-III-R differentiate between personality traits and personality disorders by stating that the former are "enduring patterns of perceiving, relating to, and thinking about the environment and oneself, and are exhibited in a wide range of important social and personal contexts," while personality disorders are traits that are inflexible, maladaptive, and a source of impairment and distress interpersonally or occupationally (p. 305).

The vagueness of this distinction has left more than ample room for the individual clinician with his or her preexisting biases to interpret certain personality traits as disordered, however, while exempting other traits, perhaps equally as dysfunctional, from being described as a form of psychopathology. Additionally, the DSM-III and DSM-III-R encourage diagnosticians to list personality traits on Axis II even if they do not clearly approach the level of psychopathology; this increases the likelihood that bias in clinical judgment may lead to inappropriate stigmatization of certain types of behaviors.

Millon (1969, 1981) has posited a model of psychopathology, heavily reflected in the DSM-III and DSM-III-R Axis II diagnoses, that examines the degree to which an individual manifests adaptive inflexibility, tendencies to foster vicious circles or self-defeating behavior, and tenuous emotional stability under conditions of stress. This model assumes that each of these is a continuous variable, with greater pathology being manifested as an individual behaves in ways that place her or him further along the continuum. Although it is not clearly stated, it appears that Millon assumes some covariance of these factors. Also unstated, but implied, is the presence of an objective measure of these dimensions, with their expressions holding across such variables as gender, race, class, and experiences of abuse or victimization. Good functioning is good functioning, irregardless of the context in which the behavior is formed or expressed. The questions, "Inflexible compared to what? Tenuously stable in relationship to what measure of consistency? Self-defeating by whose terms?" are not raised, thus ignoring the possibility that such descriptors radically change their meaning depending upon context. Technically, this model is meant to be atheoretical and of use to the clinician and diagnostician of any theoretical perspective. However, as a conceptual model, it owes much to certain theoretical perspectives on personality and psychopathology that predate the DSM-III.

Classical theorists of personality development have looked to a variety of sources as possible etiologies of personality growth and development. Most models look, with varying emphasis, at biological or constitutional factors, actual and/or symbolic learning experiences, and the social context in which the person develops. To the degree that any one of these elements is perceived as central, and others as tangential, the meaningfulness of deficits in that area will be emphasized in that particular personality theory's conceptualization of psychopathology. The perceived centrality of a factor will also be reflected in the degree to which its moderating influence will be taken into account in assessing the degree and quality of psychopathology manifested. Thus, for instance, a theorist who relies heavily on the meaning of early childhood experiences may downplay the impact of the social and interpersonal context of adult life on the distress being manifested, while a cognitive–behavioral theorist might attend more closely to those current reinforcement contingencies as they interact with prior learning. A feminist theorist would attend very strongly to the meaning and expression of gender roles at all life stages, while a biological theorist would be interested in gender primarily as the source of physiological and hormonal differences in brain development.

Traditional approaches to personality development and psychopathology have tended to place emphasis on early experience, perhaps in synergy with biologically determined temperament, as the primary factor in the development of personality and psychopathology. While it is possible to find some variability along the dimension of which periods of early life and what kinds of external learning events are the most salient (e.g., object relations theories will pay closest attention to the first few years of life, classical psychoanalytic theory focuses on the Oepidal struggle, an Eriksonian will observe how particular developmental tasks are accomplished at different age-based stages, and so on), it is unusual for a theory of personality to ask direct and critical questions about the meaning of gender roles and gender-role socialization as expressed in a variety of social and interpersonal contexts. This is not to say that traditional theories do not comment on the development of gender identity or gender role. Rather, this commentary is conducted with a complete acceptance of the status quo, and a lack of curiosity about the effect of gender-role socialization upon later manifestations of psychopathology. Gender membership is, however, often seen as a source of psychopathology (via the classical psychoanalytic perspective on female psychology by which women qua women are perceived as passive, masochistic, and castrated).

Additionally, traditional theories of personality and psychopathology often join with the culture at large in their devaluation of certain characteristics of normative female gender-role socialization. Both early research by Broverman and her colleagues (1970) and a more recent attempt to replicate that study by Rosencrantz, Delorey, and Broverman (1985) indicate that judgments of psychopathology are greatly influenced by gender-role norms and stereotypes. While male gender-role normative behavior continues to be perceived as the human criterion for healthy psychological functioning, much of the female gender role continues to be perceived as pathological or potentially pathological in some way.

This sexism in the assessment of psychopathology can have particularly powerful impact when viewed in the light of the personality disorders concept. Since gender role does constitute a series of core and enduring personality traits that are expressed transituationally over the life span, gender-role characteristics that, while normative, are stigmatized by mental health professionals may lead the clinician to diagnose personality disorders of certain types at much greater frequency in women than in men. Landrine (1989) has found that nonclinician subjects are indeed more likely to ascribe pathology to Axis II diagnoses that resemble female-gendered behaviors (borderline, histrionic, or dependent personality disorders) than to those that described male-gendered behaviors (obsessive-compulsive and narcissistic personality disorders).

Finally, research in the area of personality and psychopathology has been historically tied to the theoretical perspectives of the various personality theorists. In more recent years, research in the United

States has been conducted in the context of funding agencies such as the National Institute of Mental Health; research that reflects a bias common to that of grant reviewers is more likely to be funded, and thus carried out, than research that posits hypotheses that run counter to current biases. Thus, as Rothblum, Solomon, and Albee (1986) point out, the assumption of a biological basis for schizophrenia and the affective disorders has led to funding for research that assumes that hypothesis as given, and data appears to support it. However, the tendency for research that eschews a biological model to not receive funding means that there is less such research, and less data with which to critique the biological model.

Even more basic questions, such as that of whether what we call "psychopathology" or "mental illness" is in fact that, or some other phenomenon, for example, manifestations of cultural inequities or social injustice, are barely addressed or actively ignored by the mainstream of thinking regarding psychopathology. Sickness or dysfunction are assumed to be within the person; the health of the social norms, as Rothblum, Solomon and Albee (1986) point out, is rarely questioned. Syndromes that might constitute a normative, if not frankly normal response to abnormal events in the social and interpersonal environment, continue to be construed as forms of psychopathology if their manifestations bring a person into psychotherapy (Robert Spitzer, personal communication, 1988).

Research on the personality disorders has been conducted within a similar set of constraints and contaminated by similar biases. For instance, when a field trial was conducted by the American Psychiatric Association to attempt to develop criteria for the proposed new diagnostic category first called "masochistic personality disorder" (now self-defeating personality disorder), the taken-for-granted notions about the development of psychopathology held by the researchers in this case had profound impact on the research process. Although many of the diagnostic criteria for this proposed new diagnostic entity greatly resembled the symptoms of battered women's syndrome (Walker, 1984), the researchers did not collect any information on the abuse histories of the patients in their field trials. The assumptions regarding etiology that guided this study, for example, that behaviors that are sources of intense distress must be the result of an underlying personality disorder, were so strong as to make the issue of abuse literally invisible to this group of researchers.

Additional attempts by Robert Spitzer, the primary author, and his colleagues to validate masochistic personality disorder as a diagnostic entity demonstrated similarly the failure to attend to appropriate methodology that had been criticized by Kutchins and Kirk

(1986) in regard to already available Axis II diagnoses. In the validation study, a questionnaire was sent to psychiatrists who indicated an interest in personality disorders, asking if they believed that an entity called "masochistic personality disorder" did exist. If not, they were directed to not respond further. If such a belief did exist for the respondent, he or she was directed to indicate whether the diagnostic criteria listed made sense. This study and its results were presented as "empirical validation" of the existence of masochistic personality disorder (Kass, MacKinnon, & Spitzer, 1986). Caplan (1986) published a critique of this "empirical study" that demonstrated the persistent failure of scientific research methodology contained in this so-called empirical validation; the implication is that other Axis II diagnoses may be supported by equally spurious research efforts. The very public nature of the debate over this particular diagnostic category allowed a view of the process by which diagnoses are reified, which confirmed suspicions raised earlier regarding the biases inherent in, at the very least, the Axis II diagnoses under discussion here.

Finally, interviews with the primary authors of this particular highly controversial diagnosis would lead one to suspect that an entirely unexplored variable in the development of this category was the feelings of the psychiatrists themselves (Lenore Walker, personal communication, 1986; Intelligence in Media, 1987). Such interviews are liberally sprinkled with comments regarding how frustrating such patients are, how unwilling to take the help offered to them by psychiatrists, how blind such patients are to the caring shown by their therapists. A critical listener must begin to question the degree to which therapists' frustration was projected upon "self-defeating" patients, simply because of the frequency with which this frustration (of therapist efforts) has been used to demonstrate the presence of the supposed disorder.

The extant mainstream theories of personality and psychopathology have generated nosological systems that, in the United States, have been codified in the APA's manuals. The most current edition, DSM-III-R, can reasonably be construed as representing the epitome of mainstream thought regarding the nature and variety of psychopathology. The concept of personality disorders was one of the major new ideas presented in the third edition, and one on which large amounts of energy and attention were expended.

Thus, the current state of research and writing in the area of severe nonpsychotic psychopathology will tend to strongly support the concept of personality disorders. Millon (1986) comments that the presence of the DSM-III, with its clearly delineated diagnostic criteria, will lead to greater reliability of diagnosis; "the borderline pattern will no longer be characterized one way at Massachusetts General Hospital, another at the Menninger Clinic, a third at Michael Reese Hospital and a fourth at Langley Porter Institute" (pp. 52–53). This greater conformity of diagnostic usage, which is seen as a positive outcome of current systems of classification, and particularly of the reification of the personality disorders, may also lead to the narrowing of focus and the increase in "false positives" that is of concern to critics of the Axis II diagnoses. Additionally, this pride in reliability, which itself is founded on shaky ground, obscures questions of lack of validity and clinical meaningfulness in these diagnostic entities that have yet to be adequately addressed by the framers of DSM-III and DSM-III-R.

To summarize, the problems inherent in Axis II of the DSM-III and DSM-III-R, the personality disorders, fall into two major categories. The first consists of problems of methodology, reliability, and validity of these diagnostic entities. In particular, it should be noted that the statistical methods developed to measure reliability were invented solely for the purposes of the DSM-III, and cannot be compared in particularly meaningful ways to more standard measures of reliability, and that standard guarantees of methodological soundness were not protected. The claims to a scientific basis for these diagnoses hang upon an extremely slender thread.

The second broad category of criticisms, which will be expanded upon in the second section of this chapter, is that the Axis II diagnoses are contaminated by a variety of cultural biases, including, although not limited to, sexism. While the DSM-III-R comments upon the higher rates of many of these diagnoses in women, that comment is made in a conceptual vacuum. What is the meaning of this higher prevalence of such diagnoses as borderline personality disorder, histrionic personality disorder, or dependent personality disorder among women? At a time when the diagnosis of borderline personality seems to have become extremely common and a large industry of books and training workshops has developed to aid practitioners in working with borderline individuals, what does it mean that so many of those being described in terms of this severe characterological pathology are women? This question regarding the high rates of women so diagnosed is the starting point of a feminist analysis. If certain forms of what is presumed to be severe pathology are observed among women, a feminist analysis should lead us to ascribe quite different meanings for what is observed than might be found among mainstream thought. A feminist therapist will see the same behaviors; however, a feminist analysis will generate different conclusions.

TOWARD A FEMINIST PERSPECTIVE ON
SEVERE PSYCHOPATHOLOGY

Kaplan (1983) pointed out that many of the disorders of higher prevalence in women among the DSM-III diagnoses were caricatures of the
normal feminine gender role. This observation follows a decade of
such commentary by other authors (Chesler, 1972; Gove, 1980). A
feminist perspective and analysis of so-called "severe nonpsychotic
psychopathology," the behaviors and experiences encompassed by
the Axis II diagnostic categories in the DSM-III and DSM-III-R, thus
must begin with an analysis of the contribution of gender-role
socialization to that which is observed clinically. Such a feminist
perspective would also avoid categorizing all of what is so observed
as core psychopathology. A significant point of departure from the
perspective of the DSM-III-R concepts of personality disorders could
be found in the careful differentiation of gender-role socialization and
the behavioral, cognitive, and affective artifacts of gender-related
forms of high-frequency and psychologically traumatizing life events
from other personality traits in the assessment of disorderedness and
dysfunction.

Survey research on child sexual and physical abuse conducted in
the past decade has revealed that this abuse happens at such a high
rate in the lives of girls that it may approach normative status. Russell
(1986), in a random sample of nonpsychiatric-patient women found
that sexual abuse of some kind was reported by 37% of all participants
in the study. This finding becomes more meaningful in light of data
that hospitalized psychiatric inpatients on acute service units have
very high rates of childhood physical and/or sexual abuse histories.
Carmen, Reiker, and Mills (1984), in a review of the charts of hospitalized psychiatric inpatients, found that 43% of their sample had childhood or adult abuse histories, or both. Jacobson and Richardson
(1987) conducted structured interviews with a sample of hospitalized
psychiatric inpatients and found that 81% of those interviewed had
experienced at least one kind of major episode of interpersonal violence. They comment that these statistics do not include "minor"
experiences of interpersonal violence, such as verbal abuse, emotional abuse, or the observation of violent behaviors against objects or
other people by powerful significant others, circumstances that other
authors (Miller, 1984; Patrick-Hoffman, 1984; Walker, 1985) have
noted to have serious and potentially traumagenic impact. Bryer,
Nelson, Miller, and Krol (1987) and Herman, Perry, and van der Kolk
(1989) have found that sexual and physical abuse occur at extremely
high rates in women diagnosed as having a personality disorder.

A feminist analysis of any form of severe distress requires an understanding and contextualizing of the effects of interpersonal trauma or violence. While abuse can be a source of severe psychological distress, a feminist analysis would argue that such distress, while often resembling symptoms of a core personality pathology in its intensity and apparent resistance to a crisis intervention model of treatment, is in fact a somewhat transient phenomenon, and better conceptualized as a posttraumatic manifestation. Smith and Siegel (1985) have commented, in addition, that certain forms of behavior that may be labelled by nonfeminist clinicians as evidence of passive or dependent personality disorders are in fact appropriate and skillful manifestations of interpersonal power within a context where other, more overt and "appropriate" expressions of power may be stigmatized or penalized. When the toll taken by sexism is multiplied with the requirements for survival under abuse, an entirely different frame of reference is generated for viewing the symptoms presented by a given person.

Finally, a feminist perspective would need to consciously take into account the meaning of interpersonal context and relatedness as organizing principals in women's lives. Such a concern with the interpersonal matrix as a factor is not solely a feminist one; for example, Greene (1990) describes how Afrocentric models are also more interpersonally than individually based. However, the interpersonal, social/contextual frame has special meaning in many women's lives and in the development of female personality, as has been suggested by a number of feminist theoreticians of female personality such as Miller (1976), Surrey (1985), and Chodorow (1979). Benjamin (1986) suggests that, in order to increase diagnostic meaningfulness, it may be important to add social and intrapsychic descriptors to the diagnostic formulations in the DSM-III. Her system of coding the phenomenology and behavior of interpersonal relating, called the Structural Analysis of Social Behavior (SASB), provides a method for quantifying such phenomena, which may be useful in developing a feminist analysis of clinically observed forms of intense psychological distress.

Benjamin's (1986) model suggests that certain forms of behavior, which in isolation may appear dysfunctional or pathological, are actually appropriate and precise responses to other aspects of the interpersonal environment. This model attends to the focus of the behavior (on self, on other, or on the intrapsychic experience of self) and to the context in which it occurs. Behaviors on each of these dimensions are described on a circumplex, in which an appropriate response is one that is complementary to the focus and stimuli being

218   Psychopathology

attended to. Benjamin points out that behaviors in psychotherapy patients that appear "crazy" or meaningless tend to become easier to comprehend and more apparently goal-directed when viewed within the SASB model. Her research also suggests that very fine and precise aspects of interpersonal functioning may serve to more successfully differentiate between different clinical syndromes than do other measures that fail to take both interpersonal and phenomenological experiences into account. Such a model, which attends both to the importance of the interpersonal context in psychological function and dysfunction and the highly individual experiences that constitute the foci of that interpersonal context, fits extremely well within a feminist analysis in which the validity of internal experience is central to the understanding of expressed behaviors.

Lerman (1986), in proposing criteria for a feminist theory of personality (which would be necessary for a complete feminist theory of psychopathology), has stated that such a theory must "encompass the diversity and complexity of women's lives" (p. 173) and "arise from women's experience" (p. 175). If we are to use these two criteria in making sense of issues of gender-role socialization, sexism, and violence in women's lives, some directions begin to emerge for alternative and clinically useful ways of conceptualizing the behaviors diagnosed by the DSM-III as personality disorders.

One such conceptual framework has been advanced by Walker (1986) and myself (Brown, 1987, 1988), specifically in regard to those problems that arise from the experience of abuse. Since such histories are being found with increasing frequency in those individuals diagnosed as personality disordered (Bryer, Nelson, Miller, & Krol, 1987; Herman, Perry, & van der Kolk, 1989), this feminist model may provide a very useful alternative. Both Walker and I suggest that there may be a diagnostic category that lies between personality disorders and clinical syndromes such as posttraumatic stress disorder, tentatively described as the abuse and oppression artifact disorders. Such phenomena are seen as being more situationally determined than personality disorders, and thus more amenable to change with intervention. However, our diagnostic concept takes into better account the repetitive nature of exposure to trauma that occurs in most experiences of interpersonal violence. While the posttraumatic stress disorder diagnosis for the most part assumes a discrete, single exposure to the traumatagenic agent, and infers that such experiences tend to lie outside of everyday reality for an individual, Walker and I both observe that victims of abuse and interpersonal violence tend to have multiple exposures to trauma, and must adapt to its presence in daily life. The etiology of abuse and oppression artifact disorder symptoms would thus lie in the traumata of abuse or cultural oppression; however, their integration into many aspects of functioning would demonstrate the impact of multiple learning trials across many situations, with severe penalties for "wrong" responses that accrue under such contextual conditions.

An individual with such a disorder might present with symptoms and ways of relating that appear on first glance to be indicative of a personality disorder within a mainstream, decontextualized diagnostic framework. However, the utilization of a feminist analysis would tend to reveal that many of the behaviors being documented are responses to experiences of interpersonal trauma. Since the presence of a powerful other, for example, a mental health professional, is a context in which the interpersonal power dynamics can strongly resemble settings in which abuse has occurred, it is likely that some of the behaviors emitted by a person with an abuse disorder are responsive to the demand characteristics of that response matrix. It is even possible that the presence of the powerful other exacerbates symptoms, and that those behaviors observed by mental health professionals are significantly more distressed than behaviors expressed by the same person in other, more power-equal interpersonal contexts.

If we assume that the learning experiences that created and maintained these behaviors were frequent, we can also appreciate the tenacity of what are now symptoms of long-term, intense psychological distress. Intermittent reinforcement of these behaviors in the natural environment, which creates patterns that change or extinguish very slowly, might lead to the conclusion that an individual with multiple experiences of interpersonal violence would require many trials of exposure to nonexploitative situations before beginning to relinquish response patterns that are means of surviving, coping with, or making sense of such abuse or oppression. Walker's (1984) description of battered women's syndrome as an expression of learned helplessness fits within this model, in which multiple trials of random interpersonal victimization lead to such characteristic behaviors of battered women as passivity, guardedness, and overcontrolled affect. Summit's (1983) concept of the child sexual abuse accomodation syndrome provides another example of a potential application of this conceptual framework. In this case, the highly sexualized and inappropriate behaviors of the sexually abused child in relationship to all adults are identified as learned accomodations to repeated experiences of sexual abuse, which may then manifest as patterns of distressed behavior in adult life.

A diagnosis proposed for possible inclusion in the DSM-IV, disorder of extreme stress not otherwise specified (DESNOS), appears to be a description of similar phenomena. This diagnosis, which would be placed in tandem with posttraumatic stress disorder and the adjustment disorders as a form of distress with a clear, external etiology, describes the social and interpersonal mental health sequelae of repetitive victimization, including styles of relating, patterns of cognition, and expressions of affect that may be long-lasting and difficult to resolve while still in a victimizing context (APA, 1990). While this diagnosis continues to describe such responses as pathological responses to external events, its placement with other stress and trauma-related diagnoses suggests that, within the mainstream, there may be some move in the directions proposed by feminist analysis.

Extrapolating this conceptual framework beyond the experience of direct abuse and victimization, a feminist analysis of severe psychological distress would take into account the lifetime learning experiences of living in a sexist, racist, homophobic, ageist, and otherwise oppressive cultural context. Most individuals who are not securely ensconced within a culturally valued and dominant group will have repeated exposure throughout their lifetime to the overt expressions of such oppression. Depending upon the particular context, the penalties for failure to respond correctly can vary from annoying (being verbally harassed on the street for simply being female, African-American, gay, or lesbian) to life-threatening (being raped for simply being female, or beaten violently for being African-American, gay, or lesbian).

White women, people of color, sexual minorities, disabled people, and elders all may experience a social and interpersonal context of forced choice in which the adoption of certain patterns of response and certain perceptions of self allow for an easier fit with an oppressive society. These patterns of behavior, affect, and cognition would appear to go beyond the concept of "negative introject," first proposed by Sullivan (1935), to include the effects of the constant interaction of that introject with new, external cultural experiences. Such accommodations to oppression are visible in the markedly higher rates at which members of oppressed groups are diagnosed with a variety of mental illnesses, including personality disorders. A feminist analysis would suggest the alternative hypothesis that such individuals are manifesting not a disordered personality but a normative, functional, and at times creative (although distressed) response to potentially dangerous situations and oppressive cultural norms.

A feminist analysis, used in the context of complete and careful history taking, might suggest that many persons currently diagnosed with personality disorders are instead manifesting the sequelae of repeated exposure to the noxious and dangerous manifestations of sexism, racism, or other forms of cultural oppression. Attempts at what might be considered "healthy" means of self-expression by members of culturally disenfranchised groups are often met with punitive responses, for example, assertive behaviors in African-Americans are often used by whites as excuses for racist actions in response. Even if a given individual has not actually experienced such negative consequences firsthand, there may also be ample opportunities for symbolic learning. Children of Holocaust survivors, for example, tend to manifest a type of concentration camp survivor syndrome that appears to be attributable to symbolic learning via the parents, who had the direct experiences. Greene (1990) points out how African-American children must be taught by their parents the appropriate strategies for coping with racism, even when those strategies are sources of distress.

Certain behaviors that are defined as pathological within a DSM-III-R personality disorder context may be culturally normative, and must be reframed within a feminist analysis to reflect their normal, different-from-dominant-culture status. For instance, it is appropriate for Native American individuals to have an identity in which there is little differentiation between self and family or tribe; ego boundaries are defined in such a manner as to include all other members of the group. Identity and sense of self are appropriately drawn from role and age cohort factors. Similar patterns obtain within traditional Japanese models of personality development (Bradshaw, 1990). While a Eurocentric diagnostic perspective might call such behaviors evidence of dependent personality, a feminist analysis would see these ways of being in persons from such groups as culturally appropriate, and therefore indicators of good psychological functioning rather than distress or pathology.

This feminist, multicultural model does not argue that no one from a nondominant group experiences distress or long-term, deeply ingrained pathologic styles of relating. Rather this model suggests a careful reevaluation and at times a markedly different perception of that distress. Its meaning may shift from the symptoms of a severe core pathology to artifacts of oppression learned within a series of interpersonal and sociocultural contexts. Rather than seeing the individual as demonstrating pathology, a feminist analysis which takes into account the profound impact of multiple trials of real and symbolic learning of danger as a result of nondominant group status would tend to redefine the meaning and ascribed degree of pathology of such distress.

Such a diagnostic framework accurately describes the degree of distress felt or the difficulties encountered in changing behavioral strategies that have been overlearned in the service of survival. However, the difference in meaning between "severe psychopathology" and "severe distress secondary to a history of lifelong hostile context" is meaningful from a feminist perspective, in that the latter more accurately describes the interactive effects of person and environment in the creation of distressed affect and less-than-functional behavior.

Can a feminist analysis incorporate the Axis II disorders as currently conceptualized? It is apparent that even when such variables as oppression, abuse, and gender-role socialization are carefully factored out over time in the diagnostic process, there will be some individuals who appear to meet the diagnostic criteria for the various Axis II diagnoses. What this suggests is that there may be some clinical usefulness to these categories in some circumstances. However, their application is, within a feminist analysis, more limited than a mainstream view of psychopathology would suggest. A feminist perspective would also suggest, following on Landrine (1989), Kaplan (1983), and Caplan (1991) that certain groups of behaviors that have not previously been considered for inclusion in the category of personality disorders be studied for possible diagnostic usefulness and possible inclusion in future editions of the diagnostic manual.

A feminist perspective would require that the process of differential diagnosis include a careful investigation of competing hypotheses such as gender-role socialization, abuse experiences, and cultural oppression prior to consideration of a diagnosis of personality disorder. Such a reevaluation of the diagnostic process would be more parsimonious and more likely to yield useful information regarding both etiology and treatment than does the current approach in which clinical syndromes that resemble personality disorders are ipso facto assumed to be personality disorders without further inquiry. This would hold equally true for the diagnosis of persons of either gender.

Table 1 demonstrates a hypothetical listing of diagnostic criteria for the alternative feminist diagnoses proposed above. Such a schema allows for the consideration, independently and in tandem, of a variety of factors that could have served as the basis for current distressed behavior. Similar to Benjamin's SASB model, this framework pays attention to the interpersonal context in which the behaviors being observed for diagnostic purposes were learned. However, it goes beyond that model by applying questions that arise specifically from a feminist analysis. Benjamin, for instance, asks us to consider the attitude with which an action is taken toward some-

Table 1. Diagnosing Abuse/Oppression Artifact Disorders

Preamble

Abuse and Oppression Artifact disorders represent the psychological sequelae of exposure to stressors that may be unusual, but often are embedded in the framework of the culture in which an individual develops. As such, the stressor may be subtle and difficult for either therapist or client to immediately identify. For example, racism in society represents the stressor for the development of internalized racism and/or internalized domination; however one of the manifestations of these disorders may be the denial of the presence of racism by the client. The following outline can be used as a guide by the diagnostician and client in determining the nature of the stressors in question. More than one stressor may be present in the life of an individual, and the effects of stressors may be synergistic and overlapping. Identification of the stressor is the first step in formulating a diagnosis of Abuse or Oppression Artifact disorder.

I. Nature of environmental/contextual stressor
   A. Interpersonal
      1. Intimate or known other
      2. Individual stranger
      3. Groups of strangers
   B. Cultural/environmental
      1. Overt/punitive phenomena
      2. Covert/systemic phenomena
      3. Lack of protection/denial of opportunity

II. Frequency of exposure to stressor
   A. Infrequent/one time only
   B. Moderate frequency, or occured during one time period only
   C. High frequency

III. Nature of consequences to person
   A. Rewarding or apparently positive
   B. Mixed, confusing, ambiguous
   C. Negative, punitive
   D. Life-threatening

IV. Source of consequences (e.g., who caused the problem)
   A. As perceived by client
      1. Self
      2. Mixed
      3. Others
   B. As perceived by diagnostician
      1. Self
      2. Mixed
      3. Others

V. Developmental phenomena interacting with stressor
   A. Boundary/identity development
   B. Trust/intimacy
   C. Sexuality
      1. Function
      2. Orientation/identity
   D. Autonomy/individuation
   E. Dependency/interdependency   (cont.)

Table 1. (cont.)

In diagnosing an Abuse or Oppression Artifact disorder, agreement should, when possible, be reached between client and diagnostician regarding the nature of the stressor(s). Problematic or painful behaviors will usually be consistent in some way with the specific stressors. Because of the high likelihood of multiple stressors in persons who belong to culturally devalued groups, care should be taken to determine all potential stressors. For example, a black woman sexually abused as a child may have both the sexual abuse and racism as stressors, and these stressors may be interactive in their impact.

Diagnostic criteria

I. Existence of a stressor as described in the preamble

II. Presence of persistent and painful behavioral patterns that represent developmental-stage appropriate survival strategies for coping with stressor(s). Examples may include:
   A. Learned helplessness
   B. Covert or indirect expressions of interpersonal power
   C. Avoidant behaviors that reduce frequency of contact with stressor or phenomena resembling stressor
   D. Caretaking/rescue behavior

III. Distortion or limitation of affective responsivity, usually in contexts resembling the original stressor. Examples include:
   A. Fear or distrust of a class of persons
   B. Emotional numbness in the presence of persons or situations resembling the original stressor
   C. Rigidly gender-role stereotyped behaviors
   D. Inability to feel or express a class of emotions

IV. Distortions of cognition that support the contextual status quo. Examples include:
   A. Self-blame
   B. Shame; strongly held beliefs in one's own badness
   C. Strongly held beliefs in one's ability to control the behavior of others.
   D. Denial or minimization of distress or abuse
   E. Persistent confusion or inability to think clearly in the absence of physiological deficits that would impair cognition
   F. Extreme pessimism, despair, or cynicism

V. This pattern of behavior appears to be persistent and long-standing in nature. It is likely to be painful and ego-dystonic for the person experiencing it. Cultural phenomena which reinforce this pattern of behaviors can often be identified by both client and diagnostician.

one, for example, helpful, hostile, or neutral. A feminist analysis adds inquiry into the gender and other characteristics of the people involved, and would attend to the power differentials between them. In addition, the repetitive nature of interactions, and the fact that abuse and oppression are usually not one-time events, can be described and delineated within such a model. In other words, the reality experiences of the person being diagnosed would be taken into conscious and deliberate account in the diagnostic process. Finally, such a feminist diagnostic process takes into account the behavioral options and limits engendered by social roles, including gender, class, and cultural roles. Diagnosis of a personality disorder would occur only after the requirements of this diagnostic framework had been exhausted.

The behavioral sciences hold in their hands enormous power; they have been given by society the task of defining normalcy in a culture in which ascribed deviance may place a person's home, job, family, and physical well-being at risk. A theory of psychopathology that uncritically embraces the current social status quo as the hallmark of normalcy risks becoming a tool in the hands of those who would justify continued oppression. Such concerns are not only theoretical; in 1986, the Supreme Court of the United States upheld the right of states to imprison people for private, consenting sexual activities between adults on the grounds that such behavior, when between two people of the same gender, was "abnormal," and thus not entitled to constitutional guarantees of privacy.

The personality disorders as currently defined do embrace the status quo of white male as norm in their definitions of psychopathology. In that regard, they depart from any claims to science. While a feminist perspective on severe distress may appear at first glance to be more overtly political in the questions raised and the analysis brought to bear upon the distress felt by psychotherapy clients, it may in fact lay closer to science in its conscious attention to the potential for contamination of data by bias.

REFERENCES

American Psychiatric Association. (1980). *Diagnostic and statistical manual of mental disorders (3rd ed.)* Washington, DC: Author.

American Psychiatric Association. (1987). *Diagnostic and statistical manual of mental disorders (3rd ed., rev.)* Washington, DC: Author.

American Psychiatric Association. (1990). *DSM-IV update.* Washington, DC: Author.

Benjamin, L. S. (1986). Adding social and intrapsychic descriptors to Axis I of DSM-III. In T. Millon & G. L. Klerman (Eds.), *Contemporary directions in psychopathology: Toward the DSM-IV* (pp. 599–638). New York: Guilford.

Blashfield, R. K., & Breen, M. S. (1989). Face validity of the DSM-III-R personality disorders. *American Journal of Psychiatry, 146,* 1575–1579.

Bradshaw, C. K. (1990). A Japanese view of dependency: What Amae psychology can contribute to feminist theory and therapy. In L. S. Brown & M.P.P. Root (Eds.), *Diversity and complexity in feminist therapy* (pp. 67–86.) New York: Haworth.

Broverman, I. K., Broverman, D., Clarkson, F. E., Rosecrantz, P., & Vogel, S. (1970). Sex role stereotypes and clinical judgements of mental health. *Journal of Consulting and Clinical Psychology, 34,* 1–7.

Brown, L. S. (1986, August). Diagnosis and the zeitgeist: The politics of masochism in the *DSM-III-R.* In R. Garfinkel (Chair), *The politics of diagnosis: Feminist psychology and the DSM-III-R.* Symposium presented at the Convention of the American Psychological Association, Washington, DC.

Brown, L. S. (1987, August). Towards a new conceptual paradigm for the Axis II diagnoses. In J. Worell (Chair), *DSM-III-R.* Symposium presented at the Convention of the American Psychological Association, New York.

Brown, L. S. (1988). Feminist therapy perspectives on psychodiagnosis: Beyond the DSM and ICD. In Stichting de Maan (Ed.), *Proceedings of the International Congress on Mental Health Care for Women.* Amsterdam: Stichting de Maan.

Brown, L. S. (1991). Commentary on the Delusional dominating personality disorder. *Canadian Psychology, 32,* 142–144.

Bryer, J. B., Nelson, B. A., Miller, J. B., & Krol, P. A. (1987). Childhood sexual and physical abuse as factors in adult psychiatric illness. *American Journal of Psychiatry, 144,* 1426–1430.

Caplan, P. J. (1986). The myth of women's masochism. *American Psychologist, 39,* 130–139.

Caplan, P. J. (1991). Delusional dominating personality disorder. *Feminism and Psychology, 1,* 171–174.

Carmen, E. H., Reiker, P. P., & Mills, T. (1984). Victims of violence and psychiatric illness. *American Journal of Psychiatry, 14,* 378–383.

Chesler, P. (1972). *Women and madness.* New York: Doubleday.

Chodorow, N. (1979). *The reproduction of mothering.* Berkeley: University of California Press.

Committee on Women in Psychology. (1985). *Critique of proposed new diagnoses for the DSM-III-R.* Unpublished manuscript.

Frances, A., & Widiger, T. A. (1986). Methodological issues in personality disorder diagnosis. In T. Millon & G. L. Klerman (Eds.), *Contemporary directions in psychopathology: Toward the DSM-IV* (pp. 381–402). New York: Guilford.

Gove, W. R. (1980). Mental illness and psychiatric treatment among women. *Psychology of Women Quarterly, 38,* 345–362.

Greene, B. A. (1990). What has gone before: The legacy of racism and sexism in the live of Black mothers and daughters. In L. S. Brown & M.P.P. Root (Eds.), *Diversity and complexity in feminist therapy* (pp. 207–230). New York: Haworth.

Herman, J. L., Perry, J. C., & van der Kolk, B. A. (1989). Childhood trauma in borderline personality disorder. *American Journal of Psychiatry, 146,* 490–495.

Intelligence in Media (1987). *Diagnosis today: Women and mental health.* New York: Author.

Jacobson, A., & Richardson, B. (1987). Assault experiences of 100 psychiatric inpatients: Evidence of the need for routine inquiry. *American Journal of Psychiatry, 144,* 908–913.

Kaplan, M. (1983). A woman's view of the DSM-III. *American Psychologist, 38,* 786–792.

Kass, F. MacKinnon, R. S. & Spitzer, R. (1986). Masochistic personality: An empirical study. *American Journal of Psychiatry, 143,* 216–218.

Kutchins, H., & Kirk, S. (1986). The reliability of the DSM-III: A critical review. *Social Work Research and Abstracts, 2,* 3–12.

Landrine, H. (1989). The politics of personality disorder. *Psychology of Women Quarterly, 13,* 325–340.

Lerman, H. (1986). *A mote in Freud's eye: From psychoanalysis to the psychology of women.* New York: Springer.

Miller, A. (1984). *For your own good: Hidden cruelty in child-rearing and the roots of violence.* New York: Farrar, Strauss & Giroux.

Miller, J. S. (1976). *Towards a new psychology of women.* Boston: Beacon Press.

Millon, T. (1969). *Modern psychopathology: A biosocial approach to maladaptive learning and functioning.* Philadelphia: Saunders.

Millon, T. (1981). *Disorders of personality: DSM-III, Axis II.* New York: Wiley-Interscience.

Millon, T. (1986). On the past and future of the DSM-III: Personal recollections and projections. In T. Millon & G. L. Kleman (Eds)., *Contemporary directions in psychopathology: Towards the DSM-IV* (pp. 29–70). New York: Guilford.

Patrick-Hoffman, P. *(1984).* Psychological abuse of women by spouses and live-in lovers. *Women and Therapy, 3,* 37–48.

Rosencrantz, P. S., Delorey, C., & Broverman, I. (1985, August). *One half a generation later: Sex role stereotypes revisited.* Paper presented at the Convention of the American Psychological Association, Los Angeles, CA.

Rosewater, L. B. (1986, August). Ethical and legal implications of the DSM-III-R for feminist therapists. In R. Garfinkel (Chair), *The politics of diagnosis: Feminist psychology and the DSM-III-R.* Symposium presented at the Convention of the American Psychological Association, Washington, DC.

Rosewater, L. B. (1987). A critical analysis of the proposed self-defeating personality disorder. *Journal of Personality Disorders, 1,* 190–195.

Rothblum, E. D., Solomon, L., & Albee, G. (1986). A socio-political perspective of DSM-III. In T. Millon & G. L. Klerman (Eds.), *Contemporary directions in psychopathology: Towards the DSM-IV*. New York: Guilford.

Russell, D.E.H. (1986). *The secret trauma: Incest in the lives of girls and women*. New York: Basic.

Smith, A. J., & Siegel, R. F. (1985). Feminist therapy: Redefining power for the powerless. In L. B. Rosewater & L.E.A. Walker (Eds.), *Handbook of feminist therapy: Women's issues in psychotherapy* (pp. 13–21). New York: Springer.

Spitzer, R. L., Williams, J. B., Kass, F., & Davies, M. (1989). National field trial of the DSM-III-R diagnostic criteria for self-defeating personality disorder. *American Journal of Psychiatry, 146,* 1561–1567.

Summit, R. (1983). The child abuse accomodation syndrome. *Child Abuse and Neglect: The International Journal, 7,* 177–193.

Sullivan, H. S. (1935). *The interpersonal theory of psychiatry*. New York: Norton.

Surrey, J. (1985). *Self-in-relation: A theory of women's development*. (Work in Progress, No. 13). Wellesley, MA: Stone Center.

Walker, L.E.A. (1979). *The battered woman*. New York: Harper & Row.

Walker, L.E.A. (1984). *The battered women's syndrome*. New York: Springer.

Walker, L.E.A (1986, August). Diagnosis and politics: Abuse disorders. In R. Garfinkel (Chair), *The politics of diagnosis: Feminist psychology and the DSM-III-R*. Symposium presented at the Conference of the American Psychological Association, Washington, DC.

Walker, L.E.A. (1985). Feminist therapy with victims/survivors of interpersonal violence. In L. B. Rosewater & L.E.A. Walker (Eds.), *Handbook of feminist therapy: Women's issues in psychotherapy* (pp. 210–221). New York: Springer.

CHAPTER TEN

Reconstructing the Impact of Trauma on Personality

MARIA P. P. ROOT

> None of us can help the things that Life has done to us. . . . They're
> done before you realize it, and once they're done they make you do
> other things until at last everything comes between you and what
> you would like to be, and you've lost your true self . . .
> —Eugene O'Neill, *Long Day's Journey into Night*

Trauma permanently changes one's personal construction of reality. Particularly after trauma is inflicted by another human being, people may begin to appear less benevolent, events less random, and living more encumbered. The attempts to prevent subsequent trauma may result in a labored and sometimes tortuous existence. Fears combined with apprehension—characteristics of vigilance so commonly found in posttrauma responding—turn life's hassles and stresses into potentially threatening events. A lack of joy and hope compromise the experience of being alive.

Trauma is qualitatively different from stress, though one might consider both to be anchor points on a nonlinear continuum of negative experiences. Negative stressors leave an individual feeling "put out," inconvenienced, and distressed. These experiences are eventually relieved with the resolution of the stressor. In contrast, traumas represent destruction of basic organizing principles by which we come to know self, others, and the environment; traumas wound deeply in a way that challenges the meaning of life. Healing from the wounds of such an experience requires a restitution of order and meaning in one's life.

The wounds of trauma wear many masks: anxiety, panic, depression, multiple personalities, paranoia, anger, and sleep problems; tendencies towards suicidality, irritability, mood swings, and odd rituals; difficulty trusting people and difficult relationships; and general despair, aimlessness, and hopelessness. Elaborate theoretical conceptualizations and constructs are evoked to explain this symptomatology outside of the context of trauma. Subsequently, these explanations become entities reified in a diagnostic system that often blames the "wounded" persons for their inability to reorganize their lives after horrible experiences.

In this chapter, a feminist reconstruction of the impact of trauma on personality is outlined. Central to this conceptualization is the tenet that trauma is a very personal experience, the upheaval, stress, and pain of which can only be judged subjectively and in a psychosocial context. As such, what is deemed traumatic is determined by the traumatized person rather than the observer. This feminist conceptualization of trauma broadens the experiences that are considered traumatic (Brown, 1991), and subsequently is more inclusive of experiences subsumed by gender, race, class, sexual orientation, and ability—variables about people who those with relatively more status have often transformed into objects of hatred and oppression. Feminist theory allows for the validity of "stories" other than the American Psychiatric Association's (APA) story of trauma, which was primarily created by men and is about men's experiences (Brown, 1991).

Rather than diluting or medicalizing the concept of posttraumatic response—a criticism raised against attempts to be inclusive of traumas that include oppression by dehumanization—feminist theory speaks to the extensiveness of horrors and atrocities that *millions* of people struggle with through a lifetime. Laura Brown (1991) notes that "a feminist analysis of the experience of psychic trauma . . . moves us to a radical re-visioning of our understanding of the human condition" (p. 132). Broadening the scope of experiences that are traumatic allows us to delve deeper into understanding trauma and to construct a more inclusive general theory of trauma, which is the goal of this chapter. Because feminist theory and subsequently empowerment are rooted in acknowledging that the individual is rooted in a sociopolitical context, I start this reconstruction by providing a brief discussion and critique of hypotheses regarding the revival of interest in the study of trauma, a discussion of obstacles to recognizing the degree to which trauma is relevant to many people's lives, and a summary and critique of current diagnosis and theory.

HISTORICAL PERSPECTIVE

The Revival of Interest in Trauma Studies

Although the concept of trauma has played a central role in dynamic formulations of personality, it is only in the last 2 decades that renewed interested has been directed towards advancing theory and treatment in this area. Both striking and integral to feminist critique of trauma theory is that the initial trauma studies, from which the theory was developed, focused largely on white men. The formal, contemporary study of trauma began approximately a century ago and was based upon a pattern of disorganization exhibited by some soldiers of war; subsequently, with the advent of the railroads, victims of railway accidents were included. Because the socialization of men and women has been divergently different and manifestations of stress are generally expressed according to gender-role and cultural prescriptions, traditional models of trauma are very specific to white men, in specific situations.

The revival of the need to understand trauma in the United States emerged within the sociopolitical era of the 1960s and '70s—an era marked by the Vietnam war, international conflict, the women's rights movement, gay liberation, and the second reconstruction of the civil rights movement. It was an era marked by a generation's search for meaning and justice.

Much of the upheaval and rebellion associated with the 1960s and '70s might be characterized as a "generational posttraumatic stress response" to the experience of profound betrayal by authority figures (the "establishment") of a generation of young people crossing the threshold of adulthood. The world for which this generation hoped did not exist. Oppression was rampant and affected major portions of the population. The civil rights of large segments the American population were being violated daily. This was a generation that witnessed the assassinations of Martin Luther King, John F. Kennedy, and Malcolm X within less than a decade. Anger and confusion were catalysts for the activism and power of this generation, who spoke about the realities and atrocities of their lives and those of previous generations. "Speaking up" through protest, music, poetry, organizing, and action validated subjective experiences. Perhaps theoretical reconstruction of posttraumatic stress response was the result of trying to establish meaning for the events of this era.

Obstacles to Recognizing the Significance and Prevalence of Trauma

Despite the revival of interest in the study of trauma, several obstacles have contributed to the narrow research focus and limited understanding of trauma: (1) As time elapses since the original trauma, it becomes more difficult to connect symptoms to the initial event. And in fact, through a complex learning process, the symptomatology that is sequelae to traumatic experiences is indeed less directly related. (2) Over time the wounds of trauma are disguised by crises that require immediate attention. (3) Health care professionals are seldom trained in the area of victimization and trauma. (4) Researchers have approached the determination of trauma as though there are a limited number of "spaces" for what constitutes valid trauma (Horowitz, Weiss, & Marmar, 1987). (5) Our conceptual limitations may originate in a long-standing refusal to believe that atrocities initiated by other people indeed occur and do so with alarming frequency. Nowhere are these limitations more profound for theory than in the development of elaborate psychological theories to dismiss children's descriptions of sexual abuse (initially documented by Freud) as a product of normative developmental fantasies, lies, and complexes (Lerman, 1986; Masson, 1984). Thus, many emotionally and psychically wounded individuals are subsequently blamed for their experiences and subsequent symptomatology. What we still lack in theories of trauma is a perspective that includes the atrocities sustained by people and communities of color, both currently and historically.

Perloff (1983) suggests that most people operate on a *just world hypothesis* (you get what you deserve) as a defense against vulnerability. Mythic explanations that imply systemic participation, such as the "seductive child" (child sexual abuse); "she dressed provocatively" or "she should have known better than to go there alone" (rape); or "she should know better than to speak up when he's had a bad day" or "she's a nag" (woman battering) convey the extent to which the victim is held responsible for traumas, and conversely, to which the victimizer is attributed minimal if any responsibility. Lerner suggests that the tendency to "blame the victim" (Lerner, 1980) and denial of the prevalence of atrocities in women and children's lives, particularly, maintains the nonvictim's (usually male) sense of invulnerability.

Current Diagnosis and Theory

Attempts in the last 2 decades to understand trauma might be considered a second reconstruction of theory, as women and children's experiences are being acknowledged for the first time. The contemporary delineation and labelling of separate trauma syndromes—*battered woman syndrome* (Walker, 1979), the *rape–trauma syndrome* (Burgess & Holmstrom, 1974), the *postsexual abuse syndrome* (Briere, 1984), and the *battered child syndrome* (Kempe, Silverman, Steele, Droegemueller, & Silver, 1962)—provide a depth and breadth lacking in the initial theories of posttrauma response.

Compared with any field of inquiry and conceptualization, the study of trauma and its sequelae have the most feminist influence. Nevertheless, only one posttrauma syndrome is acknowledged by the APA (1987), *posttraumatic stress disorder* (PTSD), a syndrome primarily established on patterns of distress exhibited by male veterans of war. (This influence is evident in currently proposed revisions of the APA's *Diagnostic and Statistical Manual of Mental Disorders* [to appear in the upcoming fourth edition], which include changing the definition of what validly constitutes a stressful event that precipitates a posttrauma response.)

The current criteria for PTSD represent the refinement of a century of nosology and notably reflect Kardiner's (1941) categorization of symptoms and Horowitz's (1976) outline of positive and negative symptomatology, both primarily based on traumas of war. According to the resulting, current criteria, PTSD is estimated to affect 2% of the American population at any given time (Helzer, Robins, & McEvoy, 1987) according to the criteria set by the *Diagnostic and Statistical Manual of Mental Disorders, third edition* (DSM-III) (APA, 1980).

Trauma appears to have both psychological and physiological signatures. Initial theories of trauma, dating back a century, postulated a neurophysiological basis for symptomatology. The reader is referred to an excellent review of neurophysiological models and hypotheses of posttrauma responding by Krystal et al. (1989). It is significant to note that the impact of trauma on neurophysiological functioning should have profound implications for children, since the central nervous system undergoes maturation through adolescence. The literature on trauma, however, reflects a consistent deficit in addressing what is traumatic to children and how it impacts them.

Current neurophysiological theories observe that trauma and high levels of stress affect many brain structures and neurotransmitters that ultimately dysregulate noradrenergic activation and metabolization (Krystal et al., 1989). Central noradrenergic activation triggers brain alarm and fear centers (e.g., freezing, cognitive and behavioral shutting down, and startle responses). Krystal et al. (1989) suggest that the pattern of results emerging from animal and human studies have two important implications. First, a singular exposure to trauma may result in permanent microstructural neuronal modifications, such that an indelible memory may be established. Second, findings from animal studies suggest that more severe response to minor stressors will follow exposure to trauma (McIntyre & Edson, 1981). Exposure to chronic stress increases sensitivity to stress, which contributes to further noradrenergic activation and eventual depletion, which, in turn, involves more systems in the sensitization to stress.

Contemporary psychological theories use an integration of learning, psychodynamic, and information processing models to explain anxiety. Mowrer's (1960) two-factor learning theory explains the symptomatology of posttrauma responding through an interaction of classical and instrumental conditioning. A repeated process of higher-order classical conditioning results in the generalization of response; instrumental conditioning explains negative symptomatology, that is, avoidance responses are reinforcing.

Contemporary theory also reflects three of Horowitz's (1976) contributions that are derived from a psychodynamic theory base (and are also esconced in a Western notion of healing and psychic functioning). The first of these is the notion that it is necessary to reexperience cognitive and affective memories associated with the original trauma for healing. However, this observation may be culturally circumscribed. Second, positive symptomatology (intrusive reminiscence, rumination, anger, and nightmares) reflect an innate *completion tendency*. Negative symptoms (avoidance, defensive strategies) are a response to the anxiety and pain evoked by the positive symptomatology. The combination of positive and negative symptomatology gives rise to a "cycling" of symptomatology, the third element frequently borrowed from Horowitz.

Lastly, Lang's (1979) influence is notable in the salience of *propositional networks*, semantic structures that reflect rules, beliefs, and expectations that affect the assignment of meaning to stimuli. These propositional networks are unique for their multimodal representation of somato–visceral, visual, affective, and behavioral information with attendant positive and negative valence information. The emotional and somato–visceral networks are mutually influential and inhibitory.

The most recently evolved, comprehensive models propose that perception of meaning (cognition) is a powerful mediator of posttrauma responses (e.g., Foa, Steketee, & Rothbaum, 1989; Chemtob, Roitblatt, Hamada, Carlson, & Twentyman, 1988). These theories are mechanistic, and as such they lend themselves to laboratory testing but lose the conveyance of the qualitative difference between stress (anxiety) and trauma. For example, Foa and colleagues highlight the centrality of a threat–safety meaning that can activate propositional fear networks. Whereas Chemtob and colleagues describe a similarly mechanistic theory, they introduce the notion of a *mode shift* that occurs in response to threat, which captures some of the qualitative difference between anxiety and posttrauma responding. They suggest that this mode shift is much broader than activation of a single cognitive schema; it is a state of mind characterized by a *confirmatory bias* that increases vigilance and sensitivity to threatening stimuli as well as a tendency to interpret stimuli as threatening.

Even though our understanding of trauma has more breadth and depth now than 20 years ago, it is significantly limited by the narrowness of experiences that have been considered traumatic by professionals. This problem is maintained by the tendency to evaluate an individual's experience from the perspective of the observer or "outsider" (which is subjective, being gender, culture, class, and sexual-orientation biased) rather than the experience of the victim. Additionally, theory has been primarily developed on the subculture of men; given that expressions of distress are culturally bound, current theory and criteria are likely to be similarly culturally limited. Lastly, although the conceptualization of posttrauma responding lends itself to analysis of traumas inflicted on minority groups of people and the subsequent impact on the development of shared behaviors of a group of people (e.g., consequences of the Holocaust, internment of Japanese Americans, dislocation and decimation of Native American peoples and cultures, etc.), it remains—as with the rest of conventional psychopathology—a theory of individual distress in a limited reality. As such, the breadth of traumata and their impact relevant to women, children, and minority groups have received minimal consideration in the development of theory.

The diagnostic manual of the American Psychiatric Association has tremendous impact on research direction, theory, and treatment. Its atheoretical base excludes our conceptualization of the differential impact of trauma across the life span. The only diagnoses that recognize a developmental basis are *Axis II disorders,* which include the personality disorders frequently applied to individuals who have been victims (Herman, Perry, & van der Kolk, 1989; Putnam, 1989). As such, the implicit model that guides treatment of the wounded individual is one that is a personal deficit model that is ahistorical, lacks a life span perspective, and is esconced in a broader American culture that proposes a duality between mind and body and tends to ignore the intangible human spirit. Current theories do not account for the interaction between the environment and an individual (mind, body, and spirit) as it shapes the development of posttrauma responding and healing.

Those individuals who are able to reconstruct their lives and maintain an optimistic outlook for the future are exceptional. Trauma, by definition, creates upheaval and disorganization. It is too simplistic to attribute an individual's inability to reorganize and restore themselves to pretrauma functioning to her or his coping-skill deficits or characterological weaknesses—two popular explanations of the manifest disorganization subsequent to trauma. Such expectations ignore the effects of living in daily traumatic environments (e.g., poverty, threat to life, persistent denial or abrogation of human rights, etc.) or the effects of cumulative trauma. The strategies for coping and constructive reorganization following many traumas may not be within immediate, typical human capacity or possible through conventional individual therapy. Those transcendant survivors should be used for hope but not as standards for comparison.

Feminist theory always considers the interplay between sociopolitical factors and phenomenological experience. As such, feminist theory allows us to consider the social environment's contribution to the maintenance of posttrauma symptoms, e.g., how victims of interpersonal violence tend to be blamed, isolated, and questioned as to the accuracy of their reports or feelings, thus compounding the experience. A feminist analysis of sociopolitical and phenomenological experience allows us to extend the notion of trauma by understanding sources of secondary trauma, insidious trauma, and indirect trauma, as will be discussed in this chapter.

The remaining pages of this chapter are dedicated to developing a conceptualization of trauma that rests pivotally on the individual's subjective experience and evaluation of events. It assumes a developmental perspective that includes not only experiences that shatter assumptions of the world (Janoff-Bulman, 1985) but includes experiences as they shape a view of the world. I make the assumption that mind, body, and spirit are integrally and essentially connected in the reconstruction of meaning in life following traumatic experiences.

FEMINIST RECONSTRUCTION OF TRAUMA THEORY

Feminist perspectives validate multiple, distinct methodologies for gathering information (Belenky, Clinchy, Goldberger, & Tarule, 1987; Ballou, 1990) consistent with anthropology and sociology, such as observation, self-report, and semistructured interviews. Thus, we develop theory from a broad data base that includes very concrete data on one end (e.g., visible physical wounds) and very abstract experience on the other end (e.g., spiritual losses); scores from psychological tests represent something in between. The construction of theory in this chapter will draw on a range of sources of data. My concern is not to present a theory constructed for laboratory testing, but to construct one that explains the broadest range of posttrauma functioning across people by age, class, gender, experience, ability, and culture. This theory does not significantly contradict findings from laboratory studies, but ventures into areas where we have not collected data and areas that are not subject to empirical study by conventional methods.

Significant Strengths and Contributions of Feminist Theory

Feminist perspectives allow for many significant contributions to the understanding of trauma. Five characteristics of the feminist perspective are briefly summarized below. In combination, these characteristics unquestionnably make a feminist perspective for conceptualizing trauma unique and broadly encompassing of many persons' experiences.

Significant contributions include, first of all, placing a prominent value on an individual's subjective experience of an event or series of events. Perhaps nowhere is this more salient than in the determination of what is traumatic. The victim's perception is at least equally important to the observer's perception and evaluation of an event. When we open our exploration of trauma to those events defined as such by the individual, very profound implications arise for understanding styles of perception, reactivity, and coping (and the glaring omissions of conventional nosology and psychiatric theories).

The second significant contribution is that it depathologizes normal responses to horrible experiences that transcend daily and developmental hassles and stresses. In the instance of trauma, this means that we acknowledge that everyone has a breaking point; disorganized and unusual behavior following horrible experiences are normal responses to traumatic events. Many of the behaviors we see after trauma are manifestations of specialized coping behaviors for survival, but are not usually recognized as such and thus are pathologized. Similarly, conventional designations of how long post-trauma responding is "tolerable" are arbitrary and are neither guided by research results, sensitivity to environmental factors, or flexibility in the development of individual theories based on general theory and the uniqueness of the individual.

In line with this perspective is a consideration of the social environment's contribution to additive trauma or to obstacles to healing following the trauma. Feminist theory acknowledges and addresses the role of environmental factors that might indeed be an environmental criterion list for individual trauma. Factors such as isolation, blame, loss of social status, and effect on ability to take care of one's self and/or family add to the trauma of the original event.

Next, a feminist conceptualization of trauma moves the analysis of the problem beyond an individual perspective to a larger sociopolitical, systemic framework of conceptualization. This difference from other theoretical perspectives is important, because no matter how sensitively proposed an individual theory is, it still tends to talk about the victim's characteristics in a way that lends itself to blaming the survivor of trauma. Moving from the individual to the sociopolitical level is consistent with feminism's initial proclamation that the "personal is political" and allows us to consider that trauma can be experienced by groups or communities of people.

Lastly, feminism has been open to considering the role of spirit in the wholeness of a human being. This characteristic of feminism is important to trauma, because one of the prominent wounds of trauma is the crushing of the human spirit (i.e., dignity, respect), which may indeed be the hardest wound to heal. Ultimately a recognition of spirituality allows one to consider the effects of events that disconnect an individual from life through the isolation that follows denigration, blame, and decreased social worth. Feminist portrayals of spirituality may be connoted by the premium placed on our interrelatedness, conveyed in words such as dignity, respect, empowerment, humanity, and hope. Damage to this connectedness or larger sense of being in this world is connoted in words like oppression, evil, isolation, and dehumanization. The feminist value on spirituality has been observed not only in the connections among people but through the validation of intangible senses and intuition.

Reconstructing one's life following the pain and deep wounds of trauma necessitate an integration of mind, body, and spirit in the healing process. This view stands in contrast to contemporary theories of trauma that reside in a mind–body duality and totally ignore the intangible spirit, which may play a prominent role in finding meaning in one's life, instilling hope in the future for oneself or people or humanity, and connecting one with a larger sense of life.

Expanding the Conventional Notion of Trauma

The feminist conceptualization of trauma that follows expands the conventional notion of trauma to include more than "direct blows." A model for understanding the difference between person-perpetrated versus accidentally sustained traumas is outlined. Subsequently, I propose two ways of reframing trauma-related response. This foundation allows a broader conceptualization for understanding variations in the experience of traumata and their sequelae.

Conventionally, only some direct traumas have been acknowledged as such and researched, for example, combat trauma, rape, and natural disasters. The conventional notion of trauma offers a very narrow definition that excludes the reality of many persons, particularly dispossessed members of society. Both our acknowledgment of the pervasiveness of trauma and understanding its many masks are enhanced by considering three categories of traumatic impact: *direct, indirect,* and *insidious.*

Direct traumas generally include certain forms of maliciously perpetrated violence, war experiences, industrial accidents, and natural disasters. Direct trauma includes being the target of the trauma as well as being forced to commit atrocities that one otherwise would not. For example, soldiers in Vietnam were ordered to kill civilian women and children. These experiences created tremendous dissonance, and, subsequently, disorganization of meaning for many soldiers, particularly after returning to a civilian environment. Only recently, sexual abuse, emotional abuse, and other forms of interpersonal violence have been considered "valid" traumatic experiences. Other direct traumas previously not conceptualized as such include sudden life threatening or debilitating physical illness and destruction of cultural communities. Several cultural and ethnic communities have been traumatized for generations by dislocation (e.g., internment of Japanese Americans [Krell, 1988; Nagata, 1990; Loo, in preparation] and removal of Native Americans and Native Hawaiians from their homelands [Parker, 1989]), and genocide and decimation of ethnic populations (e.g., Jews, Native Americans, Native Hawaiians, and African-Americans).

Direct traumas to individuals usually meet with convergent validation of the horribleness of the stressor. It is the easiest type of trauma for the observer and traumatee to link to symptomatology, in part, because the normative expectation is that these events are followed by upheaval and distress. Feminist theory extends the concept of direct traumas in considering how communities as a unit can sustain direct trauma.

Indirect trauma has largely been neglected in trauma research, reflecting a lack of understanding of the impact of secondary trauma. It includes being traumatized by the trauma sustained by another, with whom one identifies in some significant way (e.g., trauma to a friend, family member, friend of a friend, another woman, a community member), witnessing trauma (e.g., workers pulling dead and/or maimed bodies out of wreckage or rubble, a mother being beaten, an execution), and receiving general information about devastation or violence (e.g., continuous news reports of violence—rape, murder, assault). Therapists who work with victims of violence are also subject to indirect trauma as they repeatedly hear stories of atrocities that challenge a benevolent view of human beings.

Females might be more likely than men to experience indirect trauma during the course of a lifetime for at least two reasons. First, women's socialization, as well as our less privileged position in this society, makes us mutually interdependent with others and more likely to feel threatened or even wounded when someone with whom we feel connected is hurt. Second, women are more likely than men to be victims of direct violent traumas. For example, many women I work with report feeling increased fear and anxiety and/or curtailing their activities outside of their homes in the evening for fear for their personal safety. Public forms of violence in the form of "hate crimes," which are increasing toward racial and ethnic minorities (Berk, 1990) and gays and lesbians (Berrill, 1990), similarly increase these groups' vulnerability to indirect trauma. Dehumanized as individuals to become objects of "symbolic" threat (Berk, 1990; Sears, 1988) and mutually interdependent within and between groups by cultural socialization and social necessity, violence against a friend or stranger that shares a "symbolic" similarity may become an indirect trauma or at least a severe stressor (Garnets, Herek, & Levy, 1990).

Because the experiences subsumed under indirect trauma are often not recognized as traumatic, it has been more difficult both to accept the emergence of symptomatology that persists after such experiences and to link the symptoms to the indirect experience. Subsequently, the reactions to indirect trauma may be attributed to minor stressors that make the posttrauma responding seem magnified out of proportion.

Lastly, *insidious trauma* is an experience of trauma that has been totally neglected. While its impact shapes a worldview rather than shatters assumptions about the world, over time it may result in a picture of symptomatology similar to that of direct or indirect trauma, particularly involving anxiety, depression, paranoia, and substance abuse. Insidious trauma is usually associated with the social status of an individual being devalued because a characteristic intrinsic to their identity is different from what is valued by those in power, for example, gender, color, sexual orientation, physical ability. As a result, it is often present throughout a lifetime and may start at birth.

As a rule, insidious trauma's effects are cumulative and directed toward a community of people. In effect, it encompasses some very "normative," yet nevertheless traumatic, experiences of groups of people. Insidious trauma incurred by minority groups usually starts early in life before one grasps the full psychological meaning of the maliciousness of the wounds, for example, a child is told he or she is not the right kind of person to play with—too poor, wrong color, etc. It does not typically include physical violence, yet leaves a distinct threat to psychological safety, security, or survival, for example, the "terrorism of racism" (Wyatt, 1989) and fear of decimation experienced by some children of Holocaust survivors (Danieli, 1985). In 1970, the Joint Commission on the Mental Health of Children clearly pointed to the profoundly disabling effects of racism by stating that the racism and poverty with which many children of color live "cripples the minority-group child in body, mind, and spirit" (p. 215).

Three types of insidious trauma can be observed. One type includes, but is not limited to, racism, anti-Semitism, poverty, heterosexism, and ageism. A related but different type of insidious trauma is the transmission of unresolved trauma and attendant defensive behaviors and/or helplessness that is transmitted transgenerationally as the result of an ancestor's direct trauma, during, for example, the Holocaust, the Japanese-American internment during World War II, the removal of Native Americans and Native Hawaiians from their homelands, and many refugees' experiences. The experiences of the previous generation result in the teaching of a worldview that incorporates the traumatic experience (Danieli, 1985; Nagata, 1990). Insidious trauma may also occur together with the experience of significantly declining health, progressive debilitating illness, or markedly decreased ability to function independently (e.g., in AIDS, diabetes, multiple sclerosis, some cancers).

The frequency of insidious traumas results in a construction of reality in which certain dimensions of security are not very secure; as such, the individual is often alert to potential threat of destruction or death and accumulates practice in dealing with threat, especially insidious experiences like ageism, homophobia, racism, and sexism. Subsequently, activation of survival behaviors, heightened sensitivity, paranoid-like behavior, and hostility are frequently observed in response to seemingly "minor" stressors by outsiders. In effect, the sensitized individual tends to risk false positives. The individual quickly moves through the stages of response to threat of danger or destruction, as will be described later.

The nature of insidious trauma also illustrates the importance of understanding that behavior is situation specific. Assessing a history of insidious trauma is imperative when considering the pretrauma functioning of persons who have experienced direct trauma. As such, styles of interacting and coping may be placed in context rather than more simply labelled as personality disorders.

The interpretation or perception of trauma type, by the categories already described, can be influenced by a person's age and the characteristics of the trauma. For example, woman battering is a direct trauma that, in chronic patterns, also entails a form of insidious trauma—psychological threat. On the other hand, a child witnessing his or her mother being battered may sustain all three types of trauma. He or she not only sustains indirect trauma in witnessing the event, but may fear the loss of the mother. And at an age when a child can begin to imagine another person's perspective, he or she may feel beaten, too.

The three categories of trauma are proposed as tools from a feminist lens. These heuristic devices help us to expand our definition of trauma beyond conventional definitions and include the experiences of many more members of our society, who sustain traumas that are unrecognized because the sequelae may not appear to be what the observer is familiar with. Subsequently, the signature of trauma tends to be labelled as a character deficit or a negatively stereotyped minority-group trait. In combination with understanding the dimensions of security (outlined below), we now have a way of helping traumatized individuals understand the disorganization that follows their experience(s) and how these experiences shape their subsequent perception and interaction with self, others, and the world.

Person-Perpetrated Versus Accidental Trauma

The feminist value placed upon the intrinsic meaning of an experience to the individual or community leads me to consider two prominent dimensions that always interact and by which we may group traumatic experiences: (1) the *perceived intent* of the source of the trauma (i.e., malicious or accidental); and (2) the *interpersonal context* within which the trauma is experienced (i.e., whether the experience occurred in isolation or with companion victims).

Intent of an accidental nature, whether or not it is perpetrated by a person, is more likely to be attributed by society, and subsequently by the victim, to the circumstances rather than the characteristics of the victim. Perloff's (1983) concept of *universal vulnerability* is relevant: "It could have happened to anyone including me." Accidental traumas (e.g., fire, miscarriage, hunting accident, natural disasters) tend to be infrequent, the victim less isolated during their recovery, and social support forthcoming. People will talk about these types of experiences and subsequently not be isolated in their experience.

Even when an accidental trauma is perpetrated by a person, observers and survivors of this type of trauma are likely to be angry at and attribute blame to the person who caused the problem (e.g., hunting or car accident). Attributions of carelessness, thoughtlessness, drug habit, etc., enable the wounded person and observers to construct an explanation for the event that does not blame the victim. The person heals whether or not the event happens in isolation or in an environment of companions, supporters, and believers (see Figure 1). Again, however, the intrinsic meaning of the event must be determined by the person experiencing it, rather than the observer.

In contrast, malicious intent is almost always perceived by the person experiencing an event and is perpetrated by a person or entity, such as a stranger, familiar person, corporate body, government, or "supreme force." Whereas persons in the support system may have sympathy for the victim, the nature of these crimes often frighten not only the victim, but also the people around them. Perhaps, in an effort to feel less vulnerable to similar traumas, people engage in "blaming the victim." Perloff's (1983) concept of *unique vulnerability* is reinforced: "There is something about you which attracts this kind of trouble." Survivors of sexual assault must often undo these oppressive attitudes, by which they have devalued themselves. An additional pervasive type of thinking described by Ler-

| | | Intent | |
		Malicious	Accidental
Context	Isolation	Rape Child sexual abuse Child physical abuse Battering Vietnam experience Racial discrimination	Car accident Avalanche Hunting accident Burglary Miscarriage
	Companion	Hostage experience Concentration camp Experience of war Dislocation	Fire Flood Earthquake Death of a child Train derailment Nuclear disaster

FIGURE 1. Phenomenological categorization of traumatic events by perceived intent and perceived context.

ner's (1980) just world hypothesis also reinforces blame: "you get what you deserve." For example, poor people are often blamed for their poverty; people of color are blamed for "not getting ahead" by their own initiative. These sorts of perspectives add insult and trauma to the original event; support by outsiders is often ambivalent, and the outsiders may hold the power to determine the distribution of resources. Victims may not report their wounds. For example, an African-American child is tormented and threatened at school, but doesn't report this to his or her teacher. Survivors of these types of traumas may socially and emotionally withdraw to avoid being secondarily traumatized by blame and isolation; sometimes the victims lash out in anger.

Our perception of intent, subjective experience of traumata, and resolution are all influenced by prior experiences, cultural factors (Parson, 1985), and stage of psychological development. For example, in children and other persons whose emotional development is very egocentric, even natural disasters (e.g., earthquakes) may be personalized. (Some religious and philosophical orientations may make this dimension artificial. In this case, the individual has been socialized to have symbolic meanings of events that may very well change their intrinsic meaning to the individual.) For many minority groups, the repeated and/or chronic experience of traumatic events makes it difficult for the individual to believe in anything but unique vulnerability (Parson, 1985). This latter type of vulnerability is reinforced in persons who are subject to repeated discrimination or threat, such as with anti-gay/lesbian violence (Comstock, 1989), racist motivated violence (Parson, 1985), anti-Semitic violence (Danieli, 1985), chronic torture experienced by many Southeast Asian refugees (Cheung, 1984; Mollica, 1988; Mollica & Lavelle, 1988), and repeated interpersonal sexual assault and violence.

The interpersonal and political context in which a trauma is experienced further determines how blame is attributed, the support one receives, and how the survivor is able to reconstruct his or her life following trauma. The context is isolated in most maliciously inflicted traumas (e.g., rape, sexual abuse, battering, mugging, terrorism), but sometimes includes companion victims (e.g., concentration camp experiences, car accidents, natural disasters) (see Figure 1).

The isolated context within which most victims of interpersonal violence are traumatized perpetuates a sense of unique vulnerability (Perloff, 1983). Isolation is often perpetuated by the victimizer, who essentially uses it as a brainwashing technique (NiCarthy, Merriam, & Coffman, 1985). In chronic traumatization, such as child sexual and physical abuse and battering, coercive techniques are used to insure isolation. The victim is often told something to reinforce his or her blame for the experience of trauma. Young victims are particularly vulnerable to these techniques, because their egocentrism places them at the center of responsibility for everything. Women are also historically particularly vulnerable, as they may have been held accountable for failures of interpersonal interactions or even for their partner's mistakes.

In contrast, having at least one companion victim with whom one can talk about traumatic experiences decreases the likelihood of feeling uniquely vulnerable, increases the likelihood that one can refuse blame for the traumata, and provides a unique type of social support. For example, communities of color have empowered their members by sharing experiences with one another and rendering a sociopolitical analysis that removes blame from the victim, places the experiences in a meaningful context (though the irrational context of racism), and validates the individual's experience. Companion victims in natural disasters, accidents, and war experience allow the individual to know there are others. More recently, the feminist movement has used this concept to empower survivors of rape and other forms of interpersonal violence by providing opportunities for group discussion, sharing, and support. The companionship of other victims allows for the possibility of absolving oneself of blame by absolving the other person(s). It further allows for bonding and a concern for someone else, which decreases one's isolation and the reverberation of the traumatic event to the exclusion of all else. Feminist perspectives have again held in high regard the value and healing power of connection in contrast to the destruction rendered by isolation. Affirmation to speak about one's experiences is one way to connect and find others who have suffered similarly.

If whole groups of people sharing a common identity have been traumatized (e.g., Holocaust victims, Japanese-American internment camp survivors, blacks, Native Americans, Native Hawaiians), there is a dual context. The group or community is isolated from the rest of society and blamed for the atrocities experienced in some way, while simultaneously having companion victims. The experience of shame over guilt, consistent with communities that are mutually interdependent (Sue & Sue, 1990), may perpetrate silence and the subsequent isolation of a community within itself such as the case with survivors of the Holocaust, Japanese-American internment, and American Indian survivors of genocide. There is a coexistence of both universal vulnerability (of all members) and unique vulnerability (of the group). Repeated traumatization or chronicity of trauma as sustained by many minority groups (Parson, 1985) further impairs resiliency by reinforcing a unique sense of vulnerability and increases the likelihood that the traumatic events acquire an intrinsic malicious value of intent that other people might consider accidental.

Stages of Vigilance

The experience of trauma affects a person in a permanent way. Research suggests that trauma's impact on the central nervous system in fact renders one more reactive to subsequent minor stressors (Krystal et al., 1989) for an unspecified period of time following the trauma. The behaviors that follow trauma suggest that humans may have innate survival templates that, once activated, guide one in filtering subsequent environmental events. After a traumatic experience, one is more likely to be sensitive to threatening cues in the environment that are associated with the original trauma, or, through a process of higher-order conditioning, are associated indirectly.

The response to threatening cues appears to occur at three qualitatively different levels: *readiness, alert,* and *survival.* The level might be determined by the independent value of individual cues, as well as the summative effect of a constellation of cues. These levels are not necessarily sequential, but are proposed as a heuristic by which both the therapist and the wounded individual may better understand posttrauma responding.

Although an individual who has been traumatized may subsequently reorganize their internal world in a way that allows them to deal with the hassles of daily living, they may never return to a complete resting state; there is always a readiness to detect threatening activities, sensory experiences, events, and people. Animal research finds this increased reactivity following trauma or chronic stress (McIntyre & Edson, 1981). Cognitive action theory (Chemtob et al., 1988) would hypothesize that an individual who has been traumatized is always "weakly potentiated."

Readiness poses both advantages and disadvantages to the survivor. On the constructive dimension, an individual may appear quick, anticipate well, and be able to "think on their feet." The disadvantages include being quicker to interpret some events as threatening, being angered or stressed more easily than persons without a history of trauma, and finding it very difficult to totally relax. For example, many individuals subject to insidious traumas react angrily (survival response) to interactions and policies that devalue or negate their existence as human beings (invisibility) because these stances may represent a subtle psychological form of annihilation. The meaning of an experience is largely determined by the historical experiences of an individual or community. For example, the ways in which a person traumatized in childhood subsequently responds to threatening stimuli, while adaptive, may not be constructive for soliciting support.

The threat value of a variable may be acquired by its conscious or unconscious linkage to the original traumatic event or vicariously by learning what has happened to other people, for example, in movies or news stories. Internal and external stimuli have differential abilities to put the system on alert or survival status as they acquire different values through experience and association with destruction of dimensions of security.

Alert is a state of heightened vigilance in response to threatening stimuli. In this state, attention and energy is harnessed and focused on signal detection, which renders the individual less able to efficiently process simultaneous events and interactions because energy is directed toward the more threatening experience or cues. The individual, however, is conscious of her or his vigilance in the alert state or easily made aware of it. Perhaps less reliably than in the readiness state, one is able to assess the reliability and validity of environmental cues based on other contextual factors, and subsequently modulate their response. It is important to note that the cues do not need to be visible, concrete cues. Many persons have developed their ability to detect negative or threatening feelings from other people. This ability may be part of the connectedness that feminist perspectives allow discussion.

Survival is a state in which the individual no longer is able to voluntarily assess the contextual validity of perceived threatening cues. It is a survival state predicated on the assumption that it is better to risk a false positive than a false negative, which could be devastating. When the survival state is activated, the individual's perceptual, decisional, and relational processes are transformed; survival consumes and redirects all energy toward defensive strategies that may rapidly alternate. Subsequently, behavioral interactions appear unsocialized. The individual can no longer direct energy toward (unnecessary) socially desirable behaviors: no taking the other person's perspective, no considerateness, no generosity, no forgiveness, no humor.

All three states, readiness, alert, *and* survival, presuppose a corresponding aroused physiological status mediated by norandrenergic activation. With each state, there is increasing demand on the body. In the event that the individual continues to receive equal or increasingly threatening stimuli, physical depletion predicts that he or she will eventually seek to withdraw (which may include dissociating) from the environment until they have enough reserve to continue their strategies with less threat to their self. This feminist interpretation of what Horowitz (1976) terms *negative symptomatology* reframes avoidance or withdrawal as adaptive to the goal of survival during the trauma. Whereas the observer might suggest that these strategies are no longer adaptive outside of the traumatic event, the observer needs to listen to the traumatee's experience of life—the trauma story remains very much alive because it is activated by cues in the environment. These stages, once again, are proposed as a tool, and I do not hypothesize that they are marked by clean shifts between stages, but rather form a continuum of behavior along which an individual may progress in response to threat.

Survival Behaviors

The data from literature, anecdotes, and clinical experience suggest that we are born with a template for survival that is activated by a single trauma. Subsequently, a repertoire of survival responding is shaped by cumulative traumatic experiences. A repertoire of nonsurvival responding (i.e., social interaction, other-inclusion, "considerate" behavior) also develops, but the responses specific to survival are reinforced and refined, thus maintaining salience in the repertoire of responding, particularly when an individual feels threatened. In the absence of trauma (extinction), the prominence of survival responses recede as the repertoire of nonsurvival-mode responding acquires breadth and salience.

One of the contributions of feminist perspective is to de-pathologize normal behavior. In this section several survival behaviors are described in just this context. These behaviors, conventionally viewed as regressive behaviors, signs of instability, or impaired emotional functioning, are cast as self-preservation behaviors, the presence of which indicates that the individual has the capacity for self-preservation.

Several processes and patterns observed in survivors of trauma exist early on in our development: egocentrism and self-referencing; quickness to anger (fight); social and emotional withdrawal (flight); perseveration (rumination); and shutting down (dissociation). The relevance of these responses as part of a "survival mode" are briefly discussed below.

Self-referencing behavior reflects active information processing and assessment of environmental events for the presence of threat. It is a form of social vigilance. This behavior also serves to decrease the likelihood of being caught off guard. As such, self-referencing behavior is a manifestation of signal detection. When self-referencing behavior is activated, the traumatee tries to ascertain how events and comments, even seemingly unrelated to the observer, are relevant to her or him. Despite the energy this process may consume, the individual is capable of redirecting his or her attention and engaging in socially desirable behaviors.

Egocentrism reflects an even narrower focus of attention than does self-referencing. Energy is withdrawn from socially desirable responding, which is unessential to survival. The person's behavior is characterized by "only thinking of themself," which appears self-centered and immature to the observer. However, in the context of having experienced trauma, this perspective of "what does this mean to me?" is directed toward self-preservation.

Perseveration indicates that an unsolved problem remains contemporary in internal experience. We all exhibit perseveration in problem-solving. If someone has confused us, we find ourselves ruminating on the experience. However, perseveration in the traumatized person is qualitatively transformed by the unwelcomed intensity and frequency of the involuntary recollection of the trauma story (Mollica, 1988), which may overshadow or even prevent simultaneous or sequential processing of any other information. Additionally, because the trauma story can be recollected in all three representational systems—visual, sensorimotor, and propositional thought—the contemporary experience can be very vivid (flashback). Without environmental cues to anchor the individual to present time, it becomes difficult to distinguish past and present experience; connections become loose and fragmented. Other unfinished trauma stories may become simultaneously current, which increases the intensity and disorganizing impact of the experience. (Therapy attempts to help the individual "schedule" the recall of the trauma story and integrate pieces of the story along unifying themes to extract relevant meaning. The therapist provides a salient cue for retaining contact with current time and distinguishing current from past experience.)

Anger is both a fighting and protective response to environmental threat. When threatened one may retort or express anger by shouting, name calling, threats, and physical striking out.

Withdrawal and *shutting down*, both flight responses, are protective survival responses that may involve some form of dissociation (Briere, 1989). They allow an individual to withdraw and restore energy to be ready to "fight" again; they are also responses to being overwhelmed and unable to comprehend or organize meaning out of experience. This latter observation would lead us to predict that children would be more likely to shutdown or withdraw from the trauma scene because of a less developed capacity for coping. As such, this method of self-defense is reinforced and may become a generalized way of responding.

Splitting, that is, dichotomizing people as good and bad, reflects a separation of threatening cues from safe cues. It may be a form of self-defense and preservation of attachment characteristic of trauma perpetrated by another person when a person is young—experiences that introduce extreme views of the dangerousness and badness of important figures (e.g., authorities, parents, "friends") that the child is not capable of integrating. This self-defense is a way of keeping order and safety in one's world; it can be viewed as a form of signal detection where there has to be an absolute criterion for designating dangerousness. It is likely to be a protective behavior that is hard to change, because it requires that an individual give up their "life raft."

The prominence of the survival schema is determined by the interaction of several factors that may not be amenable to a formulaic understanding, nor be predictive, except for a specific individual, for example, health status, age at trauma(s) (ways of knowing and remembering experience, central nervous system maturation), destruction of dimensions of trauma, history of cumulative trauma, societal view of trauma, and preparedness for trauma. Viewing survival behaviors as a reflection of a healthy capacity for self-defense provides an expanded view of the normative range of human functioning in context.

Dimensions of Traumatic Experiences

The conventional approach to trauma as a unidimensional construct (though complex) makes it difficult to compare similarities and differences between traumatic experiences, the impact of traumatic experiences at different ages, and the differential impact of trauma on survivors of similarly labeled trauma. Different theories emphasize different dimensions, all important, but derived from the area of trauma theorists are most familiar. For example, the sexual abuse literature points to the destructive impact of betrayal when the sexual abuser is known to the victim (Courtois, 1988; Herman & Hirschman, 1981); the battering literature suggests that fear of physical safety and threats to life are important dimensions for understanding its impact (Walker, 1979); the literature on severe illness in children points to the accelerated need to deal with mortality (Peterson, 1989); the experience of Vietnam veterans suggests that moral conflict and exposure to death and destruction contributed to the impact on soldiers (Wilson, Smith, & Johnson, 1985).

Disorganization of one's world appears to be the shared experience across different traumas and a core feature of the definition of trauma (Foa et al., 1989; Horowitz, 1976; Janoff-Bulman, 1985). Carmen, Reiker, and Mills (1984) emphasize how physical or sexual abuse strains the capacity for reorganization:

> victims of physical and sexual abuse are faced with an extraordinary task of conflict resolution as they look for a context in which bodily harm and threats to life can be understood. When the assailant is an intimate or family member, this process is immeasurably complicated by the profound betrayal of trust. Such victims must also cope with ongoing vulnerability to physical and psychological danger when the abuser has continuing access to the victim. (p. 382)

The labels we use for trauma—for example, rape, sexual abuse, assault—actually represent multiple traumas, the constellations of which may vary between individuals. The new wave of feminism observes that understanding differences in fundamental experiences are as critical as acknowledging similarities. By moving away from the debate of which experiences are "valid traumas" by validating the experience of the survivor, we are more likely to be able to examine the similarities and the differences between and among traumatic experiences in a way that may increase our understanding of human behavior. Each trauma case represents a shattering or destruction of different constellations of organizing principles, or *dimensions of security*, by which we come to know ourselves, others, and the world. The destruction of each dimension of security represents a trauma. For the sake of organization and educating clients about their responses to trauma, dimensions of security can be examined by the domains of experience they impact—physical, emotional–psychological, and spiritual—which ultimately affect connectedness as manifested by interpersonal relations (see Table 2).

Our dimensions of security are primarily physical at birth. Physical pain, stimulus deprivation, injury, and starvation are the most salient threats to physical survival. The destruction of physical dimensions not only carries tremendous pain but is perceived as a threat to life, a psychological dimension strongly correlated with PTSD (Kilpatrick & Best, 1988; Wilson et al., 1985). The destruction to these dimensions particularly influences psychobiological and socioemotional growth of children (whose central nervous system

TABLE 2. Dimensions of Security

Dimension	Explanation
Physical	
Stimulus deprivation	Lack of stimulation, particularly early in life, may permanently alter or retard CNS development; stimulus input also provides a grounding in reality; SD includes restricted movement, confinement
Pain	Immediate CNS response, severe pain likely to leave "memory traces"
Injury	Almost always involves pain and may also be accompanied by visual cues, e.g., blood, auditory cues, e.g., screams, gunfire
Permanent injury	Leaves indelible visual, functional, and/or kinesthetic reminder of trauma
Starvation	Also related to pain and associated with survival behaviors: hoarding, dreams about food, hallucinations, antisocial behaviors to obtain food
Psychological	
Confrontation with mortality	Confronts reality of fragility of life and reality of death
Loss of significant other(s)	Impairs sense of belonging, existence, identity, security
Perceived malicious intent	Raises fear, anticipation of harm; injures belief in benevolent action
Isolation	Alienation, lack of opportunity to test reality or assign appropriate cause/responsibility; contributes to feeling helpless and constructing idiosyncratic meaning
Helplessness/loss of control	Resignation, cessation of hope
Witness/participant to death or destruction	Human life not valued; right and wrong nonapplicable

TABLE 2. (cont.)

Dimension	Explanation
Crushing of spirit	Emotional abuse, brainwashing, and destruction result in humiliation, perceived lack of meaning to one's existence, lack of zest for life
Dislocation	Such as in refugee experience; loss of identity, homebase, country, culture, attachment—results in disorientation and being ungrounded
Interpersonal	
Betrayal	Devastates trust and willingness to be interpersonally vulnerable
Abuse of power	Fails to provide social order and assurance of safety; impairs trust
Violation of personal space	Damages sense of control over space; alters notion of inter- and intrapersonal boundaries
Rejection	Devalues worth; negates existence; may contribute to deprivation in children
Invisibility	Ignores existence, devalues worth, sentence of "death"
Loss of significant other(s)	Impairs sense of belonging, intimacy, trust

continues to mature through adolescence). These physical experiences leave memory traces that can be reactivated through an injury or physical touch. With the development of abstract thinking, one develops associations between physical dimensions and mortality.

Psychological and interpersonal dimensions of security acquire depth and salience with the development of propositional thinking, which we acquire along with symbolic representations of the external and internal world. Hypothetically, the meaning of several dimensions of security—isolation, loss, helplessness, and perceived malicious intent—emerge earlier than others. Confrontation with one's own mortality, coercion, destruction of identity, dislocation, loss of health, and witness or participant to death and destruction might require more complex thinking and abstraction. Some of the threats to these dimensions emerge with the increasing complexity of meaning attached to environmental events.

Threats to dimensions of interpersonal security include abuse of power or authority, betrayal, invisibility, loss of a significant other, and violation of personal space. Again the establishment of these dimensions requires experience of living and is mediated by propositional thinking.

Using dimensions of security by which to compare traumatic experiences, one can hypothesize more clearly about the differences among them (see Table 3). For example, experience of war as a soldier or civilian carries possible destruction of almost all physical dimensions of security, in addition to some psychological and interpersonal dimensions. The traumas sustained by Vietnam veterans overlap but are not totally consistent with the traumas sustained by Southeast Asian refugees, which included disintegration of the family, sudden and/or brutal death of a loved one, starvation, torture (and the multiple traumas along the physical and psychological dimensions associated with the trauma of torture), dislocation, and loss of cultural identity (Rozee & Van Boemel, 1989). Female refugees often additionally sustained rape. A typical story is excerpted from Mollica (1988):

> V. K. arrived in America when she was 15 years old. She had spent the previous 5 years in Communist work camps. In these camps, she was a victim of extreme mental, physical, and sexual torture. She reports multiple beatings, being hung by her ankles from a tree for three days, and spending months in solitary confinement in an underground cell. She was repeatedly raped by the Communist soldiers when she was 11 or 12 years old. (p. 309)

Recognizing that the labeled "trauma" may represent a different, though necessarily overlapping, constellation of singular traumas may allow us to understand the higher rates of PTSD in Vietnam veterans of color (Hamada, Chemtob, Sautner, & Sato, 1988), differential impact of rape among individuals, and differential impact of traumas to ethnic or minority communities (Loo, in review).

The threats to dimensions of security also have changing salience and meaning in the course of a life span, because our capacities for taking care of ourselves and controlling outcome of events may change. In later years, several dimensions of security must be reexamined. Many individuals find themselves again in a position of increased dependence on someone else for basic needs, contending with social systems that in part may dictate their relationships and value in the world. When these changes are gradual, the individual may plan for this reorganization; then these changes are less likely to be traumatic. Sudden changes, marked by a sense of helplessness or lack of control, are traumatic—both because of their suddenness and the tendency for some traumas to occur at a time when individuals are experiencing losses of significant others, less robust health, and less status and value in our society. For example, the loss of a steady job or a disabling health condition, a terminal illness, or the death of a partner may come at a time when an individual's capacity for coping is already strained by the death of a close friend, parent or other relative.

The impact of trauma, particularly when a dimension of security has not been established in a conventional manner, shapes organizing principles in developmentally idiosyncratic and survival-oriented ways. This position may result in an absence of conventional notions of the value of human life, personal space, or order. Thus, they may appear "primitive." The permanent, pervasive shaping of subsequent reality, attentional processes, and responding ultimately influences how information is taken in.

It is interesting that several cultures that have sustained long-term endemic trauma by most members have philosophical contexts for understanding their suffering. These philosophies place traumatic experience in a context that provides meaning in relationships to culture and the universe, and thus provide a means for retaining a sense of meaningfulness and connectedness with life. Offering such an interpretation of trauma reduces the isolation, unique sense of vulnerability, and the meaninglessness inherent in our perceptions of trauma. However, there is a danger in normalizing widespread traumatic experience, as such a stance permits preventable atrocities to continue.

IMPLICATIONS OF A FEMINIST CONCEPTUALIZATION OF TRAUMA

America in this century has been witness to the elimination of many routinely sustained traumatic experiences, which have been parallel-ed by a decrease in American society's acceptance of a wide range of oppressive behaviors. However, some segments of our population continue to sustain direct, indirect, and certainly insidious traumas at alarming rates and with long-term impact. Judgment is passed on the normative, defensive behaviors of those who have not been guaranteed the safety and privileges of those in power.

TABLE 3. Dimensions of Security Destroyed by Specific Traumas

Dimension	Traumas							
	Refugee experience	Rape	Combat	Earthquake	Battering	Poverty	Car accident	Japanese-American internment
Physical								
Stimulus deprivation	+					?		
Pain	+	+	+		+	?	+	
Injury	+	+	?		+	?	+	
Permanent Injury	?	?	?		?		?	
Starvation	+		?			+		
Psychological								
Confrontation with mortality	+	+	+	+	+	?	+	?
Loss of significant other(s)	+		+	?		?	?	
Perceived malicious intent	+	+	+		+	?		+
Isolation	+	+	+		+	?		+
Helplessness/loss of control	+	+	?	+	+	+	+	+

Witness/participant to death or destruction	+		+	+	?	?	+	+
Denegration of spirit	+	+	?		+	?		+
Dislocation	+		?	?		?		+
Interpersonal								
Betrayal	?				+			+
Abuse of power	+	+	?		+	+		+
Violation of personal space	+	+			+			+
Rejection	+				+	+		+
Invisibility	+					+		+
Loss of significant other(s)	+	?	+	?		?	?	

+ = usually present
? = variable (depends on survivors perceptions of intent and context, among other variables)

The feminist construction of trauma theory offered in this chapter has several significant implications. Three of the most significant are briefly discussed. First, this conceptualization requires us to define normal behavior in a situational and historical perspective, out of the individual's perception of experience, something that the current system of nosology avoids and research methodologies seldom capture. This perspective extends the notion of trauma to be more inclusive of women, children's, and minority group's experiences (i.e., by race, ethnicity, religion, class, age, etc.).

Similarly to American historians' neglect to record the atrocities suffered by ethnic minority groups of people, psychiatry's and psychology's theoretical foundations have limited contexts and tend to be ahistorical, in a sociopolitical sense, making invisible the experiences of large segments of the population who have been historically oppressed. Some researchers and theorists are suggesting that there are sequelae to the historical traumas sustained by many groups of people in this country, for example, the enslavement and kidnapping of Africans, the decimation and dislocation of Native Americans and Native Hawaiians, transgenerational effects of the Holocaust (Danieli, 1985), internment of Japanese Americans during World War II (Krell, 1988; Loo, in review; Nagata, 1990), the reneging by the U.S. government on promises of benefits and privileges to Filipino veterans who served in World War II, and the colonizing of ethnic groups of people. These experiences, as suggested in this chapter, have transformed the lives of millions of Americans; the survival-based defensive postures that have been transmitted through the generations as a result have been subsequently used against the very same people and their descendants.

This conceptualization of trauma may change the psychosocial environment in which survivors attempt to recover and reorganize their world. It also expands options for helpful community-based interventions for the psychologically and spiritually wounded. Validating distress is possible without assigning a psychiatric label.

Normalizing sequelae to trauma may enable us to claim social responsibility for survivors through social policies, political action, and community mobilizations that support them. The destigmatization of the individual, particularly in person-perpetrated traumas, may decrease the isolation that compounds the wounds of many victims.

The last major implication of this theory impacts diagnosis. Although I suggest that we not diagnose pathology in normal responding to trauma, a subjective decision about the threshold for diagnosing abnormal responding (Horowitz et al., 1987) must be made. Although guided by data, this is always a subjective decision made upon criteria, if only guided by majority versus minority responses of a group. This presents a bind for both therapist and survivor. Many trauma survivors in distress—even a normal pattern of distress following trauma–cannot afford to seek help without the assistance of third-party payers who require a diagnosis for reimbursement. Thus, we must address the current system of diagnosis.

Although the American Psychiatric Association's diagnostic manual has accomplished a major breakthrough by outlining diagnostic criteria for PTSD, it is important that we remind ourselves that this system is not a gold standard. It is one version of how trauma unfolds and will be subject to change with each revision. It is also the story understood and largely shaped by persons who have possessed much power and privilege. It tends to only attend minimally to the effects of gender, class, ethnicity, age, and community history on manifestations of distress. While the projected DSM-IV entertains the creation of a category of stress-related disorders, the underlying assumption upon which the diagnostic system is based still attributes deficits to the individual and pathologizes normative responding to horrible situations.

Current clinical experience and research suggests that post-trauma responding takes many forms and may not always fit criteria outlined in the DSM-III-R (APA, 1987). We need optional ways of validating multiple constellations of posttrauma responding. The consequence of this situation is significant. Some therapists are forcing the facts to fit the criteria; there is economic incentive for therapists to do so for third party reimbursement. Forcing facts this way may not only inappropriately shape the way therapists approach treatment, it may be unethical. On the other hand, some therapists feel forced to make the facts fit according to another, valid code of ethics by which they avoid assigning stigmatizing diagnoses to clients, since the etiologies presumed by such diagnoses would not provide an appropriate context for understanding the client's current distress.

Before the advent of the single, situationally induced disorder of PTSD, therapists gave (as they continue to give) diagnoses that are trauma-related, but not conventionally conceptualized as such, for example, borderline personality (Briere, 1989; Herman, Perry, & van der Kolk, 1989), depression (Briere, 1989; Brown, 1989), histrionic personality (Briere, 1989), multiple personality disorder (Putnam, 1989), and substance abuse disorders (Root, 1989; 1991). Except for multiple personality disorder, diagnostic labels associated with conventional nosology provide little etiological or conceptual utility (see Chapter 9, this volume).

SUMMARY

Trauma permanently changes a person. In contrast to a stressful experience, which challenges an individual's capacity to cope, trauma destroys multiple dimensions of security and exceeds the limits of human capacity to process and integrate horrible experiences into a coherent perception of self and self-in-relationship to others and the world. The disorganization created by this upheaval motivates the individual to attempt to find meaning in the experience so that she or he can reorganize the experience and integrate it into her or his perceptions of self, and self in relationship to others and the world. The greater the number of dimensions of security that are shattered, the bigger the task of reorganization. It may be reasonable and "normal" for someone to take 10 years or more to reconstruct a life, especially if they are living in an environment that is filled with cues that, in their reality, have a basis for threat or that compounds life with insidious or cumulative traumas.

Although some traumatized persons appear able to restore their daily functioning to pretrauma functioning in most situations, each one bears a signature of his or her experience(s) hypothetically related to the dimensions of security that are traumatized: difficulty with intimacy, permanency, and trust; controlled responding and affect; pervasive or intermittent anxiety and depression; rigidity of rules and expectations or few regulators; the capacity to handle certain stressors with ease while being quick to react to others; the establishment of deeply personal rituals or the absence of conventional rituals; either a greater sense of spirituality or increased doubt or disbelief in the concept. The signature of trauma may be similar across different traumas or dissimilar across same-labeled traumas. The signature of trauma, which has until recently been ignored, creates problems of overlapping criteria with other diagnoses (e.g., depression, anxiety, etc.). This poses a problem of descriptive validity for PTSD criteria that are not well differentiated from other disorders (Horowitz et al., 1987). Feminist theorists might contend that our goal is to explore the validity of overlap, rather than trying to eliminate it. Understanding the constellations of injury to dimensions of security allows us this comparison.

When a psychologically wounded person reorganizes in the context of trauma, their initial efforts are likely to be idiosyncratic. They are likely to reorganize their perceptions of self and self-in-relationship to others and the world in ways that appear psychopathological. *These reorganizations may be temporary.* However, some of the diagnoses applied to posttrauma responding may limit the way in which health care professionals attempt to help an individual reorganize her or his environment. Some people and communities of people continue to sustain insidious traumas—which prevent a rapid recovery and reinforce defensive behaviors—that are construed out of context.

The role of subjective meaning is essential to a feminist perspective on trauma and subsequent attempts at reorganization. We might postulate that survivors of trauma are attempting to seek congruency between how they knew the world and what they know and feel now.

> People say that what we're all seeking is a meaning for life. I don't think that's what we're really seeking. I think that what we're seeking is an experience of being alive, so that our life experiences on the purely physical plane will have resonances within our own innermost being and reality, so that we actually feel the rapture of being alive. (Campbell, 1988, p. 3)

Acknowledgments

The author has literally hundreds of people to thank—many have been clients in psychotherapy, and thus remain nameless. Workshop attendees and students have formed a context within which I have developed ideas. Other people made contributions through stimulating conversation, critique, and sharing of their work. I especially want to acknowledge and thank Laura Brown, Mary Ballou, Roger Hamada, Robin LaDue, Chalsa Loo, Jeannette Norris, Paula Nurius, Py Bateman, and Claude Chemtob for stimulating conversations and feedback on the development of this manuscript.

REFERENCES

American Psychiatric Association (1980). *Diagnostic and statistical manual* (3rd ed.). Washington DC: Author.

American Psychiatric Association (1987). *Diagnostic and statistical manual* (3rd ed., rev.). Washington DC: Author.

Ballou, M. B. (1990). Approaching a feminist-principled paradigm in the construction of personality theory. In L. S. Brown and M. P. P. Root (Eds.), *Diversity and complexity in feminist therapy* (pp. 23–40). New York: Haworth.

Belenky, M. F., Clinchy, B. M., Goldberger, N. R., & Tarule, J. M. (1986). *Women's ways of knowing: The development of self, voice, and mind.* New York: Basic.

Berk, R. A. (1990). Thinking about hate-motivated crimes. *Journal of Interpersonal Violence, 5,* 334–349.

Berrill, K. T. (1990). Anti-gay violence and victimization in the United States: An overview. *Journal of Interpersonal Violence, 5,* 274–294.

Briere, J. (1984). *The effects of childhood sexual abuse on later psychological functioning: Defining a post-sexual-abuse syndrome.* Paper presented at the third National Conference on Sexual Victimization of Children, Washington, DC.

Briere, J. (1989). *Therapy for Adults Molested as Children: Beyond Survival.* New York: Springer.

Brown, L. S. (1991). Not Outside the Range: One Feminist Perspective on Psychic Trauma. *American Imago: Studies in Psychoanalysis and Culture, 48,* 119–133.

Brown, L. S. (1989, August). *The Contribution of Victimization As a Risk Factor for the Development of Depressive Symptomatology in Women.* Paper presented at the 97th Annual Convention of the American Psychological Association, New Orleans, LA.

Burgess, A., & Holmstrom, L. (1974). Rape trauma syndrome. *American Journal of Psychiatry, 131,* 981–986.

Campbell, J., & Moyers, B. (1988). *The power of myth.* New York: Doubleday.

Carmen, E. H., Reiker, P. P., & Mills, T. (1984). Victims of violence and psychiatric illness. *American Journal of Psychiatry, 141,* 378–383.

Chemtob, C., Roitblatt, H. L., Hamada, R. S., Carlson, J. G., & Twentyman, C. T. (1988). A cognitive action theory of post-traumatic stress disorder. *Journal of Anxiety Disorders, 2,* 253–275.

Cheung, F. K. (1984, September 14). *Assessment and recommendations for Indochinese refugees in Southeast Asia: Special focus on boat people suffering violence in Thailand, Philippines, Indonesia, Singapore.* Washington, DC: Bureau for Refugee Programs, U.S. Department of State.

Comstock, G. D. (1989). Victims of anti-gay/lesbian violence. *Journal of Interpersonal Violence, 4,* 101–106.

Courtois, C. (1988). *Healing the incest wound.* New York: Norton.

Danieli, Y. (1985). The treatment and prevention of long-term effects and intergenerational transmission of victimization: A lesson from Holocaust survivors and their children. In C. R. Figley (Ed.), *Trauma and its wake: The study and treatment of post-traumatic stress disorder* (pp. 295–313). New York: Brunner/Mazel.

Foa, E. B., & Kozak, M. J. (1986). Emotional processing of fear: Exposure to corrective information. *Psychological Bulletin, 99,* 20–35.

Foa, E. B., Steketee, G., & Rothbaum, B. O. (1989). Behavioral/cognitive conceptualizations of post-traumatic stress disorder. *Behavior Research and Therapy, 20,* 155–176.

Garnets, L., Herek, G. M., & Levy, B. (1990). Violence and victimization of lesbians and gay men: Mental health consequences. *Journal of Interpersonal Violence, 5,* 366–383.

Green, B. L., Wilson, J. P., & Lindy, J. D. (1985). Conceptualizing post-traumatic stress disorder: A psychosocial framework. In C. R. Figley (Ed.), *Trauma and its wake: The study and treatment of post-traumatic stress disorder* (pp. 53–69). New York: Brunner/Mazel.

Hamada, R. S., Chemtob, C. M., Sautner, B., & Sato, R. (1988). Ethnic identity and Vietnam: A Japanese American Vietnam Veteran with PTSD. *Hawaii Medical Journal, 47,* 100–109.

Helzer, J. E., Robins, L. N., & McEvoy, L. (1987). Post-traumatic stress disorder in the general population. *New England Journal of Medicine, 317,* 1630–1634.

Herman, J., & Hirschman, L. (1981). *Father-daughter incest.* Cambridge, MA: Harvard University Press.

Herman, J. L., Perry, J. C., & van der Kolk, B. A. (1989). Childhood trauma in borderline personality disorder. *American Journal of Psychiatry, 146,* 490–495.

Horowitz, M. J. (1976). *Stress response syndrome.* New York: Jason Aronson.

Horowitz, M. J., Weiss, D. S., & Marmar, C. (1987). Commentary: Diagnosis of posttraumatic stress disorder. *The Journal of Nervous and Mental Disorders, 175,* 267–268.

Janoff-Bulman, R. (1985). The aftermath of victimization: Rebuilding shattered assumptions. In C. R. Figley (Ed.), *Trauma and its wake: The study and treatment of post-traumatic stress disorder* (pp. 15–35). New York: Brunner/Mazel.

Joint Commission on Mental Health of Children. (1970). *Crisis in child mental health: Challenge for the 1970's.* New York: Harper & Row.

Kardiner, A. (1941). *The traumatic neuroses of war.* New York: Hoeber.

Kempe, C. H., Silverman, F. N., Steele, B. F., Droegemueller, W., & Silver, H. K. (1962). The battered child syndrome. *Journal of the American Medical Association, 181,* 17–24.

Kilpatrick, D. G., & Best, C. L. (1988, August). *Assessment and treatment of rape-induced psychological trauma.* Paper presented at the 96th Annual Convention of the American Psychological Association, Atlanta, GA.

Krell, R. (1988). Survivors of childhood experiences in Japanese concentration camps. *American Journal of Psychiatry, 145,* 383–384.

Krystal, J. H., Kosten, T. R., Southwick, S., Mason, J. W., Perry, B. D., & Giller, E. L. (1989). Neurobiological aspects of PTSD: Review of clinical and preclinical studies. *Behavior Therapy, 20,* 177–198.

Lang, P. J. (1979). A bioinformation theory of emotional imagery. *Psychophysiology, 16,* 495–512.

Lerman, H. (1986). *A mote in Freud's eye: From psychoanalysis to the psychology of women.* New York: Springer.

Lerner, M. J. (1980). *The belief in a just world.* New York: Plenum Press.

Litz, B. T., & Keane, T. M. (1989). Information processing in anxiety disorders: Application to the understanding of post-traumatic stress disorder. *Clinical Psychology Review, 9,* 243–257.

Loo, C. M. (in review). *An integrative-sequential treatment model for post-traumatic stress disorder: A case study of the Japanese-American internment and redress.*

Masson, J. M. (1984). *The assault on truth: Freud's suppression of the seduction theory.* New York: Farrar, Straus & Giroux.

McIntyre, D. C., & Edson, N. (1981). Facilitation of amygdala kindling after norepinephine depletion with 6-hydroxydopamine in rats. *Experimental Neurology, 74,* 748–757.

Mollica, R. F. (1988). The trauma story: The psychiatric care of refugee survivors of violence and torture. In F. M. Ochberg (Ed.), *Post-traumatic therapy and the victim of violence.* New York: Brunner/-Mazel.

Mollica, R. F., & Lavelle, J. (1988). Southeast Asian refugees. In L. Comas-Diaz and E. E. H. Griffith (Eds.), *Clinical guidelines in cross-cultural mental health* (pp. 262–302). New York: Wiley.

Mowrer, (1960). *Learning theory and behavior.* New York: Wiley.

Nagata, D. (1990). The Japanese American internment: Exploring the trans-generational consequences of traumatic stress. *Journal of Traumatic Stress, 3,* 47–69.

Nicarthy, G., Merriam, K., & Coffman, S. (1985). *Talking it out.* Seattle, WA: Seal Press.

Parker, L. S. (1989). *Native American estate: The struggle over Indian and Hawaiian lands.* Honolulu, HI: University of Hawaii Press.

Parson, E. R. (1985). Ethnicity and traumatic stress: The interesecting point in therapy. In C. R. Figley (Ed.), *Trauma and its wake: The study and treatment of post-traumatic stress disorder* (pp. 314–337). New York: Brunner/Mazel.

Perloff, L. S. (1983). Perceptions of vulnerability to victimization. *Journal of Social Issues, 39,* 41–62.

Peterson, L. (1989). Coping by children undergoing stressful medical procedures and pain: A meta-analysis. *Journal of Consulting and Clinical Psychology, 57,* 380–387.

Putnam, F. W. (1989). *Diagnosis and treatment of multiple personality disorder.* New York: Guilford.

Root, M. P. P. (1989). Treatment failures: The role of sexual victimization in women's addictive behavior. *Orthopsychiatry, 59,* 542–549.

Root, M. P. P. (1991). Persistent disordered eating as a gender specific form of post-traumatic stress response to sexual assault. *Psychotherapy: Theory, Research, and Practice, 28,* 96–102.

Rosewater, L. B. (1986, August). *The DSM-III-R: Ethical and legal implications for feminist therapists.* Paper presented at the 94th Annual Convention of the American Psychological Association, Washington, DC.

Rozee, P. D., and van Boemel, G. (1989). The psychological effects of war trauma and abuse on older Cambodian refugee women. *Women and Therapy, 8,* 23–50.

Sears, D. S. (1988). Symbolic Racism. In P. A. Katz and D. A. Taylor (Eds.), *Eliminating racism.* New York: Plenum Press.

Sue, D. W., & Sue, D. (1990). *Counseling the culturally different.* New York: Wiley.

Walker, L. E. A. (1979). *The battered woman.* New York: Harper & Row.

Wilson, J. P., Smith, W. K., & Johnson, S. K. (1985). A comparative analysis of PTSD among various survivor groups. In C. R. Figley (Ed.), *Trauma and its wake: The study and treatment of post-traumatic stress disorder* (pp. 142–172). New York: Brunner/Mazel.

Wyatt, G. (1989, August). *The terrorism of racism.* Invited address at the 97th Annual Convention of the American Psychological Association, New Orleans, LA.

INDEX